Perennials for Midwestern Gardens

Perennials
for
Midwestern
Gardens

Proven Plants
for the
Heartland

Anthony W. Kahtz

TIMBER PRESS
Portland • London

Frontis: Author's garden, including daylilies in the foreground in a variety of colors; spiked speedwell (*Veronica* 'Sunny Border Blue') in the lower center; northern sea oats (*Chasmanthium latifolium*) to the left of Siberian iris foliage, and *Liatris spicata* (both white and lavender) behind that; purple coneflower (*Echinacea purpurea*) behind liatris and to the right; *Leucanthemum ×superbum* in the center background.

Published in 2008 by
Timber Press, Inc.
The Haseltine Building
133 S.W. Second Avenue, Suite 450
Portland, Oregon 97204-3527, U.S.A.
www.timberpress.com

Printed in China

Library of Congress Cataloging-in-Publication Data

Kahtz, Anthony W.
    Perennials for midwestern gardens : proven plants for the Heartland /
Anthony W. Kahtz.
        p. cm.
    Includes bibliographical references and index.
    ISBN-13: 978-0-88192-893-8
    1. Perennials—Middle West. I. Title.
    SB434.K34 2008
    635.9'320978—dc22
                                                2007036823

To my mother, Carol;
to my fiancée, Gigi Abellana, for her many hours
accompanying me to botanic gardens and parks
and helping to carry camera equipment;
and to the memory of Ziggy

Contents

Introduction

THIS BOOK PROVIDES the reader with concise, experience-tested information about herbaceous perennials (including herbs, ornamental grasses, and bulbs) that can be grown successfully throughout a wide range of the midwestern United States. Although there are various ways to define the Midwest geographically, for this book it includes the states of Michigan, Ohio, Indiana, Illinois, Wisconsin, Minnesota, Iowa, and Missouri.

Gardening in the Midwest can be challenging. The region experiences four distinct seasons, each of which can produce climatic extremes. Periods of intense heat and humidity inevitably occur at some point during the summer, and drought can be a frequent visitor. Summer thunderstorms can be violent and are sometimes accompanied by hail. Winter is often characterized by periods of intense cold, with temperatures dropping well below zero. Average snowfall varies widely across the Midwest, even within a state. For example, Cleveland, because of its proximity to Lake Erie, receives an average 55 in. of snow a year, whereas Cincinnati receives only 14 in. So in this book, I have focused on species that can withstand our weather.

My selection of plants is based on many years of professional and personal experience. The plants are noteworthy both for their ornamental features and for the relative ease with which they can be grown. Perhaps some readers will disagree with a few of the selections. For example, northern sea oats (*Chasmanthium latifolium*) provides great ornamental value during all four seasons but can be an aggressive spreader if allowed to reseed unchecked. So in each of the plant entries, I have discussed not only the plant's attractive qualities but also its shortcomings, if any. In the book I have also included one or two plants that might be termed temperamental. How else to describe delphiniums, for example? Yet they are so popular it would not make sense to omit them. Readers who are willing and able to provide delphiniums with the appropriate cultural conditions can reasonably expect to enjoy their spectacular beauty.

The plant descriptions in the book are arranged alphabetically by botanical name. Each entry provides the plant's common name(s) and the family to which it belongs. Although common names may be easier to remember, botanical names are more helpful in establishing a plant's true identity. Knowing which family a plant belongs to can also be useful, since members of the same family often share common traits such as flower color or flower shape.

Each plant entry includes discussion of the plant's flowers, leaves, habit, soil requirements, sun or shade needs, propagation methods, insect and disease problems, outstanding

Opposite: *Alcea rosea*

cultivars and related species, recommendations on use and siting, and possible companion plants. The major plant species together with the cultivars and related species provide you with over 400 perennials to consider for your garden. A box with each entry lists the plant's hardiness zones, origin, mature height and spread, landscape uses, season of bloom, and key ornamental characteristics.

Most gardeners buy perennials for the flowers, and so I discuss each plant's floral attributes in some detail. I also pay close attention to foliage, because foliage of most perennials persists far longer than the flowers and in many cases may be highly attractive in its own right.

The majority of the plants I have chosen will tolerate a wide range of soil conditions. But if a particular species requires a certain type of soil, this is noted. The sun or shade requirements listed are those that will result in optimum growth. Typically, full sun means 6 or more hours of direct sun each day. Partial shade means 2 to 5 hours of sun each day, while full shade means the absence of direct sunlight. Judging the intensity of sunlight, however, can be tricky: 4 hours of sun from 8:00 a.m. until noon is not as intense as 4 hours from noon until 4:00 p.m., yet both could be interpreted as partial shade. Experience is the best teacher in these matters.

Most perennials sold today come with a label that specifies the USDA Hardiness Zones where the plant can be expected to flourish. This information is therefore provided in the box for each plant entry. The USDA map at the end of this introduction highlights the hardiness zones of the Midwest region, which are based on average minimum winter temperature. Of course, many other factors—summer heat, humidity, wind, rainfall, drainage—come into play in determining whether a plant will survive in your area, but winter temperatures are undeniably critical in the Midwest.

The hardiness zones present in the Midwest include Zone 3 (northern Minnesota, northwestern Wisconsin, and portions of northern Michigan); Zone 4 (southern Minnesota, central and southern Wisconsin, northern and southwestern Iowa, and northern Michigan); Zone 5 (southern Iowa, northern and central portions of Missouri, Illinois, Indiana, Ohio, southern Michigan, and eastern Wisconsin); and Zone 6 (southern portions of Missouri, Illinois, Indiana, Ohio, and portions of Michigan). Each zone is further subdivided into "a" and "b" ranges, which represent a difference of 5°F in the annual minimum winter temperature. For example, Zone 3b has an average annual minimum winter temperature that is 5°F warmer than Zone 3a.

One critical phenomenon that the hardiness zone designations do not take into account is the existence of microclimates—areas in your garden that are warmer than their surroundings because of southern exposure, protection from wind, or other factors, and will therefore nurture plants that are not officially hardy in a particular zone. Through experimentation, you will find where the microclimates in your garden are.

The resources section at the end of the book lists public gardens where you can see a wide

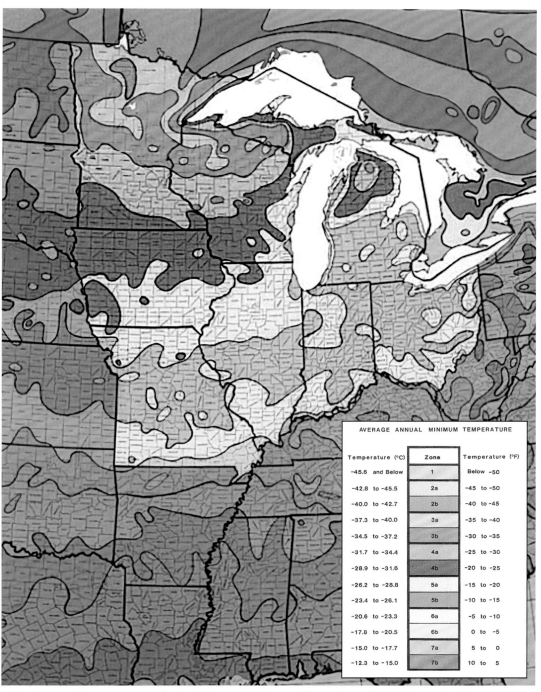

USDA Plant Hardiness Zone Map for the Midwest: Michigan, Ohio, Indiana, Illinois, Wisconsin, Minnesota, Iowa, and Missouri

Temperature (ºC)	Zone	Temperature (ºF)
-45.6 and Below	1	Below -50
-42.8 to -45.5	2a	-45 to -50
-40.0 to -42.7	2b	-40 to -45
-37.3 to -40.0	3a	-35 to -40
-34.5 to -37.2	3b	-30 to -35
-31.7 to -34.4	4a	-25 to -30
-28.9 to -31.6	4b	-20 to -25
-26.2 to -28.8	5a	-15 to -20
-23.4 to -26.1	5b	-10 to -15
-20.6 to -23.3	6a	-5 to -10
-17.8 to -20.5	6b	0 to -5
-15.0 to -17.7	7a	5 to 0
-12.3 to -15.0	7b	10 to 5

AVERAGE ANNUAL MINIMUM TEMPERATURE

selection of perennials and Web sites that carry information about perennials. A glossary is provided to assist the reader with horticultural terms. A list of selected references is included for additional reading on Midwest perennials. The index offers both scientific and common names of all plants discussed in the book.

Nothing beats actually seeing which perennials flourish in your area. Firsthand observation will reveal the range of possibilities open to you and enable you to make informed selections. Of course plant selection is a matter of personal taste. My hope is that this guide will steer you toward choices that will succeed in your garden and will help make gardening easier and more fun.

Encyclopedia
of
Perennials

Acanthus spinosus   spiny bear's breeches   acanthus family / Acanthaceae

Acanthus spinosus

Hardiness: Zones 5a to 9a
 Origin: Southeastern Europe
 Mature height: 24 to 30 in. (up to 4 ft. tall when in
   flower)
 Mature spread: 3 ft.
 Landscape use: Mid border; specimen; massed in
   large areas
 Season of bloom: Late spring to midsummer
 Key ornamental characteristics: Handsome white
   and purple flowers; deeply cut foliage

The common name spiny bear's breeches makes this plant sound like it might be appropriate for use in a children's garden. Believe me, it is not. The handsome flowers of this brute resemble oversized white and reddish-purple snapdragon blooms, but they have sharp bracts arranged in vertical rows on the large flower spikes. The floral spikes rise well above the foliage 3 or 4 ft., making an impressive display. Blooms are 1 in. wide and occur from late spring into midsummer. They can be used as fresh cut or dried flowers. When handling the flowers, be careful to avoid the thorny spines.

Shiny, arching, dark green leaves are deeply cut, and, like the flowers, provide a handsome sight in the garden. Leaves are 18 to 24 in. long, 8 to 12 in. wide, and also have spines. Foliage is basal, and this species of bear's breeches has a mounding habit.

Acanthus spinosus is easy to grow in a variety of well-drained soils. It likes part shade, but will tolerate full sun if the summer is cool. I have had the same plant in my garden for more than 10 years, and it receives shade in the early morning and late afternoon. I live in Zone 5b, and *Acanthus spinosus* is not reliably winter hardy throughout Zone 5. Providing the plant with winter mulch is recommended in its northern hardiness range.

Propagation can be accomplished by seed. Root cuttings also can be taken in early spring; they should be approximately 3 in. long and planted vertically. If you ever want to eradicate this plant from your garden, be sure to remove all the roots or it likely will resprout. *Acanthus spinosus* can spread invasively by creeping rootstock, particularly in loose soils.

Page 14: *Rudbeckia fulgida* var. *sullivantii* 'Goldsturm'

Slugs and snails are the major pests of this plant. Aphids may visit on occasion. This plant is not prone to diseases.

The cultivar *Acanthus* var. *spinosissimus* has spines that are even more wicked than those of the species. Its leaf spines are white, and the leaf dissections are narrower. *Acanthus mollis* (common bear's breeches, Zones 7 to 10), a related species, has less deeply cut leaves than *A. spinosus* and produces fewer flowers; it is also not as cold hardy.

To complement spiny bear's breeches, try growing it with *Echinacea purpurea* (purple coneflower), *Gaura lindheimeri* (white gaura), or *Geranium* (cranesbill).

The bold flowers and foliage make *Acanthus spinosus* ideal as a specimen plant in the mid border. I have also seen spiny bear's breeches massed in large areas, making a statuesque display. Its texture is so bold and dominant, the plant commands attention in any garden.

Achillea millefolium hybrids   common yarrow   daisy family / Asteraceae

Hardiness: Zones 3a to 9a
Origin: Hybrids
Mature height: 1 to 2 ft.
Mature spread: 18 in. to 2 ft.
Landscape use: Front or mid border; cottage garden; naturalized areas
Season of bloom: Early to late summer
Key ornamental characteristics: Flowers in a wide range in colors; feathery foliage

Achillea millefolium f. *rosea*

This genus was named for Achilles, a hero of ancient Greek mythology, who reportedly used the species *millefolium* to help heal the wounds of his soldiers. And so a common name of the species used primarily in England is soldier's woundweed. *Millefolium* means "many leaved" and refers to the finely dissected leaves.

Although the species is a weedy plant with small, banal, white flowers, the cultivars have larger flowers that bloom in shades of pink, red, white, and a range of pastels. The hybrids also have stronger stems and a more upright habit. Individual flowers are very small but are borne in flat corymbs 2 to 3 in. in diameter atop stalks that rise to 1 to 2 ft. Blooms usually fade as they age. They can be used in fresh or dried arrangements.

Leaves are linear-lanceolate and are alternate in arrangement. They are sessile, and have a graceful, fine, fernlike texture. Lower leaves can be up to 8 in. long. The dark green foliage has a matlike appearance. It can become tangled and may need to be cut back to basal foliage before or after the plant has flowered. When crushed, the leaves emit a slight aroma.

Achillea millefolium and its cultivars prefer full sun and well-drained soils. They are tolerant of heat and drought. The tall flower stems, however, are prone to flopping, if the plant experiences heavy rain or is sited in a windy spot. The cultivars, like the species, are reputed to spread quickly, but I have not found this to be true in my garden.

Propagation is best done by division in the spring or fall, so when you find a flower color you especially like, divide that plant. Seed can be used to propagate cultivars, but colors often vary widely from the parent plant.

Achillea millefolium 'Cerise Queen' is one of my favorite cultivars; it has bright rose-pink blooms. *Achillea millefolium* f. *rosea* has pink flowers. *Achillea* Summer Pastels Group has flowers of pastel shades of pink, rose, salmon, lavender, and orange. You may also want to check out the Galaxy hybrids of *A. millefolium* and *A. taygetea*; they have large flower heads and strong stems.

I have had good experiences with the cultivars, and they blend perfectly in my cottage-style garden. The plant is so tough it can even be mowed over in the summer and bounce right back.

Achillea 'Moonshine'   moonshine yarrow   daisy family / Asteraceae

Hardiness: Zones 3a to 8a
Origin: Hybrid
Mature height: 1 to 2 ft.
Mature spread: 1 ft.
Landscape use: Front border; specimen or in mass; cottage garden
Season of bloom: Summer
Key ornamental characteristics: Sulfur-yellow flowers; fernlike foliage

Achillea 'Moonshine' is a very attractive hybrid of *A. clypeolata* and *A. taygetea*. Beautiful sulfur-yellow flowers bloom in the summer, which are bound to enchant any gardener. The flowers are 2 to 3 in. across, flat topped, and rise above the foliage 8 to 18 in. The flowers can be used in fresh or dried arrangements.

The foliage of *Achillea* 'Moonshine' is a soft gray-green color and is feathery like a fern, making the plant attractive even when not in bloom. The foliage is also aromatic. In my Zone 5b garden, the plant foliage tends to decline after flowering, so I cut it back to basal leaves to promote new growth and possible further flowering. As the plant ages, it may lose some of its foliage; it is not uncommon for the plant to have a short life span.

Achillea 'Moonshine' prefers lean, dry to medium-wet, well-drained soil; otherwise it is prone to root rot. It thrives in full sun, and prefers sites protected from wind. The plant is more vigorous in cooler midwestern climates. It may need staking if it does not receive proper cultural care.

Pest problems are rare. The plant is susceptible, however, to a variety of leaf diseases, especially in climates with hot, wet summers. Spraying can help alleviate leaf disease problems.

Achillea 'Moonshine' is similar to the popular A. 'Coronation Gold', but it is smaller and the flower color is a lighter yellow.

Achillea 'Moonshine' looks wonderful with plants that have purple or dark blue flowers. I really like it with *Campanula glomerata* (clustered bellflower), *Geranium* (cranesbill), *Nepeta* ×*faassenii* (catmint), or *Penstemon digitalis* 'Husker Red' (Husker red foxglove penstemon). It can be used effectively as a specimen in the front border or used in mass. It also blends perfectly in a cottage garden. Since A. 'Moonshine' does not stand up well to extreme heat and humidity, gardeners in the lower Midwest can treat this hybrid like an annual in the garden.

Achillea 'Moonshine'

If you want to add an eye-catching splash of yellow to your garden or landscape, *Achillea* 'Moonshine' is the plant for you. Its gorgeous flowers and foliage make a statement in any setting.

Achillea ptarmica   sneezewort, sneezeweed   daisy family / Asteraceae

Hardiness: Zones 2b to 9a
Origin: Europe and western Asia
Mature height: 18 in. to 2 ft.
Mature spread: 2 ft.
Landscape use: Mid border
Season of bloom: Early to late summer
Key ornamental characteristics: Small, attractive flowers that bloom for weeks

Achillea ptarmica "The Pearl"

The common name sneezeweed or sneezewort does not suggest a plant you must have for your garden. But once this plant is in bloom, you will discard any preconceived notions. Sneezeweed's name may be derived from historic reports that the leaves were dried and ground to a powder that was used as snuff.

Reminiscent of baby's breath (*Gypsophila paniculata*), the flowers are small, white, and clustered in corymbs; in fact they are sometimes used in arrangements as a substitute for baby's breath. An outstanding quality of this plant is its long flowering period.

Leaves are dark green, linear to lanceolate, and finely toothed. The leaves are sessile and, unlike many other species in this genus, are not dissected.

Achillea ptarmica grows easily in moderately rich soil. It does not like overly wet soils. Unlike baby's breath, it does not need alkaline soil conditions. It thrives in full sun and will tolerate partial shade. Sneezeweed seeds freely and can be somewhat aggressive, so it works best in a cottage garden where plants are allowed to roam a bit. It is easy enough to pull up, though, especially in the early spring as the foliage emerges.

Propagation is easy by seed or division in the spring.

This plant has no serious insect or disease problems.

Achillea ptarmica has numerous cultivars with double, white flowers, which are more ornamental than the straight species. 'Perry's White' is taller and has larger flowers, and

'Ballerina' has very clear, white flowers. *Achillea ptarmica* 'The Pearl' is a cultivar I have grown for years: it blooms prolifically.

With its small, buttonlike white flowers, *Achillea ptarmica* works well with any plant. It makes a nice transition between different color schemes in the garden.

Actaea racemosa   black snakeroot, black cohosh   buttercup family / Ranunculaceae

Hardiness: Zones 3a to 8a
Origin: Eastern North America
Mature height: 4 to 7 ft.
Mature spread: 2 to 4 ft.
Landscape use: Back border; beside stream or
   pond; woodland or shade garden
Season of bloom: Mid to late summer
Key ornamental characteristics: Wandlike white
   flowers; attractive foliage; height

Actaea racemosa

Black snakeroot (*Actaea racemosa*, formerly *Cimicifuga racemosa*) has creamy white flowers on spikes that look reminiscent of a bottlebrush. Rising above the clump-forming foliage, the spikes reach up to 3 ft. long. The plant adds great architectural height to the garden or landscape, and puts on an impressive show when in bloom.

Leaves are ovate to oblong. The alternate, ternate leaves occur in 2s or 3s. The leaflets are 1 to 4 in. long, dark green, lobed, with irregularly serrate margins.

Black snakeroot performs best in soils that are rich in organic matter. It is a native woodland plant, and prefers moist soils. If sited in a location that is too dry, the leaf margins may show signs of stress by turning brown. The plant will grow in full sun or partial shade in northern zones of the Midwest, but it prefers partial shade in the lower Midwest. Too much shade may result in fewer flowers being produced. I have seen outstanding specimens growing in full sun at the Chicago Botanic Garden and in partial shade at the Missouri Botanical Garden in Saint Louis. If sited in shade, the flower spikes will bend toward the light. Flowers also have a slightly unpleasant odor, but only if you are very close.

Rust and leaf spot can be problems on occasion. There are no significant insect problems with black snakeroot.

Division is the best method of propagation and should be performed in the coolness of spring. But the process can be difficult because of the plant's deep root system. And the plants do not like to be disturbed and are difficult to establish. Seed propagation requires fresh seeds and cold stratification, and germination is difficult.

The related species *Actaea cordifolia* reaches a height of 4 to 6 ft. and has larger leaflets and flowers later than *A. racemosa*. *Actaea simplex* 'Prichard's Giant' (branched bugbane, Zones 4 to 8), a related white-flowered species, can reach 7 ft. in height. The dark foliage of some *Actaea simplex* (Atropurpurea Group) cultivars makes a dramatic statement, including 'Brunette', with purplish-bronze foliage, and 'Hillside Black Beauty', with dark purple leaves that are almost black.

Actaea racemosa is ideal for use in a woodland or partial shade garden. Try it with hostas or ferns. For an interesting mixture of white and yellow spikes, plant it with another imposing plant, *Ligularia stenocephala* (narrow spiked ligularia). The white flowers lighten up a shaded area, and the plant visually pops when sited in front of darker shrubs.

Agastache rupestris   threadleaf giant hyssop   mint family / Lamiaceae

Hardiness: Zones 4b to 9a
Origin: Southwestern United States
Mature height: 30 in. to 3 ft.
Mature spread: 18 in. to 2 ft.
Landscape use: Mid border; native plant garden
Season of bloom: Mid to late summer
Key ornamental characteristics: Salmon-orange
    flowers; fragrant foliage

Agastache rupestris

Imagine having a plant whose flowers are the colors of a sunset. That is *Agastache rupestris*. It has unique, beautiful, salmon-orange blooms. The flowers are whorled on the stem and tubular in shape. Cutting back the plant after flowering may produce another flush of flowers in fall. The genus name is derived from Greek: *agan* means "much" and *stachys* means "grain stalk," in reference to the many flowers this plant produces, a fact that bees, butterflies, and hummingbirds can verify.

The greenish-gray leaves of threadleaf giant hyssop are

opposite in arrangement and up to 2 in. long. Linear to linear-lanceolate and finely textured, when crushed the leaves emit a scent like a minty licorice. They can be used to produce tea. The plant's stems are square, which is characteristic of the family Lamiaceae.

Agastache rupestris is easy to grow in soil that is dry to moderately wet, but it requires well-drained soil. Wet-winter clay soils are especially detrimental. It prefers soils that are slightly alkaline. Being native to the southwestern United States, the plant withstands drought and poor soils, so it is ideal for xeriscaping. It performs best in full sun and is fairly tolerant of summer heat, but it also does well in light partial shade.

There are no serious insect or disease problems associated with *Agastache rupestris.*

Propagation is best by seed or division of established plants in the spring.

Agastache 'Apricot Sunrise' is a hybrid that has golden-orange flowers. The hybrid 'Desert Sunrise' has pinkish-orange-lavender blooms. 'Summer Breeze' and 'Tutti Frutti' both have pink flowers. These hybrids may not be reliably winter hardy in Zone 5, so use mulch and site them in an area that receives winter sun.

Threadleaf giant hyssop is perfect for the mid border or for a native plant garden. I like to place it in front of *Foeniculum vulgare* 'Purpureum' (bronze fennel). It also looks spectacular when placed near plants of a coarser texture like *Sedum spectabile* (showy stonecrop sedum) or *Rudbeckia fulgida* (black-eyed Susan).

Agastache rupestris is a subtly charming plant with an upright habit. There are other attractive *Agastache* species, but *A. rupestris* is the most cold hardy and has the ability to withstand midwestern winters.

Ajuga reptans   common bugle weed   mint family / Lamiaceae

Hardiness: Zones 3a to 9a
Origin: Europe
Mature height: 3 to 6 in.
Mature spread: Indefinite
Landscape use: Ground cover; slopes
Season of bloom: Spring
Key ornamental characteristics: Blue-violet flowers; attractive, quickly spreading
   foliage

If you have a large, open area or slope that would need mowing if planted with lawn grass, common bugle weed could be the plant for you. *Ajuga reptans* is stoloniferous, so it spreads easily over a wide area. The species name *reptans* refers to the "reptant" or the creeping spread of this plant.

The plant has flowers that are typically violet-blue, but they can also be shades of red,

Ajuga reptans

purple, or white. Flowers are arranged in whorls on spikes that rise above the foliage, putting on an eye-catching display in the spring. To remove spent flowers and tidy up the appearance of the plants, just set the lawn mower on a high setting and mow!

The foliage of *Ajuga reptans* is attractive: basal leaves are elliptic or ovate, with entire margins that can be slightly wavy. Leaves can be crinkly. Leaf color can range from green to bronze-red with reddish-pink-white markings, depending on the cultivar. Some cultivars' leaves may revert to green. The best foliage color is attained when the plant grows in sun.

Common bugle weed adapts to a wide range of soil types. It prefers even moisture and will tolerate dry locations. It prefers full sun but performs well in partial shade. While the foliage forms a dense carpet that spreads rapidly, shutting out most weeds, the plant does not like heavy foot traffic. Evergreen in most climates, the plant may die back in the colder hardiness zones.

Crown rot can be a problem for *Ajuga reptans*, especially in heavy soils and humid conditions. It can also destroy large areas of the plant's spread, leaving gaps. Otherwise, there are no disease or insect problems with bugle weed.

Propagation is easy by division in spring or fall. Seed is also a viable way to grow more plants, but why sow seeds when the plant is so easy to divide?

Many cultivars of *Ajuga reptans* exist. *Ajuga reptans* f. *albiflora* 'Alba' has green foliage and white flowers. *Ajuga reptans* 'Burgundy Glow' is a popular cultivar with green, pink, and white foliage. 'Catlin's Giant' has bronze-green foliage and blue flowers. 'Jungle Beauty' has purple flowers and purple-green foliage tinged with white and pinkish-red. 'Pink Elf' is a dwarf with pink flowers. 'Pink Spire' has green leaves and pink flowers.

The plant is primarily used as a ground cover. It will fill in large, shady expanses where lawns are difficult to establish. But it can encroach on lawn grass and within the garden. If you really like common bugle weed but do not want the worry of it being aggressive, plant it in pots with annuals.

Alcea rosea   hollyhock   mallow family / Malvaceae

Hardiness: Zones 2b to 9b
Origin: China
Mature height: 3 to 8 ft.
Mature spread: 18 in. to 2 ft.
Landscape use: Back border; against a fence or
    wall; cottage garden
Season of bloom: Summer
Key ornamental characteristics: Attractive flowers
    in wide color range; great architectural height

Alcea rosea

Hollyhock is a classic garden plant if there ever was one. I would venture to say that a garden is not really a garden without a few hollyhocks. Hollyhock's flowers and height make them spectacular. The flowers just announce that summer is here.

Flower colors range from white to shades of pink, lavender, red, yellow, and nearly black. Some flowers can be up to 5 in. in diameter. They are borne in terminal racemes or on spikes that can be as tall as a fishing pole.

Leaves are orbicular and have 3, 5, or 7 shallow lobes. Alternate in arrangement, they have a rough texture and gradually become smaller as they ascend the stem. Stems are unbranched and hairy.

Hollyhocks thrive in full sun and perform admirably

in light shade. They will grow in a variety of soil types but the site must be well drained. Wet winter soils are a recipe for death. Considered a biennial or short-lived perennial, hollyhocks easily self-sow and can establish colonies in the garden that persist for years, as if they were long-lived perennials. Larger plants will probably need to be staked if grown in windy sites.

By August, the leaves are often tattered looking, with anthracnose, rust, leaf spot, spider mites, or Japanese beetles doing damage. I have also found that Japanese beetles like to devour the flowers. Many leaf diseases can be treated with a fungicide spray program. Cultivars have been developed that are somewhat resistant to leaf diseases.

Propagation is best accomplished by seed. If you want plants to flower the following year, plant seeds in the summer. Every spring, I find hollyhocks popping up somewhere new in my garden. I just move them to a suitable spot, or pull up unwanted plants.

There are many *Alcea rosea* cultivars to select from. Chaters Double Group comes in a range of colors, and the flowers are reminiscent of a peony. 'Indian Spring' also comes in many colors and produces plants 6 to 8 ft. tall. 'Nigra' is a favorite of mine: it has deep maroon flowers that are almost black. It also grows 6 to 8 ft. tall. Powder Puff Group is 3 to 4 ft. tall and comes in a variety of colors.

Hollyhocks can be spectacular in the back border or intermixed in a cottage garden, providing height, contrast, and carefree charm. They are also particularly effective when grown against fences or walls.

Alchemilla mollis lady's mantle   rose family / Rosaceae

Hardiness: Zones 3a to 7a
Origin: Europe
Mature height: 8 to 10 in., with flower stems up to 18 in.
Mature spread: 2 ft.
Landscape use: Front border; mass plantings
Season of bloom: Late spring to early summer
Key ornamental characteristics: Attractive flowers; outstanding leaves; moundlike
   growth habit

Alchemilla mollis is a beautiful, low-growing plant with a mounded habit. The flowers are chartreuse or light yellow-green and occur from late spring to early summer. Apetalous and ⅛ to ¼ in. wide, they are very attractive but not overly showy, and give the illusion of floating above the foliage. They make nice cut flowers and are useful in dried arrangements.

To me, the leaves are the best feature of lady's mantle, and they are among the most attractive of perennial foliage. Lime green in color, they have soft, pubescent hairs on both sides of the leaf. If you observe lady's mantle in the early morning, a layer of beaded dew will

Alchemilla mollis

probably be on the leaves because of the pubescence. The same effect occurs after a rain or watering, and gives the plant a delicate appearance. The leaves are orbicular, 2 to 4 in. wide, and have 7 to 11 shallow-toothed, serrate lobes. Leaves can be cut back hard in midsummer to produce new growth.

Lady's mantle thrives in climates that are cool in the summer, and it will even grow in full sun. But it requires partial to full shade and moist soil conditions in warmer regions, so it will not burn. Flowering season is also shorter in warmer climates.

Although this species has been reported to freely self-sow, this has not occurred in my garden. If self-sowing becomes a problem, just remove the seed heads before they mature. This plant is easy to divide in the spring before flowering, and is slow to spread.

Lady's mantle prefers rich soil conditions. It will also grow in clay soil if its moisture needs are met. It prefers well-drained soils in the winter, and will rot if placed in an overly wet site.

I have grown this plant for more than 10 years in Zone 5b and have never experienced any disease or insect problems. However, in warmer climates, fungal and mite problems may arise.

Alchemilla mollis is a magnificent plant for the front border, and can be used as a ground cover along pathways. It can also be used in mass plantings. It works with just about any plant. Try it with *Corydalis lutea* (yellow corydalis) or *Platycodon grandiflorus* (balloon flower).

Allium giganteum   giant onion   onion family / Alliaceae

Hardiness: Zones 4b to 8b
Origin: Central Asia
Mature height: 3 to 5 ft.
Mature spread: 2 ft.
Landscape use: Back border; small groupings; specimen
Season of bloom: Late spring to early summer
Key ornamental characteristics: Eye-catching, spherical flowers; height

The genus *Allium* contains over 700 species. Culinary favorites such as chives, garlic, and edible onions are members of this genus. In addition to species that add flavor to cooking, there are many species that do not have culinary value but instead offer an ornamental aspect to the garden. One of my favorite ornamental plants in this genus is *A. giganteum*.

Like something out of a science fiction movie, the flowers are borne in a rounded, 4- to 6-in.-diameter umbel that sits atop an upright, sturdy, 3- to 5-ft. scape. The individual florets of the umbel are many in number, lilac-purple, and star shaped. They make very interesting cut and dried flowers.

Allium giganteum

Basal, pale green leaves break ground in early spring. They are 1 to 2 ft. long and 3 to 8 in. wide. Leaves are smooth and straplike, and if crushed or cut, emit a strong onion smell. After the flower scape emerges, the leaves start to wither and eventually die when the flowers start to bloom. This characteristic is a maintenance bonus, because the gardener does not have to wait for the foliage to die back, unlike for many spring flowering bulbs like tulips and daffodils.

Allium giganteum is easy to grow in a wide range of soil types. It requires well-drained soil, and it prefers full sun. Although the scapes are strong, they can be damaged by a storm. So site the plants in an area that is protected from wind. The bulbs are roughly 2 to 3 in. across and should be planted at twice that depth and 10 to 18 in. apart.

No serious insect or disease problems are associated with giant onion. But it is susceptible to bulb rot, which can occur with damp, moist conditions.

Giant onion propagation is best accomplished by division of the bulblets, and is also possible by seed. The bulblets should be removed from the base of the mature bulb in the fall and replanted. Plant seed in the spring; it will take 2 to 3 years before the plant flowers.

Numerous other *Allium* species can provide wondrous ornamental value in the garden. *Allium christophii* (star of Persia, Zones 5 to 8), also known as *A. albopilosum*, grows to 2 ft. tall and has dark lilac flowers in an umbel that is 8 to 10 in. in diameter. *Allium sphaerocephalum* (drumstick chives, Zones 4 to 9) has 2-in. purple flowers and a mature height of 18 to 36 in. Flower buds are green before turning purple, giving the umbel a 2-tone appearance. *Allium tuberosum* (Chinese chives, Zones 4 to 8) grows to 12 to 18 in. and has white flowers in a 2-in. umbel. It blooms from late summer into fall, and is a great addition to any late-season garden.

Giant onion is spectacular in the back border. It makes a dramatic statement when used in groupings. If you have a small garden, use it as a single specimen to provide a focal point. After the plant has finished flowering, just fill in the area with annuals or plants in containers. *Allium giganteum* is so remarkable, it works with any plants.

Amsonia tabernaemontana   willow blue star   dogbane family / Apocynaceae

Hardiness: Zones 3a to 9a
Origin: Eastern United States
Mature height: 2 to 3 ft.
Mature spread: 2 to 3 ft.
Landscape use: Front or middle border; shade garden; native garden; woodland garden
Season of bloom: Late spring to early summer
Key ornamental characteristics: Light blue flowers; fall foliage color

Attractive, starlike, powder blue flowers are the highlight of *Amsonia tabernaemontana*. The beautiful blue color of the blossoms is distinctive in the perennial plant gardening world. This native plant is very easy to grow.

The flowers of willow blue star are densely borne in cymelike panicles that make a showy display without commanding too much attention.

Medium green leaves are elliptic to lanceolate. Alternate in arrangement, they are sessile,

Amsonia tabernaemontana

1½ to 3 in. long, and 1 in. wide. Few perennials have foliage that produces color, but the leaves of willow blue star turn a handsome yellow in the fall and last until first frost.

The plant grows well in medium-wet soils that have good drainage, and will tolerate some drought. It prefers rich, loamy soil. The plant has an upright habit. If grown in full sun, staking will probably not be needed. It performs well in partial shade, but may need to be staked. To help the plant keep a tidy appearance, especially for shade-grown plants, cut back stems halfway after flowering to reduce flopping and promote a bushy habit.

This plant has no serious insect or disease problems. Rust is reportedly a problem on rare occasion, but I have not observed any infected specimens.

Propagation is easy by division in the spring or fall. The plant is a slow spreader, though, so it does not require frequent division. Seed can also be planted in spring, and the plants will flower the second year. Cuttings can be taken in early summer.

Several cultivars are available. *Amsonia tabernaemontana* var. *montana* is shorter than the species and does not require staking or pruning. The leaves of *A. tabernaemontana* var. *salicifolia* are noticeably longer than they are wide. The plant is not as upright as the species and has blue flowers with a white throat. *Amsonia hubrechtii* (Arkansas amsonia, Zones 4 to 9) is a related species with feathery foliage and sky blue flowers. It grows 2 to 3 ft. tall and 2 ft. wide. It is hardy only in the more southern USDA Zones of the Midwest.

Willow blue star is a versatile plant that fits into a wide range of landscape situations. Try it in a woodland or shade garden with *Pulmonaria saccharata* (Bethlehem sage), hostas, or ferns. Or use it in the front or middle border in small, massed groupings. Place it in front of coarse-textured plants like *Eupatorium purpureum* subsp. *maculatum* (Joe-Pye weed) in the perennial border to create foliage contrast. The shrub *Caryopteris* also creates interesting foliage contrast.

Anemone ×hybrida   Japanese anemone   buttercup family / Ranunculaceae

Hardiness: Zones 4a to 8a
Origin: Hybrid
Mature height: 2 to 4 ft.
Mature spread: 2 ft.
Landscape use: Mid border; shade garden; woodland garden
Season of bloom: Late summer to fall
Key ornamental characteristics: attractive pink or white flowers; handsome
    foliage

Anemone species in bloom are a sight to behold. Flowering time can be spring, summer, or fall. *Anemone ×hybrida* blooms in the late summer into the fall. If you are looking for a plant to add color and elegance to the garden at the end of the growing season, Japanese anemone is an excellent choice.

Flowers of white or shades of pink or lavender are borne on branching stems that gracefully rise above the foliage. Delicate, round blooms are 2 to 3 in. across and typically have 5 petals, with a noticeable center ring of yellow stamens.

The dark green, trifoliate, serrate leaves have long petioles. The attractive foliage will burn if cultural conditions are too hot, dry, and sunny.

Japanese anemone is easy to grow in medium-wet, organically rich, well-drained soil. It does not like dry locations. Wet winter soils are sure to cause a quick demise. A layer of mulch is advisable for colder climates. Protection from wind is also recommended. As a general rule, the plant prefers morning sun and filtered afternoon shade. The overall height of the foliage is up to 2½ ft. The plant occasionally may need staking.

Propagation can be accomplished by division in the spring. Root cuttings are also possible. Cut a 3- to 4-in. section of root in winter when the plant is dormant. Orient it vertically in a rich medium and place in a cold frame or unheated greenhouse. New plants can be slow to establish. But if grown in the right conditions, they may naturalize.

Anemone ×hybrida

There are no serious insect or disease problems associated with *Anemone ×hybrida*.

A number of *Anemone ×hybrida* cultivars exist. 'Alba' has magnificent, clear white flowers. 'Bressingham Glow' has dark rose-pink flowers; it should probably be listed as a cultivar of *Anemone hupehensis* (Chinese anemone, Zones 5 to 8). 'Honorine Jobert' is a popular cultivar with clear white flowers that blooms heavily. *Anemone hupehensis* is basically indistinguishable in appearance from *A. ×hybrida*; it blooms slightly earlier. My favorite spring-blooming species is *Anemone sylvestris* (snowdrop anemone, Zones 4 to 8), which has white flowers and grows to 12 to 18 in.

When growing Japanese anemone, *Rudbeckia fulgida* (black-eyed Susan) and *Epimedium ×rubrum* (red barrenwort) are excellent contrast plants. Japanese anemone is also a good choice in the shade or woodland garden.

Aquilegia **hybrids**   columbine   buttercup family / Ranunculaceae

Hardiness: Zones 3a to 9a
Origin: Hybrid
Mature height: 1 to 3 ft.
Mature spread: 12 to 18 in.
Landscape use: Mid border; specimen; rock garden;
    woodland garden
Season of bloom: Mid to late spring
Key ornamental characteristics: Handsome flowers
    in a wide color range; attractive foliage

Aquilegia hybrids

The Latin word *aquilegia* means "eagle," and refers to the flower's spurs that somewhat resemble an eagle's talons. Columbine provides uniquely shaped, richly colored flowers for the garden.

Aquilegia hybrids offer a wide range of flower colors, including shades of purple, blue, yellow, pink, red, and white. Showy flower petals have backward-pointing spurs. The 5 sepals are the same color as the petals.

Each leaf is made up of 2 or 3 leaflets, with incisions at the apex, giving the foliage a fernlike appearance. The leaf petiole is long and pubescent. Foliage is an attractive bluish-green. It can become haggard by midsummer, so you may want to cut the plant back to encourage new growth and a mounded habit.

Columbine tolerates a wide range of soil conditions except dry sites and heavy, poorly drained soils. It performs well in full sun or partial shade. I have found in my Zone 5b garden that plants perform better and live longer if placed in light to partial shade, especially afternoon shade. Shade also extends the bloom period. If placed in full sun, supply adequate moisture or the foliage will burn or slowly turn brown. In fact, columbine should not be placed in full sun in the lower Midwest. Removing the spent blooms may encourage further flowering. If you have the appropriate cultural conditions, the self-sowing nature of this plant will keep it in your garden for many years.

Several insect and disease problems can affect columbine. Leaf miner is a major problem; remove leaves disfigured by leaf miner activity. Leaf spot, aphids, columbine borer, crown rot, and rust can also be nuisances. A spraying program started in early spring can help control problems.

Columbine freely cross-pollinates, and propagation can be done by seed. Plants grown from spring seeding usually do not flower until the following year. Division can also be done immediately after flowering or in the fall.

There are many wonderful *Aquilegia* cultivars. McKana Group comes in a variety of colors and reaches 30 in. tall. 'Musik' series offers a multitude of different colored flowers; the plants are relatively compact in growth. 'Songbird' ('Dynasty'), a series with beautifully colored flowers, grows to 2 to 3 ft. tall; plants include 'Blue Bird', with light blue and white blooms, and 'Cardinal', which has red and white flowers. *Aquilegia canadensis* (Canadian columbine, Zones 3 to 8), which is native to eastern North America, has yellow sepals and red spurs and grows to 2 to 3 ft. tall. Under the right conditions the plant will colonize an area; it requires the same cultural conditions as the hybrids.

Columbine works nicely in the mid border and is perfect for a woodland garden. I have planted it with *Brunnera macrophylla* (summer forget-me-not), and it looks particularly attractive with variegated cultivars of that species. Or use it with *Geranium* spp. (cranesbill).

Arabis alpina **subsp.** *caucasica*   wall rock cress   cabbage family / Brassicaceae

Hardiness: Zones 4a to 7b
Origin: Mediterranean region
Mature height: 8 to 12 in.
Mature spread: 12 to 18 in.
Landscape use: Stone walls; rock garden; slopes; front border
Season of bloom: Early spring
Key ornamental characteristics: Abundant white flowers; grayish foliage

Wall rock cress is a prolific bloomer in the spring. At the peak of its flowering time, the 4-petaled flowers form a carpet that almost obscures the foliage. Fragrant, white blooms occur on racemes. After being spent, the plant should be cut back heavily to help maintain a tidy appearance throughout the growing season.

The foliage is toothed, and has a grayish-green cast primarily because of a pubescent layer. Basal leaves are obovate, and stem leaves are auriculate. After flowering, the foliage is approximately 6 in. tall. If grown under optimal conditions, the foliage will form a dense, attractive ground cover.

Long periods of high heat and humidity will cause wall rock cress to decline over the summer and possibly die. Soils need to be well drained for best growth, and the plant prefers dry to moderately wet conditions. Full sun is a must for best results. Overly wet winter soil conditions can lead to root rot.

Arabis alpina subsp. *caucasica* 'Schneehaube'. Global Book Publishing Photo Library

Downy mildew, rust, and aphids may be minor problems. Otherwise, wall rock cress is not susceptible to disease or insect issues.

Propagation may be done by division, cuttings, or seed. Divide the basal rosettes in fall. Softwood stem cuttings can be taken in early summer after blooming. Seed may be planted in a cold frame in the fall.

Several cultivars of *Arabis alpina* subsp. *caucasica* are available. 'Flore Pleno' produces double white flowers that are longer lived than the species. 'Schneehaube' ('Snowcap') has large white flowers. 'Variegata' has leaves with creamy yellow stripes. *Arabis blepharophylla* 'Fruhlingszauber' ('Spring Charm') has pink-tinted blooms.

Wall rock cress is a perfect companion plant for early spring flowering bulbs. Try it in the rock garden with *Saponaria ocymoides* (rock soapwort) or *Sempervivum tectorum* (hen and chicks). The species makes a dramatic impact when planted in mass on slopes. Wall rock cress also lives up to its name: it is perfect for rock walls. Or it can simply be used as an edging plant in the front border.

Armeria maritima   sea pink, sea thrift, common thrift   leadwort family / Plumbaginaceae

Hardiness: Zones 4a to 8a
Origin: Europe
Mature height: 3 to 4 in.; scapes 6 to 12 in.
Mature spread: 3 to 4 in. (additional spread can occur over time)
Landscape use: Rock garden; pathways; front border
Season of bloom: Spring
Key ornamental characteristics: Gorgeous pink or white flowers; dark evergreen foliage

The globe-shaped, pink or white flower heads of *Armeria maritima* are borne on leafless scapes that rise artfully above the foliage. Consisting of many tiny florets, the flower head is ½ to 1 in. in diameter. If the spent blooms are cut back, the plant may rebloom later in the summer. Blooms may be used in dried flower arrangements.

Sea pink's evergreen foliage has a dense, mounded habit resembling a clump of unmowed grass in the spring. The dark green leaves are flat, linear, and approximately 4 in. long with a center midrib. Do not cut back foliage in the fall or you may sacrifice spring blooms.

Armeria maritima needs full sun in northern regions of the Midwest and prefers some shade in the warmer regions. This plant thrives in dry and infertile soils; rich, moist soils will cause rot. As the common name implies, sea pink is highly tolerant of salty conditions and will even grow along roads where salt is spread in winter. If a friend who lives on the salt water asks for plant advice, you can heartily recommend this species.

Armeria maritima

Propagation is by seed or division. Seeds must be soaked in water for 6 to 8 hours before planting. Divide plants only if the clump becomes open in the center.

There are no serious disease or insect problems associated with sea pink.

Several cultivars of *Armeria maritima* are available. 'Alba' has creamy white flowers. 'Bloodstone' is probably a hybrid of *Armeria alliacea* (plantain thrift) and *A. maritima*; it produces dark reddish blooms on 10-in. scapes. 'Ruby Glow' is a popular cultivar with ruby-pink flowers that reach 10 in. in height.

Sea pink is a low-growing plant, which makes it ideal for rock gardens or along pathways. It can also be used in the front border of small gardens. To achieve full effect, group plants. Sea pink looks wonderful when planted with silver-leaved plants like *Santolina chamaecyparissus* (lavender cotton) or *Artemisia schmidtiana* 'Nana' (silvermound). It also works nicely with other delicate-looking perennials like *Pulsatilla vulgaris* (pasque flower).

I really like the ornamental qualities of sea pink, and have placed many of them in my garden. They tend to be short lived in my clay-based soil, but I recommend that you try this very attractive plant.

Artemisia ludoviciana   white sage   daisy family / Asteraceae

Hardiness: Zones 4b to 8a
Origin: Western United States
Mature height: 2 to 3 ft.
Mature spread: 2 ft.
Landscape use: Mid border; herb garden
Season of bloom: Summer
Key ornamental characteristics: Outstanding silvery
    foliage

Artemisia ludoviciana

White sage gets its name from the pubescent, silvery-whitish-gray color of the leaves. They are alternate in arrangement, and at quick glance resemble those of *Salvia officinalis* (common sage). The lanceolate leaves can be up to 4 in. long. They are aromatic when crushed. Leaf margins may be notched toward the apex, and be slightly serrate or entire. Stems are white.

The flowers of *Artemisia ludoviciana* are white or pale yellow, and are considered of little ornamental value. You may want to consider removing flower buds when they appear. Most species in the genus *Artemisia* are grown primarily for their outstanding foliage production.

White sage prefers poor-quality to moderately fertile soils that have good drainage. It likes soils that are dry to slightly moist. If the soil is too wet, the roots will probably rot. Being a native of the western United States, the plant needs and performs best in full sun. Shade will cause the plant to flop over. High humidity is also not to this plant's liking and will cause the foliage to decline slowly. Shearing the plant back in summer often rejuvenates it. This clump-forming plant can spread aggressively, so be alert. You could place white sage in a container and sink it in the ground. On the other hand, the plant is useful for those areas where many other plants do not grow well or at all.

Leaf rust is the primary disease concern with white sage. There are no other disease or insect problems.

Several quality cultivars of *Artemisia ludoviciana* are available. 'Silver King' is very hardy in the upper Midwest (to Zone 3). It is more compact than the species, at 3 ft. tall, and can spread aggressively. The foliage gets a red cast in fall. The Royal Horticultural Society lists this cultivar as *Artemisia ludoviciana* subsp.*mexicana* var. *albula*, with the common name of silver king. 'Silver Queen' has leaf margins that are deeply cut, and the overall growth is a little more compact than 'Silver King'. 'Valerie Finnis' is not as invasive as the species or the mentioned cultivars, and reaches a height of 2 ft.

The outstanding foliage of *Artemisia ludoviciana* especially complements plants that have green, reddish, or variegated leaves. It effectively accents and blends with just about any plant. Try it in the mid border or herb garden. I like it with plants that have blue flowers, such as *Veronica spicata* (spiked speedwell), or pink flowers, like *Saponaria ocymoides* (rock soapwort).

Artemisia schmidtiana 'Nana'   silvermound, wormwood,
mugwort   daisy family / Asteraceae

Hardiness: Zones 3a to 7a
Origin: Japan
Mature height: 12 to 18 in.
Mature spread: 18 in.
Landscape use: Front border; specimen; rock garden
Season of bloom: Summer
Key ornamental characteristics: Silvery-white foliage; mounded habit; scented leaves

The common name wormwood relates to this plant's use in the past to rid people of intestinal worms. In fact, some species of *Artemisia* contain the chemical santonin, which is still utilized for this purpose.

The flowers are yellow and barely noticeable. The plants are appreciated for their habit and foliage. Pruning the flowers before they open will help postpone this plant's losing its attractive habit.

One of the best features of *Artemisia schmidtiana* 'Nana' is its mounded habit, which it retains only in cooler zones of the upper Midwest. In warmer zones, the plant will flop and becomes open in the center. Warm climates can also lead to the foliage rotting. I really like

Artemisia schmidtiana 'Nana'

this plant, but in my hardiness zone, Zone 5b, because of the summer heat and humidity in the lower Midwest, I treat it as an annual.

Leaves are alternate and palmately divided into linear segments, which gives the plant a beautiful, fine texture. Leaves have a silvery-white cast and are silky soft to the touch. If leaves are crushed, they emit the tangy, fragrant odor characteristic of all members of this genus. In fact, smelling the leaves is one way to distinguish this genus from other silver-leaved genera.

Wormwood should be grown in full sun to partial shade. It prefers poor soils. In fact, rich soils promote the plant's opening up and becoming leggy. Cut back the stems to ground level in late fall, and mulch around the plant's base to help prevent rotting.

The main reported disease problem is rust. I have not encountered any disease problems with this plant.

Wormwood is a great plant to use in the front border or a rock garden. I like it intermixed with *Heuchera sanguinea* (coral bells) and *Pulsatilla vulgaris* (pasque flower). Try planting it in front of *Veronica spicata* 'Sunny Border Blue' (spiked speedwell). The silvery-white foliage works with all colors, from red and blue to yellow and white. It is a perfect foil for species that have coarse-textured or dark maroon foliage.

The foliage of *Artemisia schmidtiana* 'Nana' is so handsome that if you live in a cool enough climate, I highly recommend planting it. It adds charm and style to any garden.

Aruncus dioicus   goat's beard   rose family / Rosaceae

Hardiness: Zones 3a to 7a
Origin: North America
Mature height: 4 to 6 ft.
Mature spread: 4 to 6 ft.
Landscape use: Back border; woodland garden; shade garden
Season of bloom: Late spring to early summer
Key ornamental characteristics: Plumelike white flowers; attractive leaves and
    growth habit

In its leaves and flowers, goat's beard resembles astilbe. But it is much larger in size—so much so that it may be mistaken as a shrub. And unlike astilbe, it is native to the United States. *Aruncus dioicus* has handsome ornamental qualities.

Showy, creamy white flowers are borne in panicles rising above the foliage up to 1 ft. This species is dioecious. Male plants have more noticeable flowers of a creamy white color, while female flowers have a slight greenish cast. At times, though, it can be difficult to distinguish a male plant from a female plant.

Aruncus dioicus

Leaves are dark green, 2 to 3 ft. long, bipinnately or tripinnately compound, and alternate in arrangement. Leaflets are lanceolate, doubly serrate, and 2 to 4 in. long.

Aruncus dioicus needs moist soil conditions. It requires partial to full shade in the lower Midwest. In my Zone 5b garden, plants need ample shade. The plant grows better in the upper Midwest. In areas that have cool summers, it may be grown in full sun. If the plant is grown in conditions that are too dry, the leaflets will turn brown on the edges.

This plant has few disease or insect problems. Leaf spot may occasionally occur.

Propagation is difficult if done by division. The older the plant, the harder it is to divide plants since they have a tough root system. Transplanting goat's beard can also slow down its establishment rate. Plants may be grown from seed, but if you specifically want a male or female plant, you must wait until flowering to make that distinction.

Cultivars of *Aruncus dioicus* exist. 'Zweiweltenkind' ('Child of Two Worlds') grows to only about 3 ft., as does 'Kneiffii', whose leaflets are finely cut, giving the plant a fernlike appearance.

Goat's beard is a tremendous addition to a woodland or shade garden. The creamy white flowers visually pop in the shade. It is excellent as a specimen plant or used in small groups. Plant it beside ponds or streams. It is big enough that it can also be utilized in the shrub border. Like *Baptisia australis* (false indigo), it needs plenty of room to grow. Goat's beard is essentially an herbaceous shrub growing 4 to 6 ft. in height and spread.

The cultural requirements and mature size of *Aruncus dioicus* make it difficult to incorporate in some gardens. But if you have the right site and conditions, you will be greatly rewarded with this graceful plant. It provides a distinctive architectural element in the garden that few plants can.

Asarum canadense Canadian wild ginger   birthwort family / Aristolochiaceae

Hardiness: Zones 3a to 7b
Origin: Canada and eastern United States
Mature height: 4 to 8 in.
Mature spread: 6 to 12 in.
Landscape use: Woodland garden; shade garden; ground cover
Season of bloom: Spring
Key ornamental characteristics: Heart-shaped foliage; attractive but
    inconspicuous flowers

Wild ginger gets its name from the pungent scent of the aromatic oils contained in its leaves and rhizomes. The scent is reminiscent of culinary ginger (*Zingiber officinale*), and although early American settlers used the plant as a ginger substitute, it is not considered edible. When

Asarum canadense

Asarum canadense is happily sited, this demure plant's attractive foliage can make a lush, green carpet.

Canadian wild ginger is basically a stemless plant that has numerous pairs of light green, heart- or kidney-shaped leaves. The leaves have a downy pubescence, noticeable veins, and are up to 6 in. across. The plant is deciduous; basal leaves emerge in the spring about the time the plant blooms. While the foliage is the key attraction of this species, it can look a little tired by late autumn.

The plant's cup-shaped flowers are brownish-purple, and are borne on short stems that rise just above the ground. Because the plant blooms under the foliage growth, the flowers are inconspicuous although quaintly attractive. They are worth looking for in spring.

Canadian wild ginger is easy to grow in organically rich, moderately wet to wet, well-drained soils. Acidic soils are best, with a pH ranging from 5.5 to 6.5. It prefers full, deep shade but will withstand partial shade in the morning.

There are no serious insect or disease problems. Slugs and snails can be a problem, sometimes.

Canadian wild ginger spreads slowly by rhizomes. Therefore, propagation is best performed by dividing the rhizomes in the spring or fall. *Asarum* will self-sow, but slowly.

Asarum europaeum (European wild ginger, Zones 4 to 8) is a related species that has shiny, dark green leaves. In milder climates, it remains evergreen. It is slower growing than *A. canadense* but has the same cultural requirements.

Canadian wild ginger makes an ideal ground cover in shady areas and is literally a natural for woodland gardens. It is an elegant companion to other native plants such as *Phlox divaricata* (woodland phlox), *Tiarella cordifolia* (foamflower), and *Trillium grandiflorum* (white trillium).

Asclepias tuberosa   butterfly weed   milkweed family / Asclepidaceae

Hardiness: Zones 4a to 9a
Origin: Eastern United States
Mature height: 1 to 3 ft.
Mature spread: 2 ft.
Landscape use: Mid border; prairie, native, or
    butterfly garden; specimen; mass
Season of bloom: Summer
Key ornamental characteristics: Bright orange,
    yellow, or red flowers

Asclepias tuberosa

The vibrant flowers of *Asclepias tuberosa* are so stunning that I have picked out a single plant in a roadside garden while I was driving by at 70 miles per hour. There is variability in flower color, from orange to yellow-orange, red-orange, and pastel orange. This native plant certainly lives up to the common name butterfly weed; it is a favored source of nectar for butterflies of all types. The flowers are only ¼ in. across but are borne in umbels up to 4 in. in diameter. Cutting spent blooms will encourage additional flowering later in the season.

Leaves are lanceolate or oblong and sessile or short petioled. The foliage has a rough, hispid texture. The leaves are a source of food for monarch butterfly larvae. Stems are hairy. Unlike many other members of this genus, stems do not emit a milky sap when snapped. Butterfly weed has an upright, clump-forming habit.

Asclepias tuberosa is drought tolerant and ideal for dry, infertile soils. It thrives in full sun. The plant is slow to emerge in the spring and can be tricky to establish, so have patience until growth begins. Although the plant has "weed" in its common name, it is not aggressive and requires little maintenance. You may want to remove the seedpods prior to their splitting open, to avoid self-propagation. The seedpods are often used in dried flower arrangements.

There are no serious insect problems with butterfly weed. Wet soils can lead to crown rot. It is susceptible to rust and leaf spot.

Propagation can be easily accomplished by seed, but it may take 2 to 3 years before the plant flowers. In addition, variability in flower color will occur from seed. Division is not a good option since butterfly weed has a deep taproot and does not transplant well. The plant is best left undisturbed once established in the garden.

Asclepias tuberosa Gay Butterflies Group is a cultivar that can have orange, yellow, or red flowers. The related species *Asclepias incarnata* (swamp milkweed, Zones 3 to 8) has pinkish or white flowers. The blooms have a faint vanilla scent, and their stems exude a milky sap when cut, making the flowers difficult to use in arrangements.

Since butterfly weed has a long bloom period, it is invaluable in the mid border throughout the summer. Use it in mass groupings to create an eye-popping display or as a specimen for accent in the garden. I have planted it with the subshrub *Buddleja davidii* (butterfly bush), a fine combination for a butterfly garden. It also looks attractive with pale blue or lavender-flowering plants such as *Nepeta* ×*faassenii* (catmint). For a dramatic show, plant it with *Kniphofia uvaria* (red hot poker).

Asphodeline lutea   king's spear   asphodel family / Asphodelaceae

Hardiness: Zones 6a to 9a
Origin: Mediterranean region and Turkey
Mature height: 2 to 4 ft.
Mature spread: 1 to 2 ft.
Landscape uses: Mid to back border; wild garden; specimen
Season of bloom: Late spring to early summer
Key ornamental characteristics: Yellow, scented flowers; grasslike foliage

King's spear has scented, yellow, star-shaped flowers that are approximately 1 in. across. Flowers are borne on erect spikes that rise above the basal foliage 6 to 18 in. They open from the bottom to the top, and lower flowers are often spent before the top blooms open, especially if the weather is overly warm.

Leaves are bluish-gray, linear, and remind me of ornamental grass. Basal foliage ranges from 8 to 10 in. long. Stem leaves, which run up to the inflorescence, are 2 to 4 in. long. Cut the flower spikes back after blooms are spent to keep the plant looking tidy.

King's spear prefers full sun. It requires soils that are well drained and tolerates slightly dry sites. While soil conditions that are a little sandy and rocky are ideal, king's spear is not a xeriscape plant. Mulch the plant before winter to help it survive the cold in its northern zone limits.

There are no serious disease problems associated with king's spear. Slugs, snails, and aphids can be occasional problems.

Propagation can be done by seed or division. The fruit appears in midsummer and looks like a marble-sized watermelon. Plant seed in spring in a cold frame. Divide the plants in the fall, making sure that each rhizome has at least 2 growing points.

Asphodeline lutea 'Flore Pleno' is a cultivar with double, yellow flowers. *Asphodeline liburnica* (Zones 6 to 9), a related species, has bluish-green leaves, pale yellow flowers, and reaches a maximum height of 3 ft.

King's spear works well in the mid or back border and makes an excellent specimen plant. This clump-forming plant has a slightly unkempt appearance, making it useful for a wild garden. The relatively coarse texture of the flower spikes provides an attractive contrast with the foliage. If you are looking for something that may have people asking "What is that plant?" then king's spear could be for you. It is truly underutilized and deserving of more attention.

Asphodeline lutea

Aster novi-belgii   New York aster, Michaelmas daisy   daisy family / Asteraceae

Hardiness: Zones 4a to 8a
Origin: Eastern North America
Mature height: 3 to 5 ft. (cultivars may be shorter)
Mature spread: 2 to 4 ft.
Landscape use: Mid or back border; meadow garden; specimen
Season of bloom: Late summer to fall
Key ornamental characteristics: Showy, late-blooming flowers

When many other plants are fading toward season's end, New York aster provides a late summer and fall show of color. Flower color varies from shades of pink, red, purple, and lavender-blue, to white. The blooms are approximately 2 in. in diameter and have yellow centers.

Leaves are alternate in arrangement and lanceolate to linear. Leaf margin is entire, and

Aster novi-belgii

leaves are up to 5 in. long. Leaves are glabrous, in contrast to the pubescent leaves of the related species *Aster novae-angliae* (New England aster).

Aster novi-belgii requires full sun and well-drained soils. It tolerates a wide range of soil types but will die in wet winter soils. Taller cultivars may need to be staked, and many of the plants open up as the growing season progresses. Cut the foliage back halfway in early summer to help keep the plant compact and upright.

Powdery mildew and aster wilt are the two major disease problems associated with New York aster.

Propagation can be done by division in spring. To keep the plants healthy, dig up the clumps every 2 to 3 years; replant the newer outer parts and throw away the older center. Cuttings may be taken in spring or early summer.

There are numerous cultivars of *Aster novi-belgii* with varying degrees of height and flower color. For my garden I especially like cultivars that range from 2 to 3 ft. in height. 'Blue Lagoon' has lavender-blue flowers and grows to 2 ft. and does not require staking. Plant breeder Ernest Ballard developed many cultivars; the one named after him has dark reddish-pink flowers and grows up to 3 ft. 'Peter Harrison' grows 12 to 18 in. tall and has pink flowers. Another aster worth trying in midwestern gardens is 'October Skies', an aromatic aster (*Aster oblongifolius*, Zones 3 to 7). Growing to 18 in., it is covered with lilac-blue flowers in September and October.

New York aster is a natural in the mid or back border planted with *Sedum spectabile* (showy stonecrop sedum) and *Solidago* hybrids (goldenrod). It also looks attractive by itself surrounded by the green foliage of earlier flowering perennials. I like to use it as a specimen to highlight the autumn garden. Native to North America, the plant fits perfectly in a meadow garden.

Species of the genus *Aster* add a stunning spark of color to the fall garden.

Astilbe ×arendsii   false spirea; astilbe   saxifrage family / Saxifragaceae

Hardiness: Zones 4a to 9a
Origin: China, Japan, and Korea
Mature height: 2 to 4 ft.
Mature spread: approximately 2 ft.
Landscape use: Woodland garden; shade garden; beside ponds or streams; mass
Season of bloom: Late spring to midsummer
Key ornamental characteristics: Attractive plumelike flowers; handsome, divided leaves

Astilbe is a shade-loving plant. In fact, the most important cultural requirement for this perennial is moist soil conditions. If soil dries out, foliage will turn brown on the edges or die. The best shade condition for astilbe is dappled light filtering through trees and shrubs. *Astible ×arendsii* will grow in full sun, but the soil must be moist and rich. Mulching in summer helps retain soil moisture.

Astilbe flowers are small and borne profusely on erect or slightly arching plumes lofting above the foliage. Flower colors are shades of pink, red, lavender, and white. The blooms make excellent fresh flower arrangements if cut before completely open. Removing faded flower stalks will not prolong bloom but may improve plant appearance. The dried flower stalks have ornamental value.

Astilbes are mainstays of shade and woodland gardens. Clump-forming perennials, they feature a graceful, fernlike mound of mostly basal, 2 to 3 ternately compound leaves, usually with sharply toothed leaflets. Typically, leaves are dark green.

Astilbe ×arendsii hybrids, named after German nurseryman George Arends, are a large group of plants involving crosses of *A. chinensis*, *A. japonica*, *A. thunbergii*, and *A. astilboides*.

Astilbe ×arendsii

These hybrids can vary considerably in height and width, inflorescence color and shape, and leaf shape.

No serious insect or disease problems exist with this plant. But powdery mildew and wilt can occasionally appear. Japanese beetle and white fly may also be annoyances.

To propogate *Astilbe*, divide the crowns when clumps become overcrowded, every 3 to 4 years. Seed is also a potential method, but success rate is highly variable.

There are many *Astilbe* cultivars. 'Amethyst' has lilac-purple flowers. It typically forms a foliage mound to 1 to 2 ft. tall, with panicles rising up to 3 ft. 'Deutschland' has white flowers and a height of 2 ft. 'Fanal' has dark red flowers and bronze-green leaves. It has a mature height of 2 ft. 'Rheinland' has pink flowers and rises to 2 ft. 'Sprite' was named Perennial Plant of the Year for 1994 and has pale pink flowers. Its mature height is 12 to 18 in.

Astilbe is a perfect companion plant for hostas and ferns, adding a distinctive splash of color to shady areas, especially when planted in large groups. It looks spectacular planted beside a pond or stream catching its reflection.

Astrantia major   great masterwort   carrot family / Apiaceae

Hardiness: Zones 4a to 7a
Origin: Europe
Mature height: 2 to 3 ft.
Mature spread: 12 to 18 in.
Landscape use: Front to mid border; woodland
    garden; cottage garden
Season of bloom: Late spring to early summer
Key ornamental characteristics: Showy flowers and
    bracts; attractive foliage

Astrantia major

Do you have a shady spot with moist, rich soil? Do you live in a climate that has cool summer nights? Are you looking for a plant that is a little out of the norm? Then great masterwort may be the plant for you.

The subtle, greenish-white flowers form domed umbels that rise above the foliage. Greenish-white or pinkish involucral bracts extend under and beyond the flower, which may remain attractive after the flowers are spent. Flower heads can be used in fresh and dried arrangements.

Foliage occurs in basal clumps and is medium green in color. The leaves are palmate, having 3 to 7 (usually 5) noticeable lobes. The serrate leaves remind me somewhat of a stereotypical maple leaf. Stem leaves are sessile and smaller than clump leaves.

Great masterwort performs best when summer night temperatures fall consistently below 70°F. Soils need to be well-drained, moderately wet to wet, not allowed to dry out, and rich in organic matter. Partial to full shade is recommended for best performance. Great masterwort can be planted in sun as long as the soil is wet.

Graymold and mildew are occasional disease problems. Slugs are the primary pest of this species. Aphids can be an occasional issue.

Propagation can be accomplished by division in spring or fall. Seed can also be planted, and under optimal conditions this plant will reseed freely without being invasive.

Several *Astrantia major* cultivars are available. 'Alba' has white flowers that light up a shady area. 'Lars' has deep red flowers, as do 'Ruby Cloud' and 'Ruby Wedding'. 'Roma' is a good, clear pink. 'Sunningdale Variegated' is an unusual, lovely cultivar with variegated leaves of cream, yellow, and green. It is most attractive in spring when the leaves are new. Its flowers are pinkish-white.

Astrantia major is effective in the understory of a woodland or cottage garden. It also lends itself nicely to the front or mid border. The flowers and foliage of *Pulmonaria saccharata* (Bethlehem sage) contrast well with it. Or you can plant it with the standard favorite for moist, shady conditions, hosta.

Great masterwort has long been used in European gardens. The unique flowers and attractive foliage add a quaint splash to any setting.

Aurinia saxatilis   basket-of-gold   cabbage family / Brassicaceae

Hardiness: Zones 3a to 7a
Origin: Central and southern Europe
Mature height: 6 to 10 in.
Mature spread: 12 to 18 in.
Landscape use: Front border; rock garden; rock walls; slopes
Season of bloom: Early to mid-spring
Key ornamental characteristics: Bright yellow spring flowers; attractive gray-
    green foliage

Formerly known as *Alyssum saxatile*, basket-of-gold produces a mass of showy, yellow flowers in the spring. Densely packed in panicles, the flowers are approximately ½ in. in diameter.

Aurinia saxatilis

Despite having a low-mounded habit, this plant is highly noticeable in full bloom. Cut the plant back halfway after the flowers are spent to keep it tidy.

Basal leaves are obovate, 2 to 5 in. long, and pubescent. Leaves are usually entire but on occasion are serrate. Stem leaves are smaller than basal leaves and are subsessile. The foliage is gray-green, semievergreen to evergreen, and subtly attractive.

Basket-of-gold requires soils that are well drained, moderately fertile, and slightly dry. Heavy clay soils or overly wet conditions will probably result in rot and death. The best flowering occurs in full sun, though plant foliage benefits from light afternoon shade in hot summer climates. The species also tends to have a short life span in warmer zones. In fact, in the lower Midwest, you may need to treat this species as an annual: just plant it in very early spring and remove it after flowering.

Propagation is relatively easy by sowing seed in the spring. Division is best accomplished in the fall. Cuttings can be taken any time during the growing season.

There are no serious disease or insect problems with this plant, other than aphids on occasion.

There are several *Aurinia saxatilis* cultivars. 'Citrina' has lemon-yellow flowers and grows to 1 ft. tall. 'Dudley Nevill Variegated' grows to 10 in. It features apricot-colored flowers and gray-green leaves with creamy white margins. 'Tom Thumb' is short at 3 to 6 in. tall but is a vigorous grower.

When allowed to trail over rock walls, *Aurinia saxatilis* thrives. The plant is a must for the rock garden, and adds a splash of yellow to the front border. To make a big impact, plant drifts of basket-of-gold on a slope. *Armeria maritima* (sea pink) and *Sempervivum tectorum* (hen and chicks) are excellent companions for this plant in a rock garden.

Baptisia australis false indigo, blue indigo   pea family / Fabaceae

Hardiness: Zones 3a to 9a
Origin: Eastern North America
Mature height: 3 to 4 ft. (5 ft. in bloom)
Mature spread: 3 to 4 ft.
Landscape use: Back border; shrub border
Season of bloom: Mid to late spring
Key ornamental characteristics: Blue, lupinelike flowers; gray-green foliage; black seedpods that provide winter interest.

This plant has numerous outstanding ornamental qualities. The common names blue indigo and false indigo relate to the blue dye produced by the species *Baptisia tinctoria* (yellow wild indigo). Beautiful bluish-lavender flowers appear on racemes of *B. australis* in the mid to

Baptisia australis

late spring; the flowers are reminiscent of lupine blooms. Flower stalks reach up to 1 ft. above the foliage. To encourage further flowering, pinch off spent blooms.

Handsome blue-green leaves appear on gray-green stems, providing a perfect complement for the flowers. Leaves are comprised of 3 obovate leaflets.

The plant bears a fruit pod that is 2 to 3 in. long; it turns charcoal black when mature. Many seeds usually remain in the pod as it dries, and if you shake the pod it sounds like a rattle. The dry pods are excellent for dried flower arrangements. I like using this plant for its winter landscape effects because of the attractive pods.

Baptisia australis readily grows in full sun or partial shade and requires a lot of growing space. The habit is upright. Height and width are 3 to 4 ft. The plant is tolerant of many soil types, but prefers lime-free conditions. If grown in part shade, the plant will require staking. False indigo can become large enough to appear shrublike.

I have not observed any disease or insect problems with false indigo.

The plant is low maintenance and easy to grow. It is not aggressive and should not be divided once it is established. In my garden, in some years hundreds of seedlings have sprouted around the parent plant in the spring, but most of the seedlings have disappeared once the parent plant shades them out.

Baptisia australis var. *minor* (sometimes considered a separate species, *B. minor*, Zones 3 to 9) is more compact in form, growing to 2 ft. Another indigo that deserves mention is *Baptisia alba* (white wild indigo, Zones 5 to 8), which has white flowers that appear 2 to 4 weeks after *B. australis* first blooms. Hummingbirds are highly attracted to my *B. alba* specimen. *Baptisia sphaerocarpa* (Zones 5 to 8) has spectacular yellow flowers. Its mature height and spread are 2 to 3 ft.

I planted one *Baptisia australis* in my garden nearly 15 years ago and it faithfully emerges every spring. It is excellent as a specimen plant in the back of the cottage garden, but can also be placed in a shrub border. *Alcea* (hollyhock) placed behind *Baptisia* in the garden creates a dramatic effect. *Oenothera macrocarpa* (Ozark sundrops) is also a good companion plant.

Belamcanda chinensis   blackberry lily, leopard flower   iris family / Iridaceae

Hardiness: Zones 5a to 10b
Origin: China and Japan
Mature height: 2 to 4 ft.
Mature spread: 2 ft.
Landscape use: Mid border
Season of bloom: Summer
Key ornamental characteristics: Exotic-looking,
    spotted flowers; clustered black seeds

Belamcanda chinensis

The most outstanding feature of blackberry lily is the star-shaped flowers. Dark orange blooms are heavily dotted with red spots and resemble a smaller, less showy version of lily blooms. The spots are the source of the common name leopard flower. Borne on wiry stems, the flowers can rise as much as 1 ft. above the foliage; the plant may need staking. Approximately 2 in. across, the flowers are produced for a few weeks but individually last only 1 day. Flowers later develop a fruit pod that, when ripe, reveals seeds that look like a blackberry, thus the other common name. The fruit pods provide ornamental value in the late summer and fall garden.

Leaves are flat and sword shaped, and resemble the foliage of bearded iris hybrids. They are mid to dark green in color, and approximately 1ft. long and 1 in. wide, adding a vertical element in the garden. Blackberry lily forms clumps by rhizomes.

Blackberry lily has a slightly exotic appearance, but it is easy to grow in moist, well-drained soils. Full sun is essential. Poorly drained soils are sure to be this plant's end, especially in winter. It will grow but not thrive in dry soils. Blackberry lily tends to be short lived, so a layer of winter mulch is recommended in its northern zones.

Propagation is best by seed. Blackberry lily will self-sow under optimal conditions; it will flower in the second year. Division can also be accomplished in the early spring.

The major insect problem is iris borer, which feeds on the rhizomes. Prompt removal of dead leaves and cutting the plant back in late fall will help keep this pest at bay. Rust and leaf spot can be minor disease problems.

The *Belamcanda chinensis* cultivar 'Freckle Face' has pale orange flowers and a mature height of 12 to 16 in. *Belamcanda flabellata* (Zones 4 to 9) is a related species with greenish-gray foliage. *Belamcanda flabellata* 'Hello Yello' is a handsome cultivar that has unspotted yellow flowers. A favorite of mine in this genus, it grows to 1 ft. tall.

The orange flower color of *Belamcanda chinensis* strongly complements blue flowers. So place the plant behind a blue-flowering species like *Nepeta* ×*faassenii* (catmint). Blackberry lily is ideal for the mid border in small groupings.

Bergenia cordifolia heartleaf bergenia, pigsqueak saxifrage family / Saxifragaceae

Bergenia cordifolia

Hardiness: Zones 3a to 8a
Origin: Siberia and central and eastern Asia
Mature height: 12 to 18 in.
Mature spread: 1 ft.
Landscape use: Front to mid border; rock garden; ground cover; woodland garden; mass
Season of bloom: Spring
Key ornamental characteristics: Bold foliage; early pink flowers

Pigsqueak! This plant gets its common name from the adage that when you rub a wet leaf of this plant between your thumb and finger, it will make a squeaking noise like a pig.

The shiny, dark green foliage has a leathery feel and a coarse, attractive texture. Leaves are toothed, rounded, heart shaped at the base, and up to 10 in. long. Evergreen in warmer climates, the foliage can become tattered in colder zones during the winter, so remove damaged leaves. Foliage is an attractive reddish-purple during the fall and winter, adding great interest to the garden. The leaves have great ornamental value so they are often used in floral arrangements. The plant has a clump-forming habit.

The pink blooms of pigsqueak are borne on scapes that rise a few inches above the foliage. Remove spent blooms to keep the plant tidy.

Pigsqueak is easy to grow in a wide range of well-drained soil types. But it prefers moist, organically rich soils. It grows in full sun but prefers partial shade, especially in warmer regions; it does not do well with extreme heat or drought.

Spreading slowly by rhizomes, pigsqueak is best propagated by division in the spring. Sowing seed is also viable.

There are no serious insect or disease problems with pigsqueak. Slugs and snails can be a problem. Fungal leaf spot may occur from time to time.

Many plants labeled *Bergenia cordifolia* may be hybrids of *B. cordifolia* and *B. purpurascens*. 'Bressingham Ruby' has pink blooms and great fall and winter reddish-purple leaf color. 'Morgenröte' ('Morning Red') has carmine-red flowers. 'Silberlicht' ('Silver Light') has white flowers tinged with pink that have red centers.

Use pigsqueak in shaded front borders or rock gardens. It makes an excellent edging along walks and pathways or is a good ground cover for woodland gardens. Because of its rich fall and winter foliage color, I recommend using it with other plants of winter ornamental interest: for example, *Cornus alba* (Tatarian dogwood), with its red stems in winter, or *Helleborus* (Christmas or Lenten rose). Or plant it with early spring-flowering bulbs.

Bletilla striata   Chinese ground orchid   orchid family / Orchidaceae

Hardiness: Zones 5a to 9b
Origin: China
Mature height: 8 to 12 in.
Mature spread: 10 in.
Landscape use: Front border; rock garden; woodland garden; container
Season of bloom: Spring
Key ornamental characteristics: Exotic-looking lowers; handsome foliage

---

For everyone who has dreamed of having an orchid in the garden, here is your chance. And if you live north of Zone 5, you might want to plant this magnificent perennial in a container, so you can bring it inside in the winter.

Chinese ground orchid has 3 to 10 purplish-pink blooms on racemes that artfully rise to just above the foliage. Each exotic-looking flower is up to 1½ in. wide. The gorgeous blooms last 2 to 3 weeks.

Each pseudobulb produces 3 to 5 pale green, sword-shaped leaves that are 6 to 10 in. long. The leaves are upright and have a papery texture, providing an elegant backdrop for the flowers.

Bletilla striata (also known as *Bletilla hyacinthina*) requires partial shade even in its northern zones, and needs rich, moist, well-drained soil. Dry conditions will cause a reduction in flowers the next year or may bring about the plant's demise. It appreciates a little extra fertilizer during the growing season. Chinese ground orchid may not be winter hardy in northern zones. The pseudobulbs also can be dug after the foliage has died back and replanted in spring. Otherwise, the plant needs a layer of winter mulch.

Aphids, spider mites, mealybugs, and whitefly may be occasional pests. In addition, snails and slugs may cause damage.

Propagation is by division of the pseudobulbs. Cut them in the fall. If dug and brought in

Bletilla striata

for the winter, store them in a dry, frost-free area. Chinese ground orchid will naturalize by rhizomes under ideal growing conditions.

A few *Bletilla striata* cultivars are available. 'Alba' has creamy white flowers. 'Albostriata' ('Variegata') has foliage with creamy white stripes. Flowers are the same color as for the species.

Chinese ground orchid is perfect in woodland and rock gardens. It looks attractive with *Aquilegia* (columbine), *Brunnera macrophylla* (summer forget-me-not), or ferns. I prefer to use the plant in small groupings to offer the full aesthetic impact of the flowers. It is also appropriate for use in containers, where cultural conditions can be easily satisfied.

I seldom see this attractive plant in gardens. Perhaps it is unknown to the general public. You might want to seek out this special plant so you can enjoy its showy flowers.

Boltonia asteroides   boltonia, white boltonia   daisy family / Asteraceae

Hardiness: Zones 3b to 10a
Origin: Eastern United States
Mature height: 5 to 6 ft.
Mature spread: 2 to 4 ft.
Landscape use: Back border; meadow garden;
   naturalized area
Season of bloom: Late summer to frost
Key ornamental characteristics: Profuse white or
   pink flowers

Boltonia asteroides

Boltonia asteroides puts on a big flower show at the end of summer and into fall. The plant is truly a charmer.

The daisylike flowers are white, pale pink, or lavender and have a yellow center disk. Profusely borne on panicles, they are approximately ¾ in. in diameter. The flowers are a magnet for butterflies and are attractive in dried floral arrangements.

Foliage is grayish-green. Leaves are linear to lanceolate, sessile, 3 to 5 in. long, and alternate in arrangement.

Boltonia tolerates a broad range of soil types as long it gets moderate moisture and good drainage. It also performs admirably in dry soils. Boltonia needs full sun to maintain an upright habit, and will flop if it is sited in shade and rich, moist soils. If your plant flops, cut back the stems by one-third in late spring or early summer to reduce height and the need for staking.

Propagation can be done by division in spring or fall—ideally in spring so flowering is not disrupted. Sowing seed is also viable, but the cultivars may not come true to type, or look exactly like the plant the seeds were collected from. Tip cuttings can also be taken in spring.

The straight species *Boltonia asteroides* is not frequently sold; the cultivars make for better garden plants. 'Pink Beauty' has attractive pale pink blooms and grows to 5 ft. tall. It will probably need staking. *Boltonia asteroides* var. *latisquama* 'Snowbank' has white flowers and a compact habit, growing 3 to 4 ft. tall. It may not need staking if sited in full sun.

Boltonia is relatively free of disease and insect problems. Powdery mildew may be an occasional problem.

Plant boltonia if you have ample space for it in your garden. Its size and upright habit make it a perfect choice for the back border of an informal or native plant garden. It is also excellent for use in naturalized areas. Plant it with the charming *Anemone ×hybrida* (hybrid anemone), *Aster* spp., *Perovskia atriplicifolia* (Russian sage), or *Solidago* hybrids (goldenrod).

I have seen *Boltonia* specimens at the Missouri Botanical Garden in Saint Louis with end-of-season blooms that could hardly be matched by flowers of any species.

Brunnera macrophylla   summer forget-me-not, Siberian bugloss   borage
family / Boraginaceae

Brunnera macrophylla

Hardiness: Zones 3a to 7b
Origin: Caucasus
Mature height: 12 to 18 in.
Mature spread: 12 to 18 in.
Landscape use: Front border; specimen plant;
    ground cover
Season of bloom: Early to late spring
Key ornamental characteristics: Pale blue flowers;
    attractive heart-shaped leaves

Summer forget-me-not is one of my all-time favorite plants. I love the 1/8- to 1/4-in.-diameter, azure-blue, star-shaped flowers. They remind me of *Myosotis* blooms, and have a yellow center. The tiny flowers rise on a raceme several inches above the foliage.

The dark green leaves, which can be up to 8 in. wide, have a rounded heart shape. They remain attractive throughout the summer. Leaves and stems are covered with a coarse pubescence, and are interesting to touch.

In colder climates, morning sun will be tolerated, but in the lower Midwest, *Brunnera macrophylla* requires shade. It is tolerant of different soil types, but must have moisture no matter what hardiness zone you are located in. Dry soil will bring a quick demise to this plant.

Brunnera macrophylla is excellent in the front border of a shade garden. It also fits perfectly in a woodland garden or near a stream or pond. I often plant it near or under plants that provide ample shade: for example, *Iris sibirica* (Siberian iris), or a shrub such as *Syringa* (lilac). *Brunnera macrophylla* also works well with plants that require similar cultural conditions, such as *Hosta* spp., *Polemonium caeruleum* (Jacob's ladder), and ferns.

Propagation can be accomplished by sowing seeds in a cold frame. Slowly spreading by clumps, the rhizomes can be divided in the spring.

There are only three species in this genus, with *Brunnera macrophylla* being the one of garden value. The eye-catching cultivar 'Jack Frost' is a sport of *B. macrophylla* 'Langtrees'; it has silvery-white leaves. Variegated cultivars are pricy but are worth it if you can provide proper cultural conditions.

I have not encountered any disease or insect problems. Slugs and snails can be an issue.

Summer forget-me-not reputedly freely seeds itself. But I have grown this charming plant for years, and this has not happened in my garden. *Brunnera macrophylla* is not aggressive and is easy to pull up, however, if it self-sows in your garden. It truly deserves to be used more.

Calamagrostis ×acutiflora   feather reed grass   grass family / Poaceae

Hardiness: Zones 4a to 8a
Origin: Hybrid
Mature height: 4 to 5 ft.
Mature spread: 24 to 30 in.
Landscape use: Back border; mass; wet areas
Season of bloom: Late spring to summer
Key ornamental characteristics: Feathery panicles
    of flowers; dark green foliage; upright habit;
    winter interest

Calamagrostis ×acutiflora 'Karl Foerster'

Feather reed grass is one of the earliest ornamental grasses to flower. It has interesting ornamental characteristics throughout a good portion of the year. The plant's erect habit adds vertical line to the garden or landscape, and the plant is small enough to use in small gardens.

The flowers are borne in panicles up to 18 in. long that rise above the foliage. Feathery in appearance, the flowers are greenish-purple, turning pink to golden yellow before the seeds mature and changing to a straw yellow in summer. Remaining on the plant well into winter, the blooms add interest to the landscape for much of the year. They are excellent to use in fresh or dried flower arrangements.

Leaves are dark green and hairless. Blades are finely pointed and up to 3 ft. long and ½ in. wide. Feather reed grass is coarse in appearance and rough to the touch. It turns tan in winter. In warm winter regions, it may remain semievergreen.

Feather reed grass is easy to grow in a wide range of soil types. Unlike many other ornamental grasses, it performs well in heavy clay. It prefers moist soils that do not dry out, but it will tolerate dry sites. Place this plant in full sun. It can withstand partial shade, but will likely flop and produce fewer flowers. In warmer hardiness zones, the plant appreciates light afternoon shade. Feather reed grass is a cool-season grass, so it performs well in regions where it will get enough winter chill. Cut clumps to the ground in late winter just before new shoots appear.

There are no serious insect or disease problems associated with feather reed grass.

Propagation is best done by division in spring. Unlike some grasses, feather reed grass is not aggressive and spreads slowly.

The cultivars of *Calamagrostis* ×*acultiflora* are generally sterile and will not self-sow. 'Karl Foerster' is a popular, rigidly upright cultivar frequently used in the landscape. It was named Perennial Plant of the Year for 2001. It grows to 4 ft. in height. 'Overdam' is also popular; it has white stripes on the green foliage.

I like to use feather reed grass in the back border. Place *Rudbeckia fulgida* (black-eyed Susan) or *Monarda didyma* (bee balm) in front of it for interesting contrast in texture and flower shape. It also works well as a specimen or used in mass in the landscape. Feather reed grass is at home close to the water.

Callirhoe involucrata   poppy mallow   mallow family / Malvaceae

Hardiness: Zones 3b to 9a
Origin: Western United States
Mature height: 4 to 6 in.
Mature spread: 2 to 3 ft.
Landscape use: Front border; rock garden; slopes, specimen
Season of bloom: Late spring to frost
Key ornamental characteristics: Vibrant magenta flowers; attractive leaves

This under-used species is truly a must-have for the garden. The eye-catching, bright magenta flowers are 2 in. wide and cup shaped; they close in the evening. The single flowers are borne on erect stems. Poppy mallow produces blooms nonstop all summer. The flowers of poppy mallow are similar to *Malva* but mainly differ by having petals that are irregularly cut at the apex; *Malva* has one notch at the apex. Do not let the delicate appearance of *Callirhoe involucrata* fool you; this species is as tough as it is beautiful.

The foliage is dark green and highly attractive. Leaves are alternate, hairy, and deeply cut,

Callirhoe involucrata

with 5 or 7 lobes; they have a similar appearance to leaves of *Geranium* spp. In warmer zones, foliage may remain evergreen in the winter.

Poppy mallow thrives in full sun, and in clay and well-drained soils. It is highly drought resistant because of its deep taproot, and does not like wet soils. The plant is slow to become established the first year, but the second year's growth is rapid. If it gets leggy during the growing season, cut it back, and it will quickly produce new growth.

Propagation is easy. Seeds that germinate around the parent plant can be transplanted. Stem cuttings 4 in. long should be taken in the early summer. Division is possible, but take care with the deep root system.

There are no real insect or disease problems associated with poppy mallow. Crown rot may occur in poorly drained soils.

Poppy mallow's low sprawling habit makes it ideal for use along pathways. Because it grows along the ground, plant it at least 1 ft. away from a path. It is also ideal for use in rock gardens and as a trailing plant over walls. It works well with most other plant species in the garden.

Callirhoe involucrata is a native plant that is almost foolproof.

Campanula carpatica   Carpathian harebell, Carpathian bellflower

campanula family / Campanulaceae

Campanula carpatica 'Blaue Clips'
© Ewa Brozek

Hardiness: Zones 3a to 7b
Origin: Eastern Europe
Mature height: 8 to 12 in.
Mature spread: 12 in.
Landscape uses: Front border; rock gardens;
    pathways
Season of bloom: Summer
Key ornamental characteristics: Charming blue to
    white flowers

Think of the genus *Campanula* and irresistible blue, bell-shaped flowers may come to mind. *Campanula carpatica* produces singly borne, lilac-blue flowers that are approximately 2 in. in diameter and face upward on the stem. Cultivars with white or purple flowers are also available. Of the *Campanula* species available, *C. carpatica* is one of the most popular and is the easiest to find.

Foliage is dark green, ovate or triangular, and serrate. It offers an attractive backdrop for the flowers.

Carpathian harebell performs best in cool climates that are not overly humid. So it performs better in the upper Midwest than in the lower Midwest. It tolerates a wide range of soil conditions, but it needs good drainage. It prefers full sun but will do well in partial shade, especially in warmer zones. A layer of mulch in the summer will help keep the root zone cool and will make the plant happy. Deadheading spent blooms may prolong the flowering period of this plant.

There are no disease or insect problems of major consequence with this plant. Snails and slugs can be a burden at times by munching on the foliage.

Propagation may be accomplished by division or seed. To keep plants healthy, divide them every 2 to 3 years in the early spring or fall. Seed sown in spring germinates in approximately 3 weeks.

Numerous *Campanula* cultivars are available. Two cultivars of *Campanula carpatica* f. *alba* are 'Bressingham White', compact at 6 in. in height, with beautiful white blooms; and 'Weisse Clips' ('White Clips'), with lovely white flowers. *Campanula carpatica* 'China Doll' grows to 9 in. tall and has pale lavender-blue flowers. 'Blaue Clips' ('Blue Clips') is an outstanding plant that grows to 9 in. tall, with rich blue flowers.

Try *Campanula carpatica* with other nonaggressive plants like *Coreopsis verticillata* (thread-leaf coreopsis) 'Moonbeam' or 'Zagreb', *Dianthus* spp. (garden pinks), or *Stachys byzantina* (lamb's ear). Use this plant in the front border or along pathways. Its small habit also makes it ideal for rock gardens and compact areas.

Campanula poscharskyana   Serbian bellflower   campanula family / Campanulaceae

Hardiness: Zones 3b to 7b
Origin: Southeastern Europe
Mature height: 4 to 6 in.
Mature spread: 12 to 18 in.
Landscape use: Front border; rock garden; walls; pathways
Season of bloom: Late spring to early summer
Key ornamental characteristics: Sky blue flowers; prostrate habit

There are approximately 300 species in the genus *Campanula*. Serbian bellflower is one of the low-growing species, having a prostrate, sprawling habit and reaching a mature height of 6 in. at most.

Campanula poscharskyana

Serbian bellflower has gorgeous sky blue flowers with flaring, star-shaped lobes that face upward. The flowers are up to 1 in. in diameter, and create quite an impact when planted in mass. Flowering time is longer in the cooler, upper Midwest.

Medium green leaves have long petioles and are oval-rounded to cordate. Leaf arrangement is alternate, and there is a layer of hairs on the underside of the leaves. In warmer climates, the foliage may remain evergreen or semievergreen during the winter.

Campanula poscharskyana is easy to grow in most soils with regular moisture. But the soil must be well drained, especially in winter. If you have mulched your plant for the winter, remove the mulch in early spring, or moisture might rot the crown. Serbian bellflower will grow in full sun or part shade, but prefers some shade in warmer climates. It also prefers relatively cool summer nights. The plant can spread rapidly but is not overly aggressive. If necessary, just trim it back.

Propagation is by division or seed. The clumps are best divided in spring.

There are no serious insect or disease problems with this plant. The biggest problem is snails and slugs, which like to chew on the stems.

The cultivar *Campanula poscharskyana* 'Blue Gown' is larger than the species and has light blue flowers. 'Stella' has dark blue flowers.

This native of the former Yugoslavian region is ideal for the rock garden or for use as an edging for paths or the front border. The plant can be stunning when it is allowed to sprawl over walls or along embankments. It looks attractive planted with the silvery-white-leaved *Stachys byzantina* (lamb's ear). *Heuchera sanguinea* (coral bells) also complements it beautifully. Or you can place it in a container pot.

Serbian bellflower is an excellent plant. In a genus of mostly larger species, this little gem shines.

Campanula punctata   spotted bellflower, bellflower   campanula family / Campanulaceae

Hardiness: Zones 4b to 8a
Origin: Siberia and Japan
Mature height: 12 to 18 in.
Mature spread: 10 to 16 in.
Landscape use: Front or mid border; specimen plant; naturalized areas
Season of bloom: Late spring to early summer
Key ornamental characteristics: Gorgeous, white to dusky pink flowers; attractive foliage

Few plants usher in summer like the genus *Campanula*. Of all the species, *Campanula punctata*, an upright, clump-forming, heavy-blooming plant, is one of my favorites.

Large, tubular, bell-shaped flowers are white or dusky pink. The pendulous flowers are up to 2 in. long; look closely and you will see their purple-spotted throats. Flower buds have an interesting 5-ridged shape, and are fastened to the stem by long, green calyxes.

The attractive, dark green, triangular-shaped leaves provide a perfect foil for the blooms. Noticeably serrate, the leaves are alternate in arrangement and up to 5 in. long.

Campanula punctata prefers full sun to partial shade, but requires some full shade in hotter regions. It grows in a wide range of soil types but thrives in fertile, sandy loam. The plant needs consistent moisture and it benefits from a layer of summer mulch. It is not tolerant of dry locations or poorly drained soils, and it does not like overly wet winter soils. It will not perform well where night temperatures remain above 70°F.

There are no disease or insect problems of consequence associated with *Campanula punctata*. Aphids can be a minor pest.

Propagation is best by division or seed. Under optimum growing conditions, this plant spreads vigorously by rhizomes. Division can be easily accomplished in spring or fall. Seed is viable, and the plant may self-sow in the garden.

Campanula punctata

Campanula punctata 'Cherry Bells' is an excellent cultivar; it grows about 15 to 24 in. tall and has dusky pink blooms. 'Pink Chimes' has attractive pink flowers and grows to 1 ft. tall with a slightly broader spread.

Spotted bellflower is well placed in the front or mid border. I prefer to have a few specimen plants, because it tends to be aggressive like many species in this wonderful genus. To contain it, place a root barrier around it or plant it in a sunken pot. If you have a large area, it is beautiful when allowed to naturalize. *Gaura lindheimeri* (white gaura) is an attractive companion plant for the lower Midwest, or try placing it with *Artemisia schmidtiana* 'Nana' (silvermound).

Centaurea montana   mountain bluet, perennial bachelor's button   daisy
family / Asteraceae

Centaurea montana

Hardiness: Zones 3a to 8a
Origin: Europe
Mature height: 1 to 2 ft.
Mature spread: 12 to 18 in.
Landscape use: Mid or front border; cottage garden
Season of bloom: Early summer
Key ornamental characteristics: True blue flowers

Distinctive blue flowers are the primary attraction of this species. Up to 2½ in. wide, the blossoms are essentially a larger version of the flowers of the annual *Centaurea cyanus* (bachelor's button). Solitary blooms appear in early summer on unbranched stems; they have bluish-red centers and black involucral margins. The species tends to be a light bloomer. Cut the spent flower stalks to the ground for rebloom later in the season.

Leaves are lanceolate to obovate-lanceoltae and alternate in arrangement. Lower leaves can be up to 8 in. long. Leaf margins are toothed. Young leaves have a silvery-white cast, while older leaves are grayish green.

Mountain bluet is easy to grow in average, well-drained soils. It tolerates drought and prefers alkaline soils that are dry to medium wet. It actually likes poor-quality soils; avoid planting it in rich, humus-amended sites. This plant prefers the cooler upper Midwest climates. It can be invasive, spreading by stolons.

Propagation is by division or seed. I recommend division; the plant should be divided every 2 to 3 years.

Potential disease problems include rust, stem rot, and aster yellows, but these problems do not occur often. There are no significant insect issues associated with mountain bluet.

The cultivar *Centaurea montana* 'Alba' has white flowers. 'Carnea' ('Rosea') has attractive pink flowers. *Centaurea hypoleuca* 'John Coutts' (John Coutts knapweed, Zones 3 to 7) is an attractive species with pink flowers and lobed, dark green leaves. Height and spread are similar to *C. montana*.

Centaurea montana is an upright, clump-forming plant. Because of relatively sparse flower production, it should be planted in mass to render the full impact of its unique blue blossoms. It is ideal for a cottage garden or naturalized area.

Cerastium tomentosum   snow-in-summer   carnation family / Carophyllaceae

Hardiness: Zones 2b to 7a
Origin: Italy and Sicily
Mature height: 3 to 8 in. (6 to 10 in. in flower)
Mature spread: 1 ft.
Landscape use: Front border; rock gardens; stone wall plantings; pathways
Season of bloom: Spring
Key ornamental characteristics: Abundant white flowers; gray foliage

Cerastium tomentosum is a plant with two valuable ornamental qualities. First, its profuse, clear white flowers rise above the foliage in spring, creating a stunning sight. The flower is up to 1 in. in diameter. Each of the 5 petals is deeply notched, making the blooms appear to have 10 petals. Cut back spent flowers and the foliage to keep the plant tidy.

Second, the woolly foliage is attractive. Leaves are linear in shape, up to ¾ in. long, ⅛ in. wide, and opposite in arrangement. They are fuzzy and have a silvery-gray cast. The leaf hairs help the plant conserve moisture.

Snow-in-summer performs best in the cooler regions of the upper Midwest. It prefers full sun and soil with good drainage and low fertility. The plant will rot if the soil has poor drainage. It does not perform well in heat and humidity, so in warmer regions provide plants with partial shade. In my Zone 5b garden, snow-in-summer needs some shade to survive. How-

Cerastium tomentosum

ever, the plant spreads by runners, and if planted in moist, fertile soil, it can be rampant in growth. This perennial tends to be short lived; foliage can develop dead patches as it ages.

There are no serious disease or insect problems associated with snow-in-summer.

Propagation is easy. Seed germinates readily in the spring. This species may self-sow in the garden if the previous year's spent blooms are not removed. Division can be done in spring or fall, but take great care with the root system.

The cultivar *Cerastium tomentosum* 'Columnae' has white flowers and is more compact than the species, growing to 4 in. tall. 'Yo Yo' is a popular cultivar with white flowers.

Snow-in-summer forms a mat, so it is an excellent ground cover. Use it in the front border, rock garden, stone wall plantings, or between stepping-stones. The white flowers and silver-gray foliage go well with all plants. Try interplanting spring bulbs with snow-in-summer for an early season show.

Ceratostigma plumbaginoides leadwort, plumbago leadwort family / Plumbaginaceae

Hardiness: Zones 5a to 9a
Origin: Asia
Mature height: 5 to 10 in.
Mature spread: 12 to 18 in.
Landscape use: Front border; pathways; rock garden
Season of bloom: Summer to early fall
Key ornamental characteristics: Late-blooming, bright blue flowers; attractive fall
    foliage

Leadwort is quaintly attractive. Spreading by rhizomes, it forms a dense, matlike ground cover.

Flowers are deep blue, 5-petaled, and up to ¾ in. in diameter. Resembling blooms of *Phlox divaricata* (woodland phlox), they are borne in terminal groups that rise slightly above the foliage all summer and into the fall.

Leaves are alternate in arrangement, 2 in. long, and ovate. In fall the foliage turns bronzy-red in cooler climates. This groundcover can be used like *Vinca*, *Pachysandra*, and *Hedera helix*, except it does not remain evergreen like they do.

Leadwort is easy to grow in average, medium-wet, well-drained soils in full sun to part shade. It tolerates a wide range of soil types except for overly wet, poorly drained ones. It easily withstands afternoon shade. Sometimes the plant is not winter hardy in Zone 5, so there it will benefit from a layer of mulch. Furthermore, the previous year's foliage should be cut back in the spring. The plant can be mildly invasive under optimum cultural conditions.

Ceratostigma plumbaginoides

There are no serious insect or disease problems associated with *Ceratostigma plumbaginoides*.

Ceratostigma griffithii, a related species, has red leaf margins and remains evergreen. Growing up to 2 ft. in height, it has dark blue flowers and is reliable in Zones 6 to 8 (the extreme lower Midwest).

Leadwort is ideal as a groundcover or edging plant; also place it in the front border or rock garden. The foliage is slow to emerge in spring, so it is a good choice for intermixing with spring bulbs. My neighbor has had the same leadwort planting as an edging along the front walk for over 20 years. It can also be placed under other perennials or shrubs in the border.

Chasmanthium latifolium   northern sea oats   grass family / Poaceae

Hardiness: Zones 4a to 8b
Origin: United States
Mature height: 30 in. to 3 ft.
Mature spread: 12 to 18 in.
Landscape use: Mid border; specimen; naturalized areas
Season of bloom: Summer
Key ornamental characteristics: Attractive seed heads, foliage; winter interest

Chasmanthium latifolium

Northern sea oats is a handsome species that provides ornamental interest all year. The plant provides tremendous contrast and texture in the garden. I have grown the same specimen in my garden for approximately 10 years, and I truly enjoy it as an accent plant.

This clump-forming, upright plant has flat, bright green foliage. Leaves are approximately ½ in. wide and 5 to 10 in. long. The stems are 2 to 3 ft. long. The foliage turns cooper-brown in fall and natural tan in the winter. Leaving the foliage over the winter helps protect the crowns and adds winter interest. Cut it back to the ground in early spring.

Small, silvery-white flowers occur on very thin, pendulous panicles. Seed heads are flat, thin, and occur in terminal clusters. Bright green in color, they change to purplish-green-brown in late summer and tan-brown in winter. Extremely graceful in appearance, they sway in the slightest breeze. The attractive seed heads are the ornamental highlight of this plant; they are excellent for dried flower arrangements.

Northern sea oats is easy to grow in a wide range of soil types. It prefers moist soils that are well drained. It thrives in full sun, and unlike many other ornamental grass species, it grows well in partial shade. It can self-seed prolifically. *Chasmanthium latifolium* also spreads by underground runners. To contain this species, place it in a container sunk into the ground. Although highly attractive, removing the seedheads before they mature will reduce unwanted seedlings.

There are no serious disease or insect problems associated with northern sea oats.

Propagation is easily accomplished by division in spring or fall. It is also easy to grow plants from seed.

I like northern sea oats with *Sedum spectabile* (showy stonecrop sedum), for a bold winter statement. It also works well in semishade gardens, naturalized sites, and moist areas.

Chelone lyonii   pink turtlehead   figwort family / Scrophulariaceae

Hardiness: Zones 3b to 9a
Origin: Eastern United States
Mature height: 2 to 3 ft.
Mature spread: 18 to 24 in.
Landscape use: Mid border; Semishade or
    woodland garden; beside ponds, streams
Season of bloom: Late summer to early fall
Key ornamental characteristics: Unusual, clear pink
    flowers

Chelone lyonii

Reminiscent of snapdragon flowers, individual blossoms of *Chelone lyonii* resemble a turtle's head with the mouth open. The common name makes the plant an interesting inclusion for a children's garden. Flowers are clear pink and clustered around a terminal spike.

Leaves are opposite in arrangement, glabrous, and have long petioles. The dark green leaves are lanceolate to ovate, serrate, and up to 6 in. long. The plant's habit is upright and clump forming.

Pink turtlehead prefers partial shade but will also thrive in full sun if it receives adequate moisture. That is the trick with this plant: it must be sited in moist, boggy soil. It is tolerant of a wide range of soil types but thrives in rich soil conditions. If the site is too shady, the plant will flop and need staking. Pinch pink turtlehead back in spring or early summer to make the plant more compact and less likely to flop.

Propagation is easy by division in spring. Pink turtlehead spreads slowly by rhizomes to form large clumps but is not invasive. Seed is viable, and it may self-sow in moist soils. Stem cuttings can also be taken in the early summer.

No serious disease or insect problems exist with pink turtlehead. There is some susceptibility to mildew, though, especially if the plant is growing in dry soil and receiving poor air circulation.

There are several interesting related species. *Chelone glabra* (white turtlehead, Zones 3 to 8) has white flowers that sometimes have a faint pink cast. It prefers full sun and the same soil conditions as *C. lyonii*. *Chelone obliqua* (rose turtlehead, Zones 3 to 9) has veined leaves and dark pink flowers.

I have used pink turtlehead with *Astilbe ×arendsii* (false spirea), hosta, and *Pulmonaria saccharata* (Bethlehem sage). It is a natural with *Eupatorium purpureum* subsp. *maculatum* (Joe-Pye weed), since both perform at their best in moist soils and plenty of sun.

Pink turtlehead is ideal for a semishade or woodland garden. It also is at home around a pond or other water area.

Convallaria majalis lily-of-the-valley lily-of-the-valley family / Convallariaceae

Hardiness: Zones 2b to 7a
  Origin: Northern Hemisphere
  Mature height: 6 to 10 in.
  Mature spread: 1 ft.
  Landscape use: Ground cover; shade or woodland
    garden
  Season of bloom: Mid-spring
  Key ornamental characteristics: Fragrant white
    flowers; attractive foliage

This plant is much loved for its fragrant, white flowers. The delicate-looking, bell-shaped blossoms are borne on arching, leafless stems. Flowers are small at approximately ⅓ in. across. Distinctive as cut flowers, they are often sought after for wedding bouquets. A word of caution regarding *Convallaria majalis*: all parts of the plant are reported to be mildly poisonous if ingested. The red berries may be attractive to small children, so you might want to cut spent flowers before the fruit matures.

Each plant has 2 or 3 erect leaves that are 4 to 8 in. long and 1 to 3 in. wide. Lanceolate-ovate to elliptic, the leaves are medium green.

Convallaria majalis

Lily-of-the-valley is a rhizomatous plant. It spreads freely if growing in favorable conditions. It thrives in the cooler climates of the upper Midwest in partial shade and moist, rich soil. It also needs at least a few weeks of true, cold winter weather to flower at its best. If the plant gets too much sun in warmer climates and the soil is dry, leaves will become scorched, especially on the margins. If it gets too much shade, flower production may be reduced. Also, if flowering becomes sparse, the plants may need to be thinned.

Propagation is easy by division; the plants may be divided in spring or fall. A light layer of mulch applied in fall will help the plant become established.

Anthracnose, leaf spot, and stem rot are occasional problems with lily-of-the-valley. I have not encountered any insect trouble with this plant.

A few cultivars of *Convallaria majalis* are available. 'Flora Pleno', also known as 'Plena', has double white flowers that are larger than those of the species. 'Fortin's Giant' lives up to its name, having flowers that are up to ¾ in. long and foliage that is 12 to 15 in. tall. *Convallaria majalis* var. *rosea* has pale pink blooms, while *Convallaria majalis* 'Albostriata' has thin, creamy white stripes on the green leaves and white flowers.

Lily-of-the-valley makes an excellent ground cover and is ideal under shade trees. I recommend caution about incorporating it into a perennial bed because of its tendency to spread. I grow lily-of-the-valley under *Syringa* (lilac) shrubs in my garden. It makes a beautiful statement when massed, and adds appealing texture when interplanted with ferns.

Despite the plant's delicate appearance, lily-of-the-valley is a rugged perennial. It can even be mowed over without causing permanent harm. If you have the right conditions, just plant, sit back, and enjoy this romantic favorite.

Coreopsis grandiflora   coreopsis, tickseed, lance coreopsis   daisy family / Asteraceae

Hardiness: Zones 4a to 9a
Origin: Central United States; many hybrids
Mature height: 2 to 3 ft.
Mature spread: 12 to 18 in.
Landscape use: Mid border; meadow or naturalized area; specimen
Season of bloom: Late spring to summer
Key ornamental characteristics: Bright yellow flowers

Coreopsis grandiflora is planted abundantly in many landscapes. The plant is popular because of its bright yellow flowers that are produced all summer long. Flowers are up to 2½ in. in diameter and make a great show. The key to keeping this plant looking attractive is to deadhead the spent flowers to the nearest leaf. Then it will bloom in mass again. Removing spent flowers also prevents unwanted self-seeding.

Leaves are opposite and lanceolate, spatulate, or linear. The lowermost leaves are simple, while the upper ones have 3 to 5 deep lobes. If the plant develops an unkempt appearance during the summer, cut it back hard to produce a new flush of growth.

There are no serious disease or insect problems with coreopsis. But leaf spot, rust,

Coreopsis grandiflora

powdery mildew, and spotted cucumber beetle can be nuisances. Removing spent flowers can help keep disease problems at bay.

Coreopsis thrives in full sun, high humidity, and any type of well-drained soil. Avoid overly moist soil, which will result in soft, leafy growth and fewer flowers. It thrives in relatively dry locations. If coreopsis is grown in moist and overly fertile soils, it can flop.

Propagation is best done by cuttings. Seed is easy to germinate, and the plant produces many seeds. The common name tickseed comes from the fact that the black seeds resemble ticks. Division should be done in spring or fall every 2 or 3 years to keep the plant vigorous. Coreopsis tends to be short lived.

The cultivar *Coreopsis grandiflora* 'Early Sunrise' has semidouble, yellow flowers, and tends to have a short life span. 'Sunray' has double, golden-yellow flowers. 'Sundancer' is a dwarf coreopsis noted for its short height, double blossoms, and spreading growth habit. The related species *Coreopsis tripteris* (Zones 3 to 8) grows 4 to 10 in. tall and is ideal for large landscape situations. The yellow flowers have a mild anise scent.

Coreopsis grandiflora is ideal for use in the mid border. I have used it with *Perovskia atriplicifolia* (Russian sage) and *Liatris spicata* (spike gayfeather). It is effective in meadows, cottage gardens, and naturalized areas. Try it also with *Penstemon cobaea* (showy beard-tongue).

Coreopsis verticillata   thread-leaf coreopsis   daisy family / Asteraceae

Hardiness: Zones 3b to 9a
Origin: Southeastern United States
Mature height: 2 to 3 ft.
Mature spread: 18 to 24 in.
Landscape uses: Mid border; meadow or naturalized area; specimen
Season of bloom: Late spring to summer
Key ornamental characteristics: Attractive yellow flowers; bright green foliage

Coreopsis verticillata is my favorite species in this genus and it is probably the most long lived. The name is derived from the Greek *koris*, which means "bug," and *opsis*, meaning "like," and refers to the appearance of the seeds.

Gorgeous, star-shaped, yellow flowers are borne in clusters atop slender peduncles. Blooms range from 1 to 2 in. in diameter and are borne singly. To keep the plant blooming all season, remove spent flower heads. After the initial wave of flowers, shear the plant back halfway to produce new growth and more blooms.

Leaves are bright green and very attractive. The plant is bushy upright in habit, and the foliage has a fine texture, offering an appealing contrast in the garden. Leaves are palmately

Coreopsis verticillata 'Moonbeam'

divided into threadlike segments and are opposite in arrangement. The leaves are small, contributing to this plant's drought resistance.

Threadleaf coreopsis prefers to be sited in full sun and dry soil for best growth. But it will bloom in light shade. The plant will sprawl if grown in moist, rich soils.

There are no serious disease or insect problems with the species. It may get crown rot if grown in moist, poorly drained soils.

Propagation is best done by division in spring or fall. To keep the plant vigorous, divide it every 3 or 4 years. Seeds germinate easily, and the plant freely self-sows.

Several well-known cultivars of *Coreopsis verticillata* are available. The popular 'Moonbeam' is my favorite. It has butter yellow flowers and grows to 2 ft. tall. It was named Perennial Plant of the Year in 1992. 'Zagreb' has darker yellow flowers than 'Moonbeam', and I recommend it over 'Moonbeam' in areas with short growing seasons because it breaks dormancy sooner. It is also shorter in height, growing 12 to 18 in.

Threadleaf coreopsis has been part of my garden for years, and I never tire of seeing its summer show. Even when it is not in bloom, the foliage adds a soft texture to the garden. It is best used in the mid or front border as an accent, or in mass. I use it around *Campanula carpatica* (Carpathian harebell) or *Nepeta ×faassenii* (catmint), but it blends well with many plants. Try it with the ornamental grass *Festuca glauca* (blue fescue).

Corydalis lutea   yellow corydalis   fumitory family / Fumariaceae

Hardiness: Zones 5a to 7b
Origin: Southeastern Europe
Mature height: 10 to 16 in.
Mature spread: 1 ft.
Landscape use: Shade garden; rock garden; woodland garden
Season of bloom: Spring, with sporadic rebloom until fall
Key ornamental characteristics: Attractive yellow flowers; handsome fernlike
    foliage

The genus *Corydalis* contains a number of beautiful, charming species. *Corydalis lutea* is the one most often seen in U.S. gardens. Its bright lemon yellow flowers are up to ³⁄₄ in. long. Borne in axillary racemes and tubular in shape, they have a distinctive spur that flares backward; they remind me of snapdragon flowers. During spring, they are prolifically borne, and they rebloom sporadically until fall.

Foliage has an attractive grayish-blue-green color. Leaves are 2 to 3 pinnately compound with 3-lobed leaflets, which gives foliage a fine-textured, ferny appearance similar to the foliage of *Aquilegia* (columbine). Individual leaflets are obovate and are typically lobed. If the foliage looks brown or scorched over the summer, just cut it back to basal foliage to reinvigorate the plant.

Yellow corydalis prefers humus-rich soils that are well drained, evenly moist, and never dry out. But overly wet soils in winter can bring about this species' demise. It needs partial to full shade for best growth. In general, the species does not like full sun, heat or humidity, and performs best in more northern hardiness zones.

Yellow corydalis has no insect or disease problems of any consequence.

Propagation can be accomplished by collecting fresh seed and planting it immediately; germination of older seed is difficult. Try planting the seed in late summer so it can receive cold stratification over winter. Germination is erratic. In cool climates and under the right conditions, *Corydalis lutea* freely self-sows. Division can be accomplished on established plants, but transplanting has limited success, which is true for many woodland plants.

Corydalis flexuosa (blue corydalis, Zones 5 to 7) has bright blue to bluish-lavender flowers. It has a tendency to go dormant in hot weather, and is not long lived in some gardens. 'Blue Panda' is a charming cultivar with blue flowers. It grows up to 10 in. high. 'China Blue' is a taller cultivar with blue flowers. Another blue-flowered species, *C. elata* (Zones 5 to 7), tends to be more heat-tolerant and

Corydalis lutea

reliable. *Corydalis* 'Blackberry Wine' is a hybrid of unknown parentage; it has outstanding dark lavender flowers.

Utilize yellow corydalis in a rock garden, woodland garden, or shade garden setting. It likes being placed on the north side of a house or structure. The coarse leaf texture of *Asarum canadense* (Canadian wild ginger) contrasts nicely with yellow corydalis. Hellebores are also attractive companion plants.

When I worked at the Royal Horticultural Society's Wisley Gardens in England, I watched *Corydalis lutea* flourish in that cool, moist climate. It will grow easily in the upper Midwest under appropriate conditions.

Delphinium hybrids   delphinium   buttercup family / Ranunculaceae

Delphinium elatum hybrid

Hardiness: Zones 3a to 7a
Origin: Europe; hybrids
Mature height: 4 to 6 ft. (varies by hybrid and cultivar)
Mature spread: 18 to 24 in.
Landscape use: Back border; specimen
Season of bloom: Early to midsummer
Key ornamental characteristics: Gorgeous blue, white, violet, or pink flowers; attractive foliage

Delphinium is a leading candidate for diva of the perennial plant world. Delphiniums are short-lived perennials that need a lot of attention. If you can attend to their needs, their beauty will astonish you.

Outstanding flowers occur in racemes and are often paniculate. The traditional, favorite delphinium color is blue, in many shades. Flowers also occur in pink, white, violet, yellow, and red. I saw a red delphinium in a research greenhouse while working at the Royal Horticultural Society's Wisley Gardens in England. It was pretty, but confirmed for me that the color blue is best. Remove spent flower spikes to the first sprig of leaves to encourage additional bloom. The flowers are fabulous in cut arrangements but are short lived.

Basal leaves are palmate with 3 to 7 lobes. Leaves toward the apex are 3-parted. This plant's foliage provides an attractive presence in the garden.

Delphiniums need organically rich, moist, well-drained soil conditions. For best growth, they prefer alkaline soils and extra fertilization. In cooler zones, they thrive in full sun, but they need partial afternoon shade in warmer climates where heat and humidity take a toll. Delphiniums do best in the upper Midwest. Due to the stems' height and hollowness, it is advisable to support the plants, and they appreciate being placed in a location protected from strong winds. If cut to the ground after flowering and given ample water and fertililzer, you may get a second crop of flowers in late summer or early fall.

Delphiniums can have several disease and insect problems. Powdery mildew, botrytis blight, black leaf spot, crown rot, aphids, leaf miners, mites, borers, and snails and slugs all have an affinity for these plants.

Propagation is best accomplished by seed. Start seed in a greenhouse or sow outdoors in spring or summer. Delphinium may even self-sow. Division can be accomplished if you are careful. Basal cuttings may be taken in early spring.

Hybridization of delphiniums began in the mid 1800s in Europe. Breeders in America joined the fray after the First World War. *Delphinium* Belladonna Group (belladonna delphinium) and *D. elatum* (hybrid bee delphinium) are two primary hybrids for the Midwest. The *D. elatum* Pacific hybrids are magnificent, with great height and double, very showy flowers. The Pacific hybrids' flower color may vary if grown from seed. The plants have good resistance to powdery mildew.

Use delphiniums in the back border in small groupings. Space plants so that air circulates well around them, to minimize potential foliar disease. Try using delphiniums with *Papaver orientale* (oriental poppy); the leaves of delphinium contrast beautifully with poppy flowers. *Leucanthemum ×superbum* (Shasta daisy) is also a good companion.

Dianthus   garden pink, carnation   carnation family / Caryophyllaceae

Hardiness: Zones vary with species
Origin: Europe and Asia; hybrid
Mature height: 6 to 12 in.
Mature spread: 6 in. to 2 ft.
Landscape use: Rock garden; front border; pathways
Season of bloom: Spring to early summer
Key ornamental characteristics: Attractive, scented flowers; narrow foliage

Dianthus has been in cultivation for a very long period of time, because many species' flowers have an intoxicating fragrance. Description of this large genus would require its own book. There is probably a species of *Dianthus* for growth in each area of the United States.

Dianthus flowers come in shades of light pink to dark pink, crimson, and white, with an exception: *Dianthus knappi* (hairy garden pink, Zones 3 to 7), which has yellow flowers. The lower petal edges of dianthus flowers are usually serrate and some are fringed. Most dianthus flowers have a sweet, clove scent. The flowers typically rise above the foliage. Removing spent flowers may encourage light rebloom in most species.

The narrow leaves are opposite in arrangement and generally lanceolate to linear. Foliage is usually bluish-green, but it can be medium green in some species. Most species have a low, mounded habit, and if grown under ideal conditions, the foliage may form a dense mat. Foli-

Dianthus

age is evergreen and has an almost grasslike appearance, providing aesthetic value when the plant is not in flower.

All *Dianthus* prefer soil that is slightly alkaline, medium wet, and well drained. If proper drainage is not provided, the crowns may rot, especially in winter. Good air circulation is also beneficial. *Dianthus* species generally do not like heat and humidity, but *D. gratianopolia-tanus* (cheddar pink) withstands those conditions. *Dianthus* prefers full sun to partial shade.

Leaf spot and rust can be problems if grown in humid conditions. Providing the plants with plenty of space may reduce leaf diseases. There are no insect problems to speak of. *Dianthus* tends to be short lived.

Propagation is by seed, and some species freely self-sow. Stem cuttings can be taken in the summer. Division is an option in spring.

There are several *Dianthus* species worthy of mention. *Dianthus gratianopolitanus* (Zones 4 to 9) is a favorite of mine, growing up to 1 ft. tall with blue-green foliage. 'Feuerhexe' ('Fire-witch') has dark pink flowers. *Dianthus* 'Bath's Pink' has soft pink blooms that cover the foliage. *Dianthus deltoides* (maiden pinks, Zones 3 to 8) grows up to 1 ft. tall and its green leaves may take on a purplish cast in cooler months. 'Bright Eyes' has white flowers with a red center. *Dianthus* Allwoodii Alpinus Group (Allwood's pinks, Zones 5 to 7) can reach 18 in. tall; it has gray-green leaves and usually produces 2 flowers per stem. 'Robin' has bright reddish-coral flowers.

Dianthus is ideal for rock gardens, the front border, or along pathways. I have enjoyed using it for many years with Siberian irises. *Aquilegia* (columbine) also offers a wonderful complement for *Dianthus*.

Dicentra eximia   wild bleeding heart, fringed bleeding heart   fumitory
family / Fumariaceae

Hardiness: Zones 3a to 9a
Origin: Eastern United States
Mature height: 12 to 18 in.
Mature spread: 12 to 18 in.
Landscape use: Shade garden; rock border;
   naturalized area
Season of bloom: Early summer to fall if conditions
   are ideal
Key ornamental characteristics: Beautiful reddish
   to white flowers; fernlike foliage

Dicentra eximia 'Adrian Bloom'

Bleeding heart is an old-time garden favorite. It is truly the queen of the shade garden.

The distinctive, nodding, heart-shaped flowers are pink to purplish red. Inner petals protrude, so it looks like there is a drop of blood at the bottom of each flower. Blooms rise above the foliage and are borne on leafless stems. They appear in early summer, and in cooler regions may occur until fall. In warmer climates, blooms stop once the summer heat sets in, but rebloom may occur in fall.

Wild bleeding heart is easily grown in average, medium-wet, well-drained soil in part shade. Poorly drained soils will undoubtedly cause death. It prefers moist, humus-rich soils, and it is intolerant of wet soils in winter and dry soils in summer.

Leaves have a fernlike appearance, are deeply cut, and have a grayish-green color. The leaves become more finely dissected as they ascend the stem. Unlike *Dicentra spectabilis* (Japanese bleeding heart), which usually goes dormant by midsummer, the foliage of *Dicentra eximia* persists throughout the growing season and is highly attractive in its own right. The plant has a mounded habit.

There are no serious insect or disease problems with this plant. But the plant is somewhat susceptibile to aphid infestation.

Propagation is done by division in the spring. Seeds can also be sown with great success, since wild bleeding heart may naturalize in favorable cultural conditions by self-sowing.

Many *Dicentra* cultivars are hybrids of *D. eximia* and *D. formosa* (Pacific bleeding heart). *Dicentra eximia* 'Adrian Bloom' has crimson-red flowers and blue-green foliage. 'Alba' has gorgeous soft white flowers and light green foliage. *Dicentra* 'Bountiful' has dark rosy-pink flowers.

Dicentra spectabilis (Japanese bleeding heart, Zones 3 to 8) is native to Japan and is similar to *D. eximia*. But *D. spectabilis* is taller, wider, has larger flowers, and the leaves are less cut; it requires the same cultural conditions as *D. eximia*. *Dicentra spectabilis* tends to go dormant in the summer.

This North American native is ideal for the shade garden, woodland garden, or rock garden. It will also excel when allowed to naturalize. It provides attractive textural contrast when planted with hostas. Try it with *Aruncus dioicus* (goat's beard), *Pulmonaria saccharata* (Bethlehem sage), *Tiarella cordifolia* (foamflower), or *Tradescantia ×andersoniana* (spiderwort).

Wild bleeding heart truly commands attention. You are bound to be charmed by this elegant plant's fine texture and graceful beauty.

Digitalis purpurea   common foxglove   foxglove family / Scrophulariaceae

Hardiness: Zones 4b to 9a
Origin: Europe
Mature height: 2 to 5 ft. (in flower)
Mature spread: 1 to 2 ft.
Landscape use: Mid or back border; naturalized area; woodland garden; specimen
Season of bloom: Late spring to early summer
Key ornamental characteristics: Handsome pink, yellow, or white flowers; architectural height

Common foxglove is a classic garden plant and biennial that self-sows once established. The Latin word *digitalis* means "finger of a glove." Individual flowers have the appearance of cut glove fingers. *Digitalis* leaves are a source of a drug for heart disease and are very poisonous. Caution is advised if you plant common foxglove where young children or pets may come in contact with it.

Common foxglove's tubular, bell-shaped blooms are borne on spikes that rise above the foliage. Flower colors range from lavender to pink, rust, yellow, and white. The outside of the flower has the noticeable color, while the throat is generally lighter and spotted. The flowers are 2 to 3 in. long and highly attractive to hummingbirds. After the flowers are spent and seeds are released, you may remove them to keep the plant tidy if you wish.

Leaves are downy and wrinkly. They are oblong and long stalked, becoming smaller and stalkless as they ascend the stem.

Common foxglove is easy to grow in average, moderately wet soil that is organically rich and well drained. It prefers slightly acidic soils that are not allowed to become dry. If grown in a dry location, the plant's appearance will decline over time. It performs well in partial shade.

Propagation is relatively easy by seed. Seeds can be sowed directly into the garden in spring, producing a colony that may flourish for years like true perennials. When grown from seed, the plant produces only foliage the first year, with flowers occurring the second year.

Several cultivars of *Digitalis purpurea* exist. 'Alba' has white flowers. Excelsior Group's flowers are borne around the flower stalk and are more upright than blooms of the species, and plants can grow in excess of 5 ft. tall. Foxy Group produces blooms the first year of growth, which is unique to *Digitalis purpurea*.

Digitalis purpurea

Numerous disease and insect problems can arise for this plant. Powdery mildew and leaf spot can disfigure foliage if spray is not used. Crowns may rot in soggy, poorly drained winter soils. Potential pests include aphids, Japanese beetles, and mealy bugs.

The flower stalks provide brilliant color and great architectural height to the back border, and are especially effective in front of dark shrubs. They also look right at home in a woodland garden or naturalized area. Common foxglove usually reaches its peak in flower when roses begin to bloom. You may want to place common foxglove near other flowering plants, so when the flowers fade, companion plants fill in the void.

Common foxglove has been used for medicinal purposes for centuries. The first clinical study of its usefulness for coronary disease dates from the 1700s.

Echinacea purpurea   purple coneflower   daisy family / Asteraceae

Hardiness: Zones 3a to 8b
Origin: Eastern United States
Mature height: 2 to 4 ft.
Mature spread: 18 to 24 in.
Landscape use: Mid border; specimen; mass; naturalized areas
Season of bloom: Summer
Key ornamental characteristics: Pink, white, or sunset-colored flowers

Purple coneflower is one of the most reliable summer-blooming perennials. A garden may not really be a garden without at least one specimen of this plant. If you want to attract butterflies to your garden, this plant will do the trick, and bees enjoy them too.

The flowers are 3 to 5 in. wide, with a deep brownish-orange cone in the center. The petals are rosy-lavender and hang down slightly. The dried flowers can be used in arrangements

Echinacea purpurea

and craft projects. The seed cones add interest to the winter garden and attract birds in search of food. Wild canaries (goldfinches) faithfully arrive in my garden in late summer to feast on the seeds.

This drought-resistant species is native to the eastern United States and easily withstands full sun and dry conditions. It accommodates a wide range of soil types but prefers well-drained locations.

Leaves are alternate, dark green, and coarsely pubescent. Lower leaves are ovate and coarsely toothed. Leaves located toward the top of the plant are narrower in shape. Stems are also coarsely pubescent.

Purple coneflower has few disease or insect problems. I have had occasional minor problems with leaf spot and Japanese beetle.

Propagation is by clump division or seed. Division can be difficult and should only take place once the plant is fully established. Seed is easy to germinate, and in fact, I have to pull several self-sown purple coneflower plants from my garden every year. The plant is not overly aggressive in self-sowing, however, and once established, purple coneflower is pretty much trouble free.

Numerous *Echinacea purpurea* cultivars are available. 'Alba' has white blooms with a greenish center disc. 'Magnus' was Perennial Plant of the Year in 1998 and has large, rosy-lavender flowers that do not droop as much as the species. 'Rubinstern' ('Ruby Star') has deep rosy-lavender flowers and grows to 3 ft. 'White Swan' has white flowers with drooping petals and is seed-propagated. *Echinacea* 'Sunrise' lives up to its name, with bright, citron-yellow flowers. I have one planted on the east end of my garden. 'Sunset' has warm, russet-orange blooms, and I have planted one on my garden's west end. These are part of the Big Sky Series, a cross between *E. purpurea* and *E. paradoxa*, which includes numerous selections with flowers in shades of yellow, orange, and red. *Echinacea laevigata* (smooth coneflower, Zones 3 to 8) is a related species with a smooth top leaf surface.

Echinacea is popular in herbal medicine, with claims of numerous benefits including reduced cold and flu symptoms. For making herbal remedies, the root of *Echinacea angustifolia* (narrow-leaf purple coneflower) is typically used.

I cannot imagine a garden without purple coneflower, and have used it with a broad range of plants. Some of my favorite companions include *Perovskia atriplicifolia* (Russian sage), *Liatris spicata* (spike gayfeather), and *Hemerocallis* (daylily). Purple coneflower forms the backbone of my garden: I have intermittingly placed it throughout the mid border. And I have used different *Echinacea* cultivars to place subtle shades of rosy-lavender color in the garden.

Anyone can grow this intriguing plant. If you are a new gardener or just want a plant that is reliable, purple coneflower will leave you feeling like an expert.

Echinops ritro   globe thistle   daisy family / Asteraceae

Hardiness: Zones 3b to 8b
Origin: Europe and western Asia
Mature height: 3 to 4 ft.
Mature spread: 2 to 3 ft.
Landscape use: Mid border; specimen
Season of bloom: Summer
Key ornamental characteristics: Spherical steel-blue flowers

Gorgeous steel-blue flowers of globe thistle are borne on gray stems and surrounded by bristly, sharp bracts. Flower heads are approximately 2 in. in diameter. The buds have a steel-blue color before the flowers appear, which gives the plant the appearance of being in bloom longer. Flowers can be used in fresh or dried bouquets. To retain the blue color, cut them when they are young and place in a dry, warm room. Bees and nocturnal moths are highly attracted to the flowers.

Globe thistle grows best in full sun and adapts to a wide range of soils, even dry, poor soils, as long as they are well drained. It will also tolerate partial shade. Flower color intensity is greatest in northern areas where summer nights are cooler. But globe thistle is versatile and thrives in the heat of the lower Midwest. The habit is upright and the plant may need staking.

Echinops ritro 'Veitch's Blue'

Leaves are alternate, 6 to 8 in. long, with wavy margins. The upper leaf surface is smooth, while underneath it is downy gray and hairy. Leaves have a thistlelike appearance with spiny tips, but they are not as vicious as they look. As the summer progresses, lower leaves may become brown on the margins and look generally tattered.

Propagation is best accomplished by division or root cuttings in spring. New plants should flower that same year. Seed is also an option, but variability often occurs in plants grown from seed.

This rugged plant is usually free from disease or insect problems. But aphids may be an occasional problem.

Several *Echinops ritro* cultivars exist. 'Sea Stone' is smaller than other cultivars at 16 in. in height with a similar spread, making it ideal for small gardens. 'Taplow Blue' has steel-blue flowers with a silvery cast. The plants can grow up to 4 ft.. 'Veitch's Blue' has darker blue flowers than 'Taplow Blue' and is a more prolific bloomer. It grows to 3 ft. in height.

Globe thistle is ideal for the mid border. Its textural quality works nicely with *Achillea* 'Moonshine' (moonshine yarrow), *Coreopsis verticillata* (threadleaf coreopsis), and *Coreopsis grandiflora* (coreopsis).

The unusual flowers of globe thistle are uniquely attractive. They add a desirable, subtle, splash of steel-blue color to the garden. Who needs formal, dainty flowers anyway?

Epimedium ×rubrum   red barrenwort   barberry family / Berberidaceae

Hardiness: Zones 4a to 8a
Origin: Hybrid
Mature height: 8 to 12 in.
Mature spread: 1 ft.
Landscape use: Shade; woodland garden; rock garden; ground cover
Season of bloom: Mid-spring
Key ornamental characteristics: Delicate spring flowers; attractive foliage

This hybrid's parents are *Epimedium alpinum* (alpine barrenwort, Zones 5 to 9) and *E. grandiflorum* (longspur barrenwort, Zones 5 to 8). There are many quality species and hybrids of this genus, but *E. ×rubrum* probably forms the best ground cover. This plant is primarily grown because of the basal foliage.

Leaflets are heart shaped and occur on wiry stems. They are highlighted with red in the spring, fall, and cool summers. When the weather turns warm, the foliage is medium green. This hybrid is semievergreen, but if your plant develops brown leaf margins or foliage, cut it back.

Flowers rise above the foliage in spring. The inner flower sepals are crimson red while the

Epimedium ×youngianum 'Niveum'

petals are yellow or red in color. Each inflorescence has 10 to 20 flowers that are approximately 1 in. across. The spurs are turned upward.

Red barrenwort is easy to grow in soil that is moderately moist and well drained. It prefers soils that are moist and organically rich, but will withstand drought once the plant is established. The plant requires partial to full shade or a quick death will occur.

Propagation is best by division. Red barrenwort is a rhizomatous, clump-forming plant that can be easily divided in spring or fall. It spreads rapidly, but is not aggressive.

There are no serious insect or disease problems associated with red barrenwort.

Several related *Epimedium* species are highly attractive. *Epimedium grandiflorum* (longspur epimedium, Zones 4 to 8) has large flowers marked with pink, white, and red. It grows to 1 ft. tall. The foliage emerges a coppery-brown before turning green in summer and red in fall. *Epimedium ×versicolor* (bicolor barrenwort, Zones 4 to 8) has yellow flowers. The cultivar 'Sulphureum' tolerates dry sites better than many related plants; it has yellow flowers and usually remains evergreen. *Epimedium ×youngianum* (Young's barrenwort, Zones 4 to 8) is a low-growing hybrid with purplish leaves in spring and crimson foliage in the fall. The popular cultivar 'Niveum' has white flowers.

Epimedium ×rubrum is perfect for a shade or woodland garden and complements other plants that require the same cultural conditions, for example, *Astilbe ×arendii* (false spirea). Or use it all by itself: it will create a dense growth of foliage. It is also tough and will grow under trees where many perennials fear to tread.

This plant has become popular as a ground cover because it provides ornamental value in the spring, summer, and fall. Also, if you live in a warmer climate or select a related species that is evergreen, the ornamental value remains all year.

Eryngium amethystinum   amethyst sea holly   carrot family / Apiaceae

Hardiness: Zones 3b to 8a
Origin: Mediterranean region
Mature height: 18 to 30 in.
Mature spread: 18 to 24 in.
Landscape use: Mid border; specimen
Season of bloom: Summer
Key ornamental characteristics: Steel-blue flowers and stems

Amethyst sea holly is a rugged plant that thrives easily in dry, infertile, poor-quality soils that might kill other plants. It requires full sun. Native to seaside areas, this plant tolerates high salt levels, including salts used on winter roads.

Eryngium amethystinum

Steel-blue flowers are up to ¾ in. in diameter, profusely borne, and resemble those of thistle. The bracts are lance shaped, sharply pointed, and longer than the globe-shaped flower heads. The bracts are sharp, so you should wear gloves when handling this species. Blooms are excellent for use in fresh or dried flower arrangements, and will retain much of their color when dried. Stems are the same color as the flowers.

Leaves are obovate and deeply, pinnately cut. Foliage has a coarse appearance and is spiny. Lower leaves tend to be larger than those ascending the stem. The plant has a stiff, upright habit.

Propagation can be done by seed or root cuttings. Division is risky because the plants have taproots that are difficult to separate.

Amethyst sea holly has no serious disease or insect problems. The plant does not like wet winters, though, and benefits from a layer of gravel or sand placed around the plant's base to improve drainage.

There are several related species. *Eryngium alpinum* (alpine sea holly, Zones 4 to 8) has finely cut, lacy-looking bracts. This species is a prolific bloomer and has a magnificent steel-blue color. It is not quite as cold hardy as *Eryngium amethystinum*. *Eryngium bourgatii* (Mediterranean sea holly, Zones 5 to 8) has coarse leaves with noticeable white veins. The flowers have a slightly more blue-green color than other species. It also is not as winter hardy as *Eryngium amethystinum*.

The flowers and foliage of this plant provide unique color and contrast to the perennial border. Try growing it with *Platycodon grandiflorus* (balloon flower), *Heliopsis helianthoides* var. *scabra* (heliopsis sunflower), *Rudbeckia fulgida* (black-eyed Susan), and ornamental grasses.

Because of its bold, coarse appearance, *Eryngium amethystinum* is best used as a specimen or in small groups of three plants rather than in a massed planting. Amethyst sea holly adds winter interest to the garden, and the seeds are a food source for some birds.

Eupatorium purpureum subsp. *maculatum*   Joe-Pye weed
daisy family / Asteraceae

Hardiness: Zones 4a to 8a
Origin: Eastern North America
Mature height: 4 to 7 ft.
Mature spread: 2 to 4 ft.
Landscape use: Back border; naturalized areas; specimen
Season of bloom: Midsummer to fall
Key ornamental characteristics: large, attractive flower heads; great height;
    winter interest

If you want height in the garden, look no farther than Joe-Pye weed. Reaching up to 7 ft., with its imposing, erect habit, this native giant makes a bold statement in the garden.

Large flower heads make a tremendous impact from a distance or viewed up close. Highly attractive to butterflies, they are comprised of 8 to 20 florets that are reddish-burgundy-lavender in color. In late autumn, seed heads appear and add interest to the winter landscape.

Medium green leaves are lanceolate, serrate, and up to 8 in. long. Coarse in texture, they typically appear in whorls of 3 to 6 per node and may have a faint purple midrib. Stems are speckled with tiny purple spots.

Joe-Pye weed is native to damp meadows, thickets, and coastal areas in eastern North America. It thrives in moist, rich soil that does not dry out. Plants grown in a dry site will scorch. The plant is easy to grow. You will get its best performance in full sun, but the plant will tolerate light shade. Shade tends to make the plant become even taller and leggy. Plants should be cut to the ground in late winter or early spring.

Propagation is best accomplished by stem cuttings in spring. Division can be done approximately every 3 years. Seeds are also viable.

This plant knows no serious disease or insect problems.

Eupatorium purpureum subsp. *maculatum*

Eupatorium maculatum 'Gateway' is a popular cultivar that is more compact than the subspecies, typically growing 4 to 5 ft. tall and having mauve-pink blooms. It is more shrub-like and has tighter, thicker inflorescences. It also has purple-speckled stems and is more floriferous.

I use Joe-Pye weed with *Rudbeckia fulgida* (black-eyed Susan), *Solidago* hybrids (goldenrod), and *Aster novi-belgii* (New York aster). Its size and coarseness also add a remarkable texture that is appropriate in a shrub border. Joe-Pye weed is a wonderful plant to use in the back border, in naturalized areas, around ponds, or next to brick walls.

Eupatorium rugosum   white snakeroot   daisy family / Asteraceae

Hardiness: Zones 3a to 7a
Origin: Eastern North America
Mature height: 3 to 5 ft.
Mature spread: 2 to 3 ft.
Landscape use: Back or mid border; native plant
    garden; woodland garden
Season of bloom: Late summer to fall
Key ornamental characteristics: Dense corymbs of
    white flowers

Eupatorium rugosum 'Chocolate'

White snakeroot (synonymous with *Ageratina altissima*) is native to the United States. Indigenous peoples of North America reportedly used the roots of this plant to treat snakebite. It deserves to be used more in gardens.

Small, white flowers occur in dense corymbs and are ¼ in. wide. They make an attractive display, because the inflorescence can be up to 4 in. wide on densely branched plants. If you use your imagination, the inflorescence looks a little like a cauliflower head. The flowers last from late summer to frost and have an appealing fluffy appearance.

Dark green leaves are opposite in arrangement, serrate, and lanceolate to ovate. They are 3 to 6 in. long and slightly wrinkled.

White snakeroot naturally occurs in woodland areas and therefore is easy to grow in moderately wet to wet, well-drained soils. It prefers moist, organically rich sites, but will withstand dry conditions. It grows in full sun to partial shade, and is more shade tolerant than other members of the genus.

Propagation is easy by seed. In fact, you may want to deadhead spent flowers to keep the plant from reseeding, although it is only aggressive under ideal conditions. White snakeroot also spreads by rhizomes, making division easy in spring.

Powdery mildew, leaf miner, and flea beetle may be nuisances on occasion. Otherwise the plant has no disease or insect problems.

Euplatorium rugosum 'Chocolate' is an attractive cultivar, which I grow and thoroughly enjoy. It has noticeable dark burgundy-tinged stems and leaves, which provide an elegant context for the white flowers. It grows 3 to 4 ft. tall.

Grow white snakeroot in the mid or back border. *Macleya cordata* (plume poppy) and *Rudbeckia fulgida* (black-eyed Susan) are all good companions. White snakeroot is also useful in a native plant garden or a woodland garden.

All parts of *Eupatorium rugosum* contain the toxic compound barium sulphate, which, if eaten in large quantities, can bring death. It was reported that cows that ate large amounts of this plant produced poisonous milk, which resulted in the death of pioneers during the expansion west. This concern is an issue if you produce your own milk and the plant grows in the fields with the cows.

Euphorbia epithymoides cushion spurge   spurge family / Euphorbiaceae

Hardiness: Zones 4a to 8a
Origin: Eastern Europe
Mature height: 12 to 18 in.
Mature spread: 12 to 18 in.
Landscape use: Front border; specimen
Season of bloom: Early to mid-spring
Key ornamental characteristics: Bright chartreuse bracts

Euphorbia epithymoides

Cushion spurge is in full bloom when most other species are just starting to emerge from winter dormancy. Tiny, insignificant blooms are borne in a cyathium, but electric, chartreuse bracts are an eye-catching feature of the inflorescence. The color is so pronounced that it reminds me of black light paint—this plant will light up any garden.

Leaves are oblong and remain dark green through the summer. The foliage turns a dark shade of red in the fall, which is unusual for most perennials. This plant is in the same family as the beloved Christmas poinsettia, which means that when you break the stems or leaves, a milky sap usually appears. The sap can irritate the skin of some people, so I recommend wearing gloves when handling this plant.

Easy to cultivate except in wet soil, cushion spurge prefers somewhat dry conditions. In its northern hardiness areas, it withstands full sun but benefits from partial afternoon shade. In the warmer, lower Midwest, partial shade is a requirement. This plant has a beautiful mound shape, which tends to become leggy over the summer.

I have not encountered any disease or insect problems with this plant after growing it for more than 10 years in Zone 5b. But the plant reputedly is subject to wilt diseases in warm, humid regions.

The plants can be difficult to divide, so choose an established plant and make sure to provide enough root system for each division. Cushion spurge seeds germinate reasonably well and require a warm, humid environment.

Utilize *Euphorbia epithymoides* with early spring flowering bulbs. It will easily accompany tulips, daffodils, and other brightly colored bulb blooms. I place it in the front border of my garden and it is a welcome sight in early spring.

Euphorbia epithymoides (also known as *E. polychroma*) is ideal as a specimen plant in the garden.

Festuca glauca   blue fescue   grass family / Poaceae

Hardiness: Zones 5a to 8b
Origin: Europe
Mature height: 6 to 10 in. (slightly taller in bloom)
Mature spread: 8 in.
Landscape use: Front border; rock garden; accent plant; mass
Season of bloom: Summer
Key ornamental characteristics: Fine, gray-blue foliage

Although you may not realize it, blue fescue is probably growing in your lawn. For ornamental gardening purposes, *Festuca glauca* is a favorite. It is grown as a perennial for its fine-textured foliage. *Festuca glauca* is synonymous with *Festuca cinerea*, *F. ovina* var. *glauca*, and *F.*

ovina 'Glauca'. By any name, its rounded dome shape and unique color make it recognizable from a distance. The plant's small size and nonaggressive nature make it ideal for many garden or landscape situations.

Blue fescue produces numerous arching flower stems that carry tiny, blue-green, purple-tinged spikelets in late spring and early summer. The stems rise just a few inches above the foliage. I like the fine texture of the flower stems. But some gardeners prefer to remove the flowers when they appear to prevent the seed heads from developing.

Festuca glauca

The glaucous, bluish-gray leaves are linear and 3 to 8 in. long. This grass's densely tufted, clump-forming, upright, ornamental foliage is semievergreen in mild winter climates and turns brown in colder zones. I have seen it do both in my Zone 5b garden, depending on the severity of the winter. Foliage should be cut back to 2 to 4 in. in early spring to promote new growth and tidy the plant.

Blue fescue is easy to grow in a wide range of soil types. It prefers dry to moderately wet conditions with good drainage. While it is tolerant of drought and poor soils, overly wet sites will cause it to die quickly. High humidity and summer heat may cause the plant to decline; if this occurs, trim it back to rejuvenate the foliage. Preferring full sun for best foliage coloration, it will tolerate light shade.

Propagation is by seed or division. When reproduced by seed, variations in foliage color may occur. Cultivars should be divided in spring or fall to ensure true-to-type reproduction. The clumps have a tendency to die in the center, so they should be divided every 2 to 3 years.

There are no insect or disease problems of consequence for blue fescue.

A number of *Festuca glauca* cultivars are available. 'Azurit' has bluish-green foliage and is fairly tall at 12 to 18 in. 'Boulder Blue' is a heavy bloomer, with a strong blue cast. Mature height is 12 to 15 in. 'Elijah Blue' is a quality cultivar and one of my favorites. It grows 6 to 10 in. tall and has powdery blue foliage. 'Meerblau ('Sea Blue') has blue-green foliage and grows 6 to 10 in. tall. 'Platinum' has green-tinged, silvery-blue foliage and grows 6 to 10 in. tall.

Blue fescue works well in the front border, rock garden, and as a specimen plant. I prefer to use it as an accent plant in the garden, but it can be used in mass. I have seen the plant successfully massed on slopes, giving the landscape a formal appearance.

I enjoy the character of this plant: to me, it looks like a blue-gray porcupine. If you are interested in ornamental grasses but do not know where to start, I highly recommend blue fescue.

Filipendula ulmaria   meadowsweet, queen-of-the-meadow   rose family / Rosaceae

Hardiness: Zones 3a to 7b
Origin: Europe and western Asia
Mature height: 3 to 4 ft.
Mature spread: 3 ft.
Landscape use: Shade; woodland gardens; back border; ponds and streams
Season of bloom: Early to midsummer
Key ornamental characteristics: Plumelike, creamy white flowers; attractive, dark green foliage

Queen-of-the-meadow makes a statement in any setting because of its relatively large size. The mildly fragrant flowers are creamy white and borne in dense, paniculate cymes. They somewhat resemble *Astilbe* blooms; the 4- to 6-in. panicles are made up of ¼-in.-wide individual flowers.

The serrate leaves are dark green on top, with a whitish color and tomentose texture underneath. Alternate in arrangement and pinnately compound, 7 to 9 leaflets make up each leaf. Noticeable veins occur on each leaflet, giving the plant added texture.

Queen-of-the-meadow appreciates partial shade, especially in warmer regions of the Midwest. The plant may tolerate full sun in cooler zones if all other cultural conditions are met. It prefers moist-to-wet soil conditions, and cannot survive dry soils and drought. It performs better in alkaline soils.

Filipendula ulmaria is susceptible to mildew, especially if the soil is dry or the plant has experienced other stressful conditions. There are no other disease or insect problems with the plant.

Propagation may be accomplished by seed or divison. The species will self-sow, and seeds are usually viable. If seeds are purchased, make sure they undergo a warm and cool period before planting. Queen-of-the-meadow has a tough root system so you will need a sharp spade to divide the plant in spring.

Filipendula ulmaria © Hazel Proudlove

Filipendula ulmaria 'Aurea' features attractive creamy yellow foliage as an ornamental highlight. The flowers of this cultivar are insignificant and probably should be removed before setting seed. The seeds will yield green-leaved plants. 'Flore Pleno' has very showy, double, creamy white flowers. *Filipendula rubra* (queen-of-the-prairie, Zones 3 to 9), a related species, is native to eastern and central North America and has pinkish blooms. *Filipendula vulgaris* (dropwort meadowsweet, Zones 3 to 8) has creamy white flowers tinged with a pinkish-red cast.

Queen-of-the-meadow is a clump-forming species that looks tremendous when planted in groups around ponds or next to streams. It is also ideal for a shade or woodland garden. Try planting it with *Ligularia* spp. or ferns. Also consider using it with *Lobelia cardinalis* (cardinal flower), although the two plants may not bloom at the same time.

Foeniculum vulgare   fennel   carrot family / Apiaceae

Hardiness: Zones 4a to 9a
Origin: Southern Europe
Mature height: 4 to 5 ft. (up to 7 ft. in right
  conditions)
Mature spread: 18 to 24 in.
Landscape use: Back border; specimen; filler
Season of bloom: Mid to late summer
Key ornamental characteristics: Gorgeous, feathery
  foliage; sulfur-yellow flowers

Foeniculum vulgare 'Purpureum'

Fennel is not just for the herb garden. This plant provides architectural height and unusual texture in any landscape. Use this plant to introduce young children to gardening: the stems and leaves taste and smell like licorice or anise. Fennel leaves and stems are used as a flavorful ingredient in a variety of foods such as salads and fish dishes. The tasty seeds are also used in making baked goods and sausage.

Fennel leaves are repeatedly pinnately compound with thread-thin leaflets, giving the plant a fine-textured, feathery appearance. Petioles are broad and wrap around the stem joints. *Foeniculum vulgare* is very similar to dill (*Anethum graveolens*) in appearance, except its foliage is light green instead of bluish-green, and its stems are solid while dill stems are hollow.

The plant's tiny, sulfur-yellow flowers occur in large, flat umbels in midsummer and perfectly complement the delicate foliage. Butterflies are highly attracted to the flowers. Unless you grow the plant to produce seed, I suggest cutting spent flowers to prevent unwanted seedlings.

Fennel is easy to grow in moist, humus-rich, well-drained soils in full sun. It can reach a height of 5 ft. or more, and does not need staking. This sturdy plant can even remain upright after a heavy thunderstorm.

Fennel has no serious insect or disease problems. Stem and root rot may occur, especially in poorly drained soils. Aphids and slugs can be minor problems and the larvae (caterpillars) of swallowtail butterflies may munch on the foliage. I just remove caterpillars when I see them, because I value the plant. But some people grow fennel solely as a food source for swallowtail caterpillars.

Propagation of fennel is easy from seed sown directly in the garden in spring. My plants usually self-sow around the parent. Division can also be done with established plants.

In my garden, I grow the cultivar *Foeniculum vulgare* 'Purpureum' (also known as 'Rubrum'). It has gorgeous mahogany-purple-green foliage that offers a strong contrast with the green foliage of other plants. *Foeniculum vulgare* var. *azoricum* is an annual; it is a favorite in salads and as a cooked vegetable.

Fennel makes an exceptional filler plant in the garden. For something slightly out of the ordinary, add a fennel plant to your perennial garden or shrub border.

Gaillardia ×grandiflora   blanket flower   daisy family / Asteraceae

Hardiness: Zones 3a to 10a
Origin: Western United States
Mature height: 2 to 3 ft.
Mature spread: 2 ft.
Landscape use: Mid border; mass
Season of bloom: Summer
Key ornamental characteristics: Eye-catching, abundant, yellow and wine-red
    flowers

I love blanket flower. The yellow flowers have varying amounts of wine-red coloring at the base of the petals, and the center is a deep wine-red color. Truly eye-catching, the flowers range from 2 to 4 in. in diameter. They first appear in early summer and last until the end of the season. *Gaillardia* will continue to bloom without deadheading, but if you remove spent flowers, flower production is enhanced.

Leaves are coarsely toothed, gray green, and pubescent. Some gardeners develop a rash from the fuzzy leaves, so I recommend wearing gloves when handling this plant. The plant's habit is sprawling. Stems tend to flop and have an informal appearance. One of the few drawbacks of *Gaillardia ×grandiflora* is that it tends to be short lived. (The plant is a hybrid cross of *G. aristata*, a perennial, and *G. pulchella*, an annual. The introduction of annual genes enhances the bloom period while favoring a short life span.)

Blanket flower does not like heavy, clay soils because their winter wetness can kill the roots. But the plant thrives in sun, heat, and dry soils.

Disease and insect problems are few. Powdery mildew, leaf spot, aster yellows, and leafhopper can be occasional problems.

Gaillardia is easy to propagate by seed. A few cultivars, however, such as 'Goblin', cannot be reproduced in this manner. Division should be done in the spring.

There are many *Gaillardia ×grandiflora* cultivars in existence. Some cultivars have pure,

Gaillardia ×grandiflora 'Kobold' ('Goblin')

deep wine-red flowers while others have pure yellow. And there are dwarf cultivars. I have never been disappointed with any *Gaillardia* cultivar. They are all beautiful and easy to grow. 'Burgunder' (or 'Burgundy') grows up to 3 ft. tall and has wine-red flowers. 'Kobold' ('Goblin') is a dwarf growing 8 to 12 in. tall. 'Oranges and Lemons' is a recent introduction with an upright habit and soft, orange-yellow flowers. It has been a prolific bloomer in its first year in my garden. 'Summer's Kiss' has gorgeous apricot colored flowers. *Gaillardia* 'Fanfare' is very unusual and is one of my favorite cultivars. Instead of a typical daisy flower, each individual petal is tubular and resembles a trumpet; the effect is a ring of candycorn tubes.

   Gaillardia is an attractive companion of *Achillea* 'Moonshine' (moonshine yarrow), *Leucanthemum ×superbum* (Shasta daisy), *Liatris spicata* (spiked gayfeather), and *Salvia ×superba* (perennial salvia).

   This native plant is perfect for a cottage garden.

Gaura lindheimeri   white gaura   evening primrose family / Onagraceae

Hardiness: Zones 5a to 9a
Origin: Southern United States and Mexico
Mature height: 3 to 4 ft.
Mature spread: 24 to 30 in.
Landscape use: Mid border; native garden
Season of bloom: Late spring to fall
Key ornamental characteristics: Graceful, white flowers fading to pink on
   wandlike stems

My first *Gaura lindheimeri* plant was given to me 5 years ago, and it has been part of my Zone 5b garden every since. It is a charming but tough plant. The genus name, derived from the Greek word *gauros*, means "superb."

White gaura has pinkish buds that open to white flowers before slowly fading to pink. This makes for a subtly dazzling effect as older flowers fade while new ones open. Flowers have 4 petals that look like butterfly wings. They are borne on long, wandlike stems that gracefully arch above the foliage. Stems may become leggy, especially if grown in rich soils.

Gaura lindheimeri

Remove spent flower spikes to prolong the bloom period from late spring to fall. White gaura reportedly may self-sow if flower stems remain into the fall. This has not occurred in my garden, but I live in the species' northernmost hardiness zone.

Leaves are lanceolate and 1 to 3 in. long. They are sessile and alternate in arrangement. Occasionally they have maroon-colored spots. The plant is clump forming and has a vase-shaped habit.

Native to Texas, Louisiana, and Mexico, white gaura prefers sandy, loamy, well-drained soils and full sun. Good drainage is essential for its survival. The plant's long taproot enables it to tolerate drought, heat, and humidity. Once planted, it will take 2 to 3 years for white gaura to become fully established.

The cultivar *Gaura lindheimeri* 'Siskiyou Pink' has deep pink flowers. 'Whirling Butterflies' grows to 3 ft. tall and is a consistent bloomer.

Propagation is best by seed. Division is rarely needed, and because of the plant's deep root system, division is difficult and might damage the established plant.

There are no serious insect or disease problems with white gaura. Root rot may occur in heavy, poorly drained soils.

I plant white gaura around other drought-tolerant plants in the mid border. The flowers and arching stems are a nice complement to *Perovskia atriplicifolia* (Russian sage), *Ratibida columnifera* (Mexican hat), or *Nepeta ×faassenii* (catmint). It can also be used in the wildflower or native garden where it can sprawl and naturalize. Plant it against a sunny, west- or south-facing wall. White gaura easily stands up to heat. If you live in the upper Midwest, try treating it as an annual and plant it in large pots.

Geranium   cranesbill, hardy geranium   geranium family / Geraniaceae

Hardiness: Zones vary with species
Origin: Worldwide
Mature height: 6 in. to 2 ft.
Mature spread: Varies with habit
Landscape use: Front or mid border; woodland garden; mass; specimen
Season of bloom: Spring to fall
Key ornamental characteristics: Attractive blue, pink, or white flowers; handsome palmate foliage; moundlike or trailing habit

---

Plants in the genus *Geranium* are called hardy geraniums; they are distinct from annual geraniums (*Pelargonium*). The genus has more than 300 species. Many hardy geraniums are simply spectacular.

Hardy geraniums thrive in a wide range of soil types, with good moisture and drainage being primary needs. This native plant easily withstands full sun or partial shade. But in the extreme lower Midwest, I suggest providing afternoon shade.

Propagation is best done by division in the spring or fall every 3 or 4 years. Plant seed in the late summer or fall.

Leaves usually are palmate, may be deeply dissected, and grow from basal rosettes. Depending on the species, leaves can be alternate or opposite. Some species' leaves are hairy while others are aromatic. After blooming, you may cut back the foliage to encourage further flowering. In the fall, some species have attractive scarlet- or yellow-colored foliage while others remain evergreen. The foliage of this genus adds texture and ornamental interest to the garden.

Flower color ranges from shades of pink to magenta, lavender, blue, and white. Each flower has 5 overlapping petals and 10 stamens. Flowers appear in spring and last until fall with many species. The fruit is the shape of a beak, which provides the common name cranesbill.

Members of this genus are generally free of disease and insect problems. Japanese beetle may occur with some species.

Most hardy geraniums have a clump-forming, mounded, or spreading ground-cover habit. For example, *Geranium pratense* (meadow cranesbill, Zones 5 to 8) has a clump-forming habit whereas *G. sanguineum* (bloody cranesbill, Zones 3 to 8) is more mounded. The U.S. native *G. maculatum* (Zones 4 to 8) spreads like a ground cover.

Geranium 'Johnson's Blue'

Geranium 'Johnson's Blue', a hybrid of *G. himalayense* (lilac geranium, Zones 4 to 8) and *G. pratense*, is my favorite hardy geranium. The habit is floppy, but that in no way detracts from the beautiful, clear blue flowers. Blooms occur all summer because of minimal seed set. *Geranium sanguineum* is the most commonly seen species in American gardens and is a beauty. It has magenta flowers, and the small-leaved, pubescent foliage has fall color. *Geranium himalayense* has lavender flowers. It withstands shade relatively well. An outstanding recent introduction is *Geranium* 'Rozanne' (Zones 5 to 8), a hybrid of *G. himalayense* and *G. wallichianum*. Named Perennial Plant of the Year for 2008 by the Perennial Plant Association, it grows from 12 to 18 in., producing lovely, white-centered, blue-lavender flowers all summer long.

Cranesbill can be used in a variety of ways, from front to mid-border perennial gardens to woodland gardens.

Geum   avens, geum   rose family / Rosaceae

Geum 'Mrs J. Bradshaw'

Hardiness: Zones 4a to 7a
Origin: Hybrids
Mature height: 18 to 24 in.
Mature spread: 18 in.
Landscape use: Front or mid border; specimen; mass
Season of bloom: Late spring to early summer
Key ornamental characteristics: Brightly colored flowers; handsome, lobed foliage

This genus has approximately 50 species. Most plants available for the garden are hybrids of *Geum chiloense* and *G. coccineum*.

Red-orange, yellow, or orange flowers create a bright appearance in the landscape and remind me of buttercups. Flowers are approximately 1 in. in diameter and, depending on the cultivar, can be single or double. They rise several inches above the foliage. Deadheading the plant will produce rebloom later in the growing season.

Leaves are up to 6 in. long and pinnate, with 5 to 7 lobes. Much of the foliage is basal and pubescent. Depending on species or cultivar, the leaves are cut in various ways, but the terminal lobe is largest. Leaflets are unequally toothed. The foliage is subtly attractive and may remain evergreen over the winter, depending on climate severity.

There are few insect or disease problems with geum. Fungal leaf spot, powdery mildew, and spider mites can be slight problems.

This plant has a narrow hardiness range and prefers areas with relatively cool summers and warm winters. I recommend protection from the afternoon sun in the warmer regions of its range. *Geum* requires excellent drainage and moist, humus-rich soil. Wet winters may kill the plant.

Propagation is easily accomplished by division in the spring or fall. Division every 1 or 2 years helps prolong the life of the plant. Fresh seed sowed directly in the spring will quickly germinate. Cultivars should be propagated by cuttings.

Several *Geum* cultivars are available. My favorite is 'Mrs J. Bradshaw', which has eye-catching, semidouble, scarlet flowers. In addition, the leaves are very attractive. 'Fire Opal' bears scarlet-orange, semidouble blooms. 'Red Wings' has scarlet flowers. *Geum reptans* (creeping avens, Zones 4 to 7) is a low-growing (6 to 8 in.) species that prefers alkaline soils. It produces soft yellow blooms on creeping stems in the spring.

Foliage is usually low enough to the ground that geum can be used in the front border. Because flowers rise above the foliage, the plant is effective in the mid border. I have also used this plant along pathways to provide a focal point in the garden.

The flower colors contrast nicely with blue or lavender flowers. I have used this plant with *Alchemilla mollis* (lady's mantle), *Baptisia australis* (false indigo), and *Nepeta* ×*faassenii* (cat-mint). Some cultivars can be very showy in flower color, so pick a cultivar to suit your taste.

This attractive plant can be short lived. In my Zone 5b garden, many have failed after a year or two.

Gypsophila paniculata   baby's breath   carnation family / Carophyllaceae

Hardiness: Zones 3b to 7a
Origin: Europe and northern Asia
Mature height: 2 to 3 ft.
Mature spread: 3 ft.
Landscape use: Mid border; specimen; mass
Season of bloom: Summer
Key ornamental characteristics: Sprays of tiny, white flowers

Ever-present in bridal bouquets and floral arrangements, baby's breath is a mainstay of the floral industry. This plant also has great ornamental value in the garden.

The white flowers are tiny, at 1/16 in. in diameter. Borne in panicles in numbers too high to count, the blooms give this plant an airy appearance. Feel free to cut some of the flowers for bouquets, because the plant will produce more. Cut the first wave of spent flowers, and a second wave will follow in the late summer or early fall.

Leaves are narrow, opposite in arrangement, and approximately 4 in. long. The foliage

Gypsophila paniculata

provides an excellent backdrop for the sprays of flowers. Baby's breath foliage is high in calcium and magnesium; apply supplements of these nutrients to the soil to boost plant growth.

Baby's breath prefers soil that is somewhat dry and well drained. It may not survive wet winters in poorly drained soils. It needs slightly alkaline soil; a pH of 7.0 to 7.5 is ideal. Incorporate lime in the soil to raise the pH. *Gypsophila paniculata* thrives in full sun and likes to be left undisturbed once established. Once mature, it may need staking.

There are no serious disease or insect problems with this species. The plant has slight susceptibility to botrytis and aster yellows.

The cultivar *Gypsophila paniculata* 'Bristol Fairy' is an old favorite, with double, white flowers excellent for cutting. It grows 2 to 3 ft. tall. 'Compacta Plena' grows to 18 in. and produces fewer flowers than 'Bristol Fairy'. 'Flamingo' has pale pink flowers and grows to 3 to 4 ft. tall. 'Perfecta' has large, white flowers and is a vigorous grower.

Baby's breath's sprays of white flowers work beautifully with every plant in the garden. The plant's fine texture provides nice contrast to any perennial border. Utilize it as a summer filler for areas where early spring wildflowers, bulbs, or other plants have died back. It is also a fine complement for brightly colored plants like *Lychnis coronaria* (rose campion), and it adds a touch of elegance to a rose garden.

Helenium autumnale   sneezeweed   daisy family / Asteraceae

Hardiness: Zones 3a to 8a
Origin: Eastern United States
Mature height: 3 to 5 ft.
Mature spread: 2 to 3 ft.
Landscape use: Back border; center of island bed; wildflower or meadow garden
Season of bloom: Midsummer to fall
Key ornamental characteristics: Late-season flowers in a variety of warm colors

Despite its common name, this plant probably will not make you sneeze. Like the maligned *Solidago* (goldenrod), sneezeweed blooms when plants such as ragweed, the real allergenic culprit, are also in bloom. One legend has it that sneezeweed got its moniker from the flowers and leaves being dried and used as snuff. Another reports that Native Americans used the dried leaves as a remedy for allergies.

Flower colors range from yellow to orange and rusty-red-brown. Blooms are up to 3 in. in diameter, and each ray has 3 noticeable lobes at the apex. The rays often droop slightly around the prominent, darker colored center disk. Removing faded flowers will encourage additional blooms. Pruning the plant back halfway in late May or early June will result in additional

Helenium autumnale

branching and more flowers. It will also reduce the need to stake this tall, upright plant. *Helenium autumnale* blooms for weeks and lasts well into fall, often until autumn frost, hence the species name.

The dark green leaves are linear-lanceolate to elliptic, glabrous, possibly serrate, and alternate in arrangement. Stems branch toward the top of the plant and are winged, which is a distinctive identification characteristic of the plant when it is not in flower.

Sneezeweed is easy to grow in moist, humus-rich soils, but does not tolerate dry locations. This native plant prefers full sun for best performance. It tends to fall over, and too much fertilizer will surely cause the plant to flop.

Propagation can take place by division in spring or fall every 2 to 4 years. Seed is also viable, although not uniform, and will yield many seedlings. The plant can be somewhat invasive if sited in ideal conditions.

There are a few disease problems associated with this plant. The leaves are susceptible to powdery mildew, leaf spot, and rust. Cutting plants back after flowering will reduce the chance of disease or insects.

A number of *Helenium* cultivars are available. Most grown today are crosses of *H. autumnale* and *H. hoopesii* (western sneezeweed). 'Bruno' has mahogany-red flowers and grows 3 to 4 ft. tall. 'Butterpat' has gorgeous, yellow flowers and grows 4 to 5 ft. tall. 'Wyndley' is a shorter cultivar, growing to 2 to 3 ft. and having coppery-brown flowers.

Locate sneezeweed in the back border or the center of an island bed. It works especially well with *Sedum spectabile* (showy stonecrop sedum) and any ornamental grass. The flower textures of *Helenium autumnale* and *Solidago* (goldenrod) are nicely complementary.

Helenium is supposedly named after Helen of Troy, although it is a native American plant. The brilliant flowers add a show of color at the end of the summer season.

Helianthus maximiliani   Maximilian sunflower   daisy family / Asteraceae

Hardiness: Zones 4a to 9a
Origin: Central United States
Mature height: 6 to 10 ft.
Mature spread: 2 to 3 ft.
Landscape use: Back border; center of island bed; meadow or prairie garden
Season of bloom: Late summer to frost
Key ornamental characteristics: Yellow flowers; impressive height

Maximilian sunflower is essentially summer's last hoorah. Numerous yellow flowers appear on each stalk of this imposing plant. If you are looking for a plant with dramatic height, look no farther. Of the species of perennials I have grown, this has been by far the tallest.

The gorgeous yellow flowers of *Helianthus max-imiliani* are 2 to 3 in. across. The rays are a lighter shade of yellow than the center disks. Flowers are borne individually on short stalks in the leaf axils at the top 4 to 5 ft. of the stem.

Leaves are 3 to 8 in. long, tapered, and have a greenish-gray cast. They have a deep midrib and are very scabrous.

Maximilian sunflower is easy to grow and performs well in a wide range of soils from sandy to loam and clay. It prefers sites that are dry or have medium moisture and easily withstands drought conditions. A sun worshiper, it requires full sun to thrive. The stems can reach 10 ft. in height on this rapidly growing plant. If you want a more compact plant, cut it back to 2 ft. in midsummer. Taller plants may need some staking or other support, especially if sited in wind-exposed areas.

This sunflower has no serious insect or disease problems.

Propagation is very easy by seed. The plant may freely self-sow in the garden. Seed can germinate in a span of only 2 weeks. Cuttings are easy to root.

Maximilian sunflower is native to the Great Plains and tall-grass prairie regions of central North America. It is typically found today in dry, open areas such as prairies, bluffs, and along roadsides.

Helianthus maximiliani 'Lemon Yellow', a beautiful cultivar, has pale yellow flowers. 'Santa Fe' has

Helianthus maximiliani

attractive golden-yellow blooms. *Helianthus ×multiflorus* (perennial sunflower, Zones 4 to 8) is a cross of the annual *H. annuus* (the plant that displays the classic large-faced flowers) and the perennial *H. decapetalus* (thin-leaf sunflower). Its mature height is approximately 5 ft. Flowers are bright yellow and up to 5 in. across.

Plant Maximilian sunflower against a wall or fence to help provide support, if needed. It is excellent for use in a native plant garden, cottage garden, meadow or prairie garden, or in naturalized areas.

Heliopsis helianthoides **var.** *scabra*   sunflower heliopsis   daisy family / Asteraceae

Hardiness: 3b to 9a
Origin: United States
Mature height: 3 to 4 ft.
Mature spread: 2 to 3 ft.
Landscape use: Mid or back border; prairie or meadow garden
Season of bloom: Summer to early fall
Key ornamental characteristics: Bright yellow flowers

Heliopsis is smaller but similar in appearance and closely related to *Helianthus*, the true sunflower. Invaluable for its long bloom period, sunflower heliopsis has showy, daisylike, yellow flowers that can be up to 3 in. in diameter. Removing spent flowers will extend the long blooming season even more. It is an excellent cut flower for a summer bouquet.

Leaves are opposite or whorled in arrangement, up to 5 in. long, serrate, and lanceolate-ovate. Leaves and stems have a rough texture. In warmer zones, the leaves should be cut back after the plant blooms. The plant has an upright, clump-forming habit.

Sunflower heliopsis is easy to grow. It tolerates a wide range of soils including poor soils

Heliopsis helianthoides var. *scabra*

and thrives in dry to moderately wet, well-drained soil. At home in full sun, it also tolerates light shade. But if it gets too much shade, it will become leggy and need staking. Sunflower heliopsis withstands drought, but does better if regularly watered. The plant is typically short lived.

Propagation is best accomplished by division in spring or fall. The plant should be divided every 2 or 3 years. Cuttings of the cultivars can also be taken.

There are no serious insect or disease problems with this plant. However, it has some susceptibility to aphids.

The straight species *Heliopsis helianthoides,* which is frequently seen growing along country roads, is weedy and produces fewer flowers than the *H.* var. *scabra* cultivars. 'Ballerina' ('Ballet Dancer') has yellow flowers with brown centers and grows to 2 ft. 'Prairie Sunset' has purple stems and purple-veined foliage. Its flowers are yellow with maroon tinting at the base of each ray, forming a ring around the yellow-brown center disk. It grows up to 4 ft. tall. 'Sommersonne' ('Summer Sun') is a handsome cultivar with double, bright yellow flowers; it grows to 3 ft.

Utilize sunflower heliopsis in the mid or back border. Or let it go wild in a meadow garden. It is a fine companion for *Eupatorium purpureum* subsp. *maculatum* (Joe-Pye weed), *Leucanthemum ×superbum* (Shasta daisy), *Liatris spicata* (spike gayfeather), *Ratibida columnifera* (Mexican hat), or *Teucrium chamaedrys* (wall germander).

Heliopsis adds a bright, yellow splash of color to the landscape. I love to use it as a specimen to provide accent in the garden.

Helleborus ×hybridus   Lenten rose   buttercup family / Ranunculaceae

Hardiness: Zones 4a to 9a
Origin: Hybrid
Mature height: 1 to 2 ft.
Mature spread: 12 to 18 in.
Landscape use: Edging; walkway; rock garden; massed
Season of bloom: Late winter to early spring
Key ornamental characteristics: Very early, long-lasting flowers in a variety of
    colors; evergreen foliage

Helleborus ×hybridus, the Perennial Plant Association's Plant of the Year for 2005, is a catchall name for a wide range of colorful hybrids of many *Helleborus* species.

Helleborus ×hybridus flowers appear in mid to late winter and last 2 months or more. Unbelievably, this plant can bloom in temperatures below freezing, especially if snow is on the ground to act as insulation. What many people consider to be the flowers of the plant

Helleborus ×hybridus

are really sepals surrounding the flowers. Sepal colors range from lavender to pink, green, creamy white, primrose yellow, deep red, and even purplish black. Double-flowered selections are becoming increasingly available; they look like miniature peonies (to which they are related). Many hybrids are now being sold by flower color rather than by cultivar name. For example, *H. ×hybridus* red flowered has dark maroon-red flowers and deeply cut leaves.

Lenten rose has evergreen, glossy, leathery, serrate, palmate leaves. Foliage can also be deeply cut. If not protected from harsh winter winds, foliage can become scorched and ragged. If this occurs, cut the damaged foliage back just before or during a new flush of growth.

Lenten rose prefers organically rich, moist, well-drained soils. Plants thrive in soils that are slightly alkaline. They do not tolerate overly wet sites and will withstand dry locations. They prefer light to moderate shade. Amazingly, Lenten rose is tolerant of summer heat and humidity.

This plant is relatively free of disease or insect problems. Crown rot can occur if the plant is sited in an overly wet location. Black spot and slugs can also be problematic on occasion. Aphids can sometimes appear in large numbers.

Division is probably the best method of propagation. In spring, carefully separate the crown's several roots and buds. Lenten rose is slow to establish. Seed can also be used, but it will take a few years for the plant to flower and even longer to really get established. Lenten rose also self-sows, and new plants close to the parent can be transplanted easily.

A cautionary note for gardeners with small children or pets: Lenten rose has toxic properties. Any part of the plant may be poisonous, but ingestion is serious only if large amounts have been consumed. The sap can also be irritating to the skin, so gloves should be worn when handling Lenten rose.

Another attractive *Helleborus* species is *H. niger* (Christmas rose, Zones 3 to 8), which blooms very early, and has upright, relatively flat, white flowers.

Use Lenten rose along pathways or walkways. It makes an impact when massed. Other plants that work well with *Helleborus* include species of *Epimedium* (barrenwort), the winter flowering shrub *Hamamelis* (witch hazel), *Pulmonaria* (Bethlehem sage), and *Tiarella* (foam-flower). Also plant Lenten rose with early spring flowering bulbs.

Helleborus offers a unique combination of winter growth, winter flowering, shade tolerance, and evergreen foliage. Place plants close to where you come and go regularly, so you can enjoy their lively show in winter.

Hemerocallis   daylily   daylily family / Hemerocallidaceae

Hardiness: Zones 3a to 9a
Origin: Central Europe to Asia; hybrids
Mature height: 1 to 4 ft.
Mature spread: 2 to 3 ft.
Landscape use: Mid border; mass; small cultivars ideal for rock gardens
Season of bloom: Spring to fall, depending on cultivar
Key ornamental characteristics: Broad spectrum of flower colors

---

Daylilies are endlessly versatile. The varied flower characteristics make this plant ideal as a backbone for the garden. Daylily's genus name *Hemerocallis* is from the Greek words meaning "day" and "beauty," in reference to an individual flower's short life span. But an abundance of flower buds appears on each flower stalk, called a scape, and many stalks occur on each plant. So the plant displays abundant blooms over a period of several weeks. Depending on the cultivar, the scape rises 1 to 4 ft. and the flowers may be fragrant.

You may have seen the "escaped" daylilies with yellow (*Hemerocallis flava*) or orange (*H. fulva*) flowers growing along roads, on embankments, or in the yards of abandoned houses. The incredibly wide range of flower colors available today is the result of extensive hybridization. In fact, the only colors not yet available are pure white and pure blue. In addition to cultivars' solid-colored flowers, there are also bi- and tricolored forms. The center portion of the daylily flower usually differs in color from the rest of the bloom. Typically the center is a shade of yellow, orange, or green.

Flower shapes are also diverse. Blooms are available in circular, star, ruffled, trumpet, and double forms, to name just a few. In addition, there are three categories of flower size: miniature (flowers 3 in. or less in diameter), small (flowers 3 to 4½ in. in diameter), and large (flowers 4½ in. or more in diameter).

Hemerocallis bloom time varies from spring to fall, depending on which hardiness zone the plants grow in and on the cultivar. When purchasing a plant, check the bloom time of the cultivar.

Leaves are opposite in arrangement on the crown. When a plant has several fans, it forms a clump. Leaves are long and linear in shape, ranging from 1 to 2 ft. long and ½ to 1 in. wide.

Foliage color ranges from bluish-green to yellow-green. Leaves have a noticeable midrib on the underside.

Daylilies easily adapt to many types of soils ranging from sandy to clay. But they perform best in well-drained soils that are high in organic matter. They thrive in full sun but will tolerate partial shade. Pastel flowers of some cultivars tend to fade if placed in continuous sun.

There are few serious disease or insect problems with daylilies. But aphids, spider mites, thrips, and slugs and snails may cause minor problems. Also, in recent years, daylily rust has been identified in 30 states, but it is mostly a problem in Zones 7 and above. If daylily rust is a problem in your area, choose resistant cultivars.

Hemerocallis hybrids

Propagation is best by division in the fall or spring every 3 to 5 years. Plants can also be propagated by seed.

Daylilies work well with almost any plant in the garden, and are best suited for the mid border. Try them with *Echinops ritro* (globe thistle) or *Kniphofia uvaria* (red hot poker). They are dramatic when massed. Dwarf cultivars are perfect for rock gardens.

For more information on daylilies, see the American Hemerocallis Society Web site.

Heuchera sanguinea   coral bells   saxifrage family / Saxifragaceae

Hardiness: 3b to 8a
Origin: Southwestern United States; hybrid
Mature height: 12 to 30 in. (in flower)
Mature spread: 1 ft.
Landscape use: Front border; along pathways; mass
Season of bloom: Late spring to midsummer
Key ornamental characteristics: Beautiful small
    flowers; attractive foliage

Heuchera sanguinea

Heuchera sanguinea is a classic garden perennial. If sited in appropriate cultural conditions, the plant is long lasting and tough. Much hybridization has taken place within the species, and you may find it listed as *H.* ×*brizoides*.

The plant's bell-shaped flowers are ¼ to ½ in. long. They are borne in cymose panicles that rise 10 to 20 in. above the foliage. Flower colors are white and shades of red and pink. Adequate watering enhances flower production. Remove spent flower stalks for extended flowering.

The attractive leaves are basal and ovate-orbicular or heart shaped. Leaves are 1 to 2 in. across and have 5 to 7 lobes. In my protected garden in Zone 5b, the plant remains semievergreen during mild winters.

Coral bells prefers full sun but likes partial shade in hotter regions. It performs best in well-drained soils rich in organic matter and having a neutral to alkaline pH. This species needs well-drained soil for health and survival. The plant does not like heavy, clay soils.

There are no serious disease or insect problems associated with *Heuchera sanguinea*. But the plant is subject to frost heaving. During wet or alternating freeze-thaw-freeze winters, the plants push up out of the ground. Pushing the crown back down into the ground can help.

Propagation is best by division. Divide the plant when it shows signs of having a woody center, preferably in spring. Discard the woody center and plant the remaining divisions. Leaf cuttings can also be taken in the fall: Cut an entire leaf plus a portion of the petiole, then use a rooting powder and stick the cutting in sand. Seed can also be planted.

Many *Heuchera* cultivars exist. Bressingham hybrids is typically seed propagated. Flower colors are red, pink, or white. 'Chatterbox' has rose-pink blooms. 'Leuchtkäfer' has stunning, bright red flowers. 'Snowflake' has pure white flowers. *Heuchera* ×*heucherella* (foamy bells) is an intergeneric hybrid created in the early 1900s between a variety of *Heuchera* and a variety of *Tiarella*. It is generally more compact and delicate in appearance than its *Heuchera* parent. Its flower colors are pink or white.

Delicate looking when planted singly, coral bells makes a spectacular statement when planted in mass. Try it with *Geranium* (hardy geranium) in sun, or *Pulmonaria saccharata* (Bethlehem sage) in shade. Coral bells blends well with all plants.

Hibiscus moscheutos   rose mallow, common mallow   mallow family / Malvaceae

Hardiness: Zones 4a to 9b
Origin: Eastern United States
Mature height: 3 to 8 ft.
Mature spread: 2 to 4 ft.
Landscape use: Back border; specimen; near ponds
Season of bloom: Midsummer to frost
Key ornamental characteristics: Huge, eye-catching
     flowers; plant height

If you want eye-catching flowers, look no farther than rose mallow. Many species of this genus are tropical or subtropical plants. The dramatic flowers can be as large as dinner plates, measuring from 4 to 12 in. across. Flowers are shades of red, pink, and white as well as bicolor. Borne singly, blooms last but a few days, but flowers are produced prolifically throughout the flowering season. Remove spent blooms to help maintain the plant's appearance.

Rose mallow will tolerate light shade, but it prefers full sun and good air circulation to be healthy and disease resistant. It requires moist to wet soils that are organically rich, but performs admirably in typical garden soil as long

Hibiscus moscheutos

as it is not dry. Long, regular watering is advisable. Site the plant in a protected spot to reduce potential windburn. Taller plants may need staking, especially if they receive too much shade. Cut stems back to within 6 in. of the ground in late fall. Prune off the previous year's growth after new growth has emerged in spring.

Leaves are large, green, have pubescence on the underside, and alternate in arrangement. They are heart shaped with no lobes, or they have 3 to 5 shallow lobes. Leaf growth is slow to begin in spring, but rose mallow grows rapidly. The plant benefits from regular fertilization over the summer. Pinch back the plants in spring to make them more compact.

Propagation can be accomplished by division in spring or fall. Seed propagation is also possible in spring. Either method will produce a plant that flowers the second year.

Several disease and insect problems exist with rose mallow. Japanese beetle and white fly are the two primary concerns; they can quickly do their damage. Leaf spot, canker, aphids, scale, blight, and rust can also take a toll.

Numerous *Hibiscus* cultivars are available. Southern Belle Group Disco Belle Series, mixed, is a compact plant ideal for small gardens. Flower colors are red, pink, and white. Its mature height is 2 ft. The Fleming hybrids produce gorgeous, large, pink flowers with red centers. Southern Belle Group has large flowers in red, pink, white, or bicolor. Plants grow 4 to 6 ft. tall.

The flowers of rose mallow can be dominating in the garden. I use this plant as a specimen or as an accent in the back border of the perennial bed. It is vibrant enough to be planted in the shrub border as well. Its cultural requirements make it ideal for pond areas.

Hosta   hosta, plantain lily, funkia   hosta family / Hostaceae

Hardiness: Zones 3a to 8a
Origin: China and Japan; hybrid
Mature height: 8 in. to 3 ft. (varies with cultivar, hybrid, species)
Mature spread: 10 in. to 2 ft. (varies with cultivar, hybrid, species)
Landscape use: Shade or semishade gardens; mass; specimen; naturalized areas
Season of bloom: Summer
Key ornamental characteristics: Bold, handsome foliage; flowers can be fragrant

The genus *Hosta* immediately comes to mind as the one for a semishade or full-shade garden. Plants typically are long lived and easy to grow, so they are very popular in the garden world. Perennials are typically grown for their flowers, but hostas are usually grown for their handsome foliage. However, some hostas produce beautiful, aromatic blooms.

Foliage colors are diverse, ranging from green, to blue-green, yellow, gold, cream, and white. Many hybrids have foliage that is solidly colored while others have variegated leaves.

Hosta hybrid

Generally, the cultivars with green and gold leaves can take more sun than the ones with blue foliage. The leaves can be thin and narrow to broad. They can also be shiny and smooth to wavy and crinkled. There is almost endless variety in hosta foliage.

Depending on the hybrid or species, *Hosta* flowers are white or lavender and occur at some point in the summer. Flowers are borne on scapes. The flowers of *H. plantaginea* and its cultivars are white and tend to be fragrant. You may find that the flowers detract from the foliage, so remove them at your discretion.

Hostas prefer humus-rich, well-drained soil. Plants prefer light to full shade and even moisture. Some hostas can be grown in full sun, but only if they get adequate moisture and the climate is not too hot, like in portions of the Pacific Northwest or Northeast. Hostas will suffer in dry soils.

Leaf spot can be an occasional disease problem for *Hosta*. But the main problem is insects. Snails and slugs are the major problem: they can do heavy damage to a plant. You can try home remedies to control them, such as putting out a saucer of beer, but I recommend snail and slug bait. Black vine weevil can also be an occasional problem.

Propagation is best by division in spring, but *Hosta* plants do not need to be frequently divided. To be successful dividing them, be sure to dig clumps. Seeds are viable, but plants are slow to establish.

The number of hostas available today is truly dizzying. Some, however, have attained the status of tried-and-true classics, including *Hosta* 'Halcyon', a medium-sized plant with bluish foliage; 'Francee', medium-sized with white-edged, green leaves; 'Sum and Substance', a huge, gold-leaved cultivar; and 'Gold Standard', with green-edged, golden leaves.

Hostas do not need to be planted with any other plants. But if you want to add contrasting texture, try *Astilbe ×arendsii* (astilbe), *Corydalis lutea* (yellow corydalis), *Pulmonaria saccharata* (Bethlehem sage), or ferns. Ideal for shady areas, hosta looks dramatic in mass and also when used as a specimen. No genus brightens up a shaded area more than *Hosta*, especially the types with variegated leaves. Some actually appear luminous.

Iberis sempervirens   evergreen candytuft   cabbage family / Brassicaceae

Hardiness: Zones 3b to 9a
Origin: Europe
Mature height: 6 to 12 in.
Mature spread: 18 in. to 2 ft.
Landscape use: Front border; along pathways; rock garden
Season of bloom: Spring
Key ornamental characteristics: Beautiful, pure white flowers; deep green foliage

The Latin species name *sempervirens* means "always green." This popular evergreen perennial spreads, forming a low-growing, matlike mound. Evergreen candytuft announces that warm weather is soon to arrive by flowering in early spring when many other perennials are just emerging.

The pretty, 4-petaled, white flowers are the main attraction of evergreen candytuft. They completely cover the plant in spring, often obscuring the foliage. In cool climates, flowers may develop a slight pink cast as they age. After flowering, cut the foliage back halfway to encourage new growth and maintain growth habit.

Leaves are dark green, alternate, linear, leathery, and glabrous. In colder zones, foliage is

Iberis sempervirens

semievergreen, and the plant appreciates protection from the winter sun so it does not get sun scorch. Stems are semiwoody to woody; the plant is actually a subshrub.

Ibiris sempervirens requires full sun to produce lots of flowers. Partial shade will reduce the floriferous nature of the plant. Evergreen candytuft can grow in a variety of soil types. But wet, inadequately drained conditions may kill plants.

This plant has few disease and insect problems. However, club root can lead to stunted growth, and crown rot will kill the plant.

Propagation of the species can be accomplished by seed. Cuttings can be taken in midsummer to reproduce cultivars. Division can be done fall or spring. The stems may root where they touch the soil, creating new plants that can be transplanted.

Several *Iberis sempervirens* cultivars are available. 'Alexander's White' is tall, growing to 1 ft., and produces an abundance of white flowers. 'Autumn Snow' has white flowers in both spring and fall. 'Snowflake' ('Schneeflocke') has large, white flowers and grows to 10 in. tall.

The splashy, white, early spring flowers blend wonderfully with the bright flowers of spring flowering bulbs like tulip and daffodil. *Euphorbia epithymoides* (cushion spurge) is also an attractive companion plant.

Iris hybrids   bearded iris   iris family / Iridaceae

Hardiness: Zones 3a to 10a
Origin: Hybrid
Mature height: 28 in. to 4 ft.
Mature spread: 18 to 24 in.
Landscape use: Mid or back border; mass
Season of bloom: Mid-spring to early summer
Key ornamental characteristics: Gorgeous flowers in a wide range of colors

Bearded iris hybrids are longstanding, traditional garden plants. They are by far the most popular of this broad-ranging genus. Just drive down any country road in the Midwest or southern United States, and you will see them putting on their spring show.

Bearded irises have been divided into categories based on height: miniature dwarf bearded (to 8 in.), standard dwarf bearded (8 to 16 in.), intermediate bearded (16 to 27½ in.), miniature tall bearded (16 to 27½ in., with small, graceful flowers), and tall bearded (27½ in. and up). Border bearded irises are essentially a slightly smaller version of tall bearded irises. In general, the smaller varieties bloom earlier than the taller ones.

The tall bearded iris species was formerly known as *Iris germanica*, but with extensive hybridization, cultivars are not representative of the typical German iris. There are countless *Iris* cultivars; the majority falls into the tall bearded iris category. I recommend getting information from the American Iris Society (www.irises.org) to select a cultivar and get more information.

The Greek word *iris* means "rainbow," referring to the vast range of flower colors available. Flowers rise above the foliage, with one or more blossoms per stem. Bearded iris gets its name from the "beard," or hairs visible on the outer segments of some flowers. Flowers are at least 5 in. wide, and come in a vast range of colors. Leaves are light green, sword shaped, and are up to 18 in. long.

Plants must be placed in full sun to maximize flowering. Soil must have a near-neutral pH with excellent drainage. Iris will adapt to a variety of soils except heavy clay. Providing proper drainage will help reduce susceptibility to bacterial soft rot. Do not place mulch around the rhizomes, as it can contribute to decay. When planting iris, amend the soil with organic matter. Foliage should be cut back to ground level in winter to help prevent disease problems. Once established, bearded iris is drought tolerant.

Bearded irises are prone to a number of insects and diseases. The most serious insect problem is iris borer, which tunnels into the

Tall bearded iris

rhizomes, thus increasing susceptibility to bacterial and fungal infection such as bacterial soft rot. Leaf spot can also be a problem. Infected rhizomes and other plant parts should be removed quickly to prevent spread of infection. Aphids and thrips can cause damage to flowers and spread viral diseases. An insecticide spraying routine may be the best way to keep bearded iris healthy.

Propagation is best by division every 3 or 4 years. It should be done after flowering in the summer. Plant the rhizomes at an angle so a small portion is aboveground to help reduce potential rot.

Bearded irises look wonderful when massed in front of a shrub border. They also provide an abundance of color in the mid or back border. Try mixing irises with other classic garden plants like daylilies and peonies.

Iris sibirica   Siberian iris   iris family / Iridaceae

Hardiness: Zones 3a to 9a
Origin: Central Europe
Mature height: 2 to 4 ft.
Mature spread: 18 to 24 in.
Landscape use: Mid border; mass
Season of bloom: Mid-spring
Key ornamental characteristics: Purplish-blue to
    lavender, white, or yellow flowers; grasslike
    foliage; seedpods add winter interest

Iris sibirica

Siberian irises add an elegant note to the garden. They have 2 to 5 purplish-blue, lavender, white, or yellow flowers per stem held slightly above the foliage. The flowers appear in mid-spring and last for approximately 2 weeks. The relatively short bloom period of this species is its only drawback. After flowering, the stalks are topped by a 2- to 3-in. seedpod that adds textural interest, especially in winter.

Foliage is reminiscent of ornamental grass and makes an impact in the garden after the flowers are spent. The leaves are linear and about ½ inch in width, resembling an arching sword. In fall the foliage has an orange cast. The habit is upright and vase shaped, and the plant reaches 3 to 4 ft. in height.

Siberian irises perform best in full sun but will tolerate light shade. The plants I have growing in full sun are slightly larger and bloom more profusely than my plants in light shade. This perennial prefers moist soils that are slightly acidic, but it will tolerate a variety of conditions including slightly dry soils. This species generally requires little maintenance; it simply requires removal of the previous year's growth in spring.

Siberian irises do not tend to be prone to soft rot or iris borer like many bearded irises. In fact, I have grown this species for over 10 years and have never encountered any disease or insect problems.

Division is best in spring but is not frequently needed. If you do divide plants, do not let them dry out before replanting.

There are many *Iris sibirica* cultivars to select from. 'Caesar's Brother' is a favorite, with dark purplish-blue flowers and a mature height of 3 ft. While blue, purple, and white are the most common flower colors, newer cultivars offer yellow, pink, and subtle blends. Newer varieties also tend to have a longer bloom period.

I grow eight Siberian iris plants along a curved pathway in my garden. At the peak of flowering, I have counted more than 200 blooms on those plants. In front of the iris, I have pink-flowering *Dianthus*, which blooms at the same period, and the two species put on a magnificent floral display. Siberian iris also is a terrific companion to *Paeonia* (peony). It easily fits into formal or informal situations.

Kalimeris pinnatifida 'Hortensis' Japanese aster daisy family / Asteraceae

Hardiness: Zones 4b to 8a
Origin: Eastern Asia
Mature height: 2 to 3 ft.
Mature spread: 2 ft.
Landscape use: Mid border; wild or meadow garden
Season of bloom: Midsummer to fall
Key ornamental characteristics: Long-blooming, semidouble, white flowers

Are you looking for a plant that requires little if any care? Has a long bloom period? Adapts to a wide range of conditions? Japanese aster may be for you.

Kalimeris pinnatifida

Kalimeris pinnatifida 'Hortensis' bears semidouble, white flowers that are 1 in. across. Each individual flower has a yellow center. Japanese aster blooms from midsummer to fall.

The medium green leaves on the lower portion of the plant are pinnately lobed, ovate-oblong, and up to 3 in. long. Leaves toward the top of the stem are 1 in. long and sometimes entire. The foliage is alternate in arrangement on this upright, bushy plant.

Japanese aster is very easy to cultivate in just about any moderately moist, well-drained soil type. It prefers full sun in northern zones and benefits from partial shade in hotter regions.

There are no serious disease or insect problems associated with Japanese aster.

Propagation is very easy by division in the spring or fall. Spring is best so that flowering is not disrupted. Seed can also be sown.

The related species *Kalimeris mongolica* (Zones 5 to 9) has white flowers with purple-tinged rays and a yellow center. It is hardy only in the extreme southern portions of the Midwest.

Kalimeris pinnatifida (also known as *Asteromoea pinnatifida*) is best used in a meadow or wild garden because of its informal appearance. It can also be used in the mid border of an informal perennial bed. The white flowers provide a nice transition among other species. Try using it in front of *Solidago* (goldenrod) and behind *Sedum spectabile* (showy stonecrop sedum) for an effective late summer and early fall display. It also blends in well with asters and has a similar appearance.

Kirengeshoma palmata   yellow waxbells   hydrangea family / Hydrangeaceae

Hardiness: Zones 5a to 7a
Origin: Japan and Korea
Mature height: 3 to 4 ft.
Mature spread: 3 to 4 ft.
Landscape use: Back border of shade garden; specimen
Season of bloom: Late summer to early fall
Key ornamental characteristics: Handsome, maplelike foliage; pale yellow flowers late in season

This genus of two species comes from Asia. At one time, *Kirengeshoma palmata* was classified as its own family, but now it is in the hydrangea family. This unique perennial looks like a shrub at first glance. *Kirengeshoma* comes from the Japanese, and means "yellow lotus flower hat." The species *palmata* means "shaped like a hand," in reference to the leaves' maple leaf appearance.

Waxy, yellow, bell-shaped flowers droop on wiry, thin stems; flowers are typically borne in clusters of 3 blooms. The plants in the wild reportedly have flowers ranging from white to

Kirengeshoma palmata

apricot in color. Blooms do not fully open, tend to be short lived, and give way to interesting, unusually shaped fruit. The greenish-brown fruit capsule has 2 or 3 protruding horns.

The plant's major aesthetic quality is its foliage. Leaves are medium green, coarsely toothed, shallowly lobed, pubescent, and can be up to 8 in. wide. Farther up the reddish-purple stem, the leaves become smaller. Yellow waxbells has an upright habit and is clump forming.

Yellow waxbells is particular about where it is sited. It prefers moist, acidic, organically rich, well-drained soils in partial to full shade.

Propagation should be done by division after the plant has become fully established. Seed is difficult to come by and irregular in germination.

There are no serious insect or disease problems with yellow waxbells.

Kirengeshoma koreana is the other species in this genus, but there is debate as to whether the two species might, in fact, be the same species. It has been suggested that the Korean native grows slightly taller, the flowers open more fully, and it has more of a greenish stem than the species from Japan.

This unique plant is ideal for use in woodland gardens. Its late-blooming flowers add interest when many other woodland plants have faded. It also fits perfectly into a Japanese- or Chinese-style garden. Try planting it around Asiatic maples.

Although yellow waxbells has been available for years in the nursery industry, it is not widely known. Its distinctive aesthetic qualities will add interest to the shade garden.

Knautia macedonica   knautia knautia   teasel family / Dipsacaceae

Hardiness: Zones 4a to 7a
Origin: Europe
Mature height: 18 to 30 in.
Mature spread: 1 to 2 ft.
Landscape use: Front or mid border; mass
Season of bloom: Summer
Key ornamental characteristics: Attractive dark
    crimson flowers

Knautia macedonica

The distinctive, deep crimson flowers draw attention to this plant, which was formerly known as *Scabiosa rumelica*. Blooms have the same dome or pincushion shape as *Scabiosa* flowers. They are borne on stems that rise and twist from basal clumps. Each flower stem branches into several stalks. Removing spent blooms encourages flowering later in the season. Knautia makes a wonderful cut flower.

Leaves are entire or, at the base of the plant, they have a few lobes. They are 3 in. long and become more divided and feathery toward the top of the plant.

Knautia is easy to grow in well-drained, slightly alkaline, ordinary soil. It prefers full sun, but does not like heat and humidity. Even in cooler climates, the plant can look a little tired. It forms an upright clump in the spring and early summer, but may flop and need staking as the heat of summer progresses. Or you can let it lean against taller plants.

There are no disease or insect problems associated with this plant.

Propagation is best by seed. Under optimal conditions, the species may self-seed in the garden.

This plant is a good one to mass in the front or mid border of a cottage garden. Try placing it behind a silver-leaved plant like *Achillea* 'Moonshine' and in front of a burgundy-leaved specimen like *Eupatorium rugosum* 'Chocolate'.

Knautia macedonia has a short life span, 1 to 2 years, but I continue to purchase a specimen or two for my garden as needed. Its dark crimson flower color is not often found in perennials.

Kniphofia uvaria   red hot poker, torchlily   asphodel family / Asphodelaceae

Hardiness: Zones 5a to 9a
Origin: Southern Africa
Mature height: 18 to 24 in. (up to 5 ft. in flower)
Mature spread: 3 ft.
Landscape use: Mid border; specimen
Season of bloom: Late spring through summer
Key ornamental characteristics: Glowing, orange-
    red and yellow flowers

Kniphofia uvaria

I was visiting the Royal Horticultural Society's Wisley Gardens in England during the summer of 2002 and came across the most impressive example of *Kniphofia* I have ever seen. I spotted it at least 100 yards away across a clearing. The flowers blazed even at that distance. Hence, the much-deserved common names red hot poker and torch lily.

If you are intimidated by dramatic, brightly colored flowers, red hot poker is not for you. Flower stems rise 2 to 3 ft. above the foliage, and blooms are massed 5 to 10 in. at the apex of the scape. The racemes of tubular flowers change color bottom to top: flowers at the apex are orange-red and still opening as the lower ones are finished and turning yellow. This color display is eye-catching. Flower scapes should be removed when spent.

Greenish-gray foliage is linear and is 1 in. wide and up to 3 ft. long. The midrib of leaves is deeply set. Red hot poker is upright in habit and clump forming. After blooming, leaves can be cut back halfway to tidy up the plant. In colder climates, leaves can be bundled and tied over the center of the plant to protect it from winter moisture and cold. Where I live, in Zone 5b, leaves remain semievergreen if we have a mild winter.

Kniphofia prefers full sun and well-drained soils. It will not tolerate heavy, moist soils, and wet winter soils will cause root rot. The plant prefers sites protected from wind.

There are no disease or insect problems asociated with this plant.

Propagation can be by seed, but it will take a few years for the plant to establish itself and flower. Division is possible, but plants take several years to grow large enough to be successfully divided. However, division is traumatic for red hot poker; it is best if plants are not disturbed.

This species has been mostly replaced in cultivation by the many hybrids resulting from a parentage of *Kniphofia uvaria*, *K. ×praecox* (Zones 5a to 9a), *K. galpinii* (Zones 4 to 9), and *K.*

macowanii (Zones 4 to 9); the latter two species are now listed as *K. triangularis* subsp. *triangularis*. *Kniphofia* 'Alcazar' has brilliant red flowers tinged with salmon on 3- to 4-ft. stems. 'Bressingham Comet' is a compact hybrid with orange to yellow flowers rising 2 ft. above the foliage. 'Rosea Superba' has rose-red flowers. 'Sunningdale Yellow' has dark yellow flowers that rise 3 ft.

I use red hot poker in front of shrubs that complement its vibrant flowers; for example, *Itea virginica* (Virginia sweetspire). It also works well with plants that have silver-colored foliage, and is best suited for the mid border of a perennial garden. Because it is so brightly colored, I recommend utilizing it as a specimen or at most in groups of 3 plants.

Red hot poker is one of the most flamboyant perennials. Its dazzling, tall blooms put on a remarkable show.

Lamium maculatum   spotted nettle   mint family / Lamiaceae

Lamium maculatum

Hardiness: Zones 3a to 8a
Origin: Europe and west Asia
Mature height: 4 to 8 in.
Mature spread: 12 to 18 in.
Landscape use: Ground cover for shady areas; front
    border
Season of bloom: Late spring to midsummer
Key ornamental characteristics: Attractive,
    variegated leaves; pleasant pink or white flowers

Although the unique, colorful foliage of spotted nettle slightly resembles that of *Urtica dioica* (stinging nettle), it does not have stinging hairs. And *Lamium maculatum*'s unique, colorful leaves make it an attractive, friendly plant for the perennial garden.

Leaves are medium green with splotches of creamy white or gray-green near the midrib. They are ovate with a cordate base, and have crenate-dentate margins. Leaves are opposite in arrangement and 1 to 2 in. long. Foliage can be evergreen in warmer climates. Stems are square.

Mauve-pink flowers rise just above the foliage. Approximately ½ in. long, they occur in whorls at the end of stems. The blooms are 2-lipped, hooded, and slightly reminiscent of snapdragon flowers.

Spotted nettle is easy to grow in a range of soil types, but it prefers loam that is slightly acidic. The soil must be well drained and moist but not overly wet. If the soil is too dry, the foliage will decline and look ragged. The plant thrives in partial to full shade, but will scorch if exposed to too much sun. High heat and humidity may also cause the plant to look unsightly. Trim back tattered summer foliage to encourage new growth. When sited in ideal conditions, spotted nettle quickly spreads. But it is not overly aggressive and is easy to pull up.

There are no serious insect or disease problems associated with spotted nettle. Aphids, snails, and slugs are occasional visitors. Crown rot may occur in overly wet soils. Powdery mildew may also occur on occasion.

Division is the best method of propagation and is easily accomplished in the spring or fall. Stem cuttings can also be taken during the growing season.

Several *Lamium maculatum* cultivars are available. 'Beacon Silver' has silver leaves with green margins, and the flowers are dark pink. 'Chequers Board' has green leaves with a silver stripe and pink flowers. 'Roseum' has pink flowers and green leaves with white markings. 'White Nancy' has white flowers and green and silver leaves.

Lamium maculatum is grown primarily for its foliage. It is perfect for use as a mat-forming ground cover to lighten up shady areas. It provides an excellent complement for hostas and ferns. It can also be used in the front border, but does not do well with foot traffic.

Lavandula angustifolia   commom lavender, English lavender   mint family / Lamiaceae

Hardiness: Zones 5a to 9a
Origin: Mediterranean region
Mature height: 1 to 2 ft.
Mature spread: 1 to 2 ft.
Landscape use: Mid border; specimen; in mass
Season of bloom: Summer
Key ornamental characteristics: Fragrant lavender or purple flowers; attractive foliage

The soothing scent of lavender is used in a variety of household items, from soaps to candles, sachets, and potpourri. In addition, the attractive foliage and flowers of this popular perennial add a touch of elegance to any garden.

Flowers are purple to lavender and ¼ to ½ in. long. Blooms are borne on spikes, and like the foliage are highly aromatic. Honeybees are highly attracted to lavender.

Gray leaves are opposite or whorled in arrangement, while new growth is often clustered in axils. Stems are square, and the plant has a white, tomentose texture.

Lavandula angustifolia

Lavender thrives in full sun and hot weather. It prefers well-drained soils. If grown in heavy clay soils, the plant's growth can be soft, which can lead to hardiness problems in colder areas. Lavender tends to have a more compact growth habit in cooler climates. When plants begin to show new signs of growth in the spring after danger of frost has passed, cut back old stems by one-third to invigorate the plant and encourage flower production.

There are few serious disease or insect problems with common lavender. Leaf spot, root rot, and root-knot nematode may occasionally occur. The plant may be short lived in the wet winters of the northern end of its hardiness zone.

Propagation is by stem cuttings in the summer or division in the fall.

Numerous cultivars of *Lavandula angustifolia* exist. 'Alba' is a very attractive, white-flowering plant. 'Hidcote' has dark violet-blue flowers and silver-gray foliage. 'Mitcham Gray' has dark violet flowers. 'Munstead' is compact in habit, and flowers early in the summer.

Plant lavender along pathways and in other areas where you will brush against it and release the fragrance. I use it intermixed with peonies and shrub roses. Because of its gray foliage, lavender contrasts nicely with plants that have deep green leaves. It is beautiful as a specimen or in mass.

Common lavender is a must for every garden. Due to hardiness problems, especially in the upper Midwest, try placing lavender in a pot and treating it as an annual. When fall arrives, just cut it back and make some lavender potpourri.

Leucanthemum ×superbum   Shasta daisy   daisy family / Asteraceae

Hardiness: Zones 5a to 9a
Origin: Hybrid
Mature height: 1 to 3 ft.
Mature spread: 2 ft.
Landscape use: Mid border; specimen
Season of bloom: Early summer to frost
Key ornamental characteristics: White flowers with yellow centers; dark green foliage

Leucanthemum ×superbum

Shasta daisy is a hybrid of *Leucanthemum lacustre* (Portuguese chrysanthemum) and *L. maximum* (Pyrenees chrysanthemum) that was first produced by the famous horticulturist Luther Burbank. Beautiful 2- to 3-in.-diameter, white flowers with yellow centers appear in the early summer and last until frost on heavily branched plants.

The coarsely toothed, dark green leaves truly complement the flowers. Alternate in arrangement, lower leaves are oblanceolate while the upper leaves are lanceolate. Foliage provides excellent texture in the garden once the plant is established.

Leucanthemum ×superbum grows best in full sun and moist, well-drained sites—especially well drained during the winter. I have had several stands of Shasta daisy die from overly wet winter soil. Shasta daisy is very easy to maintain; deadhead as needed to help prolong bloom later in the season.

I have never encountered any disease problems with Shasta daisy. Japanese beetle will appear on occasion.

Shasta daisy is easy to propagate. It can be divided in spring or fall. Seed readily germinates, and stem cuttings can be taken in early summer.

There are many single and double-flowering *Leucanthemum ×superbum* cultivars. 'Alaska' is an old, cold-hardy cultivar that has single, 3-in., pure white flowers borne on 2- to 3-ft. stems. 'Becky' has large white flowers and was named Perennial Plant of the Year for 2003 by the Perennial Plant Association. 'Mount Shasta' is 2 ft. tall and has double flowers. 'Snowcap' is compact, growing 15 to 18 in. with a bushy habit.

Shasta daisy's attractive white flowers work with every plant in the garden. If placed in front of a dark background in the landscape, they really pop. I particularly like Shasta daisy with *Pervoskia atriplicifolia* (Russian sage), *Lavandula angustifolia* (English lavender, and *Liatris spicata* (spike gayfeather). If you need a specimen plant for the mid border or want to create a mass display of white in the summer landscape, this is the species for you. The white flowers truly have a cooling effect during a warm summer day.

Liatris spicata   spike gayfeather   daisy family / Asteraceae

Hardiness: Zones 3a to 9a
Origin: Central and eastern United States
Mature height: 2 to 4 ft.
Mature spread: 2 ft.
Landscape use: Mid border; mass; specimen; wild or prairie garden
Season of bloom: Summer
Key ornamental characteristics: Spikes of mauve-purple flowers; seed heads offer
    winter interest

Liatris spicata

Liatris spicata is totally reliable in the garden. This native plant will flower profusely year after year. It is tough but beautiful.

Spike gayfeather has mauve-purple flower heads on spikes that are 10 to 16 in. long. Flowers open from the top of the spike down, which is unusual among plants with flower spikes. Although it belongs to the daisy family, its flowers do not resemble daisies, and in fact look like a bottlebrush. The colorful blossoms appear for several weeks in the summer. They are excellent for use in fresh or dried flower arrangements. The flowers also are highly attractive to butterflies and bees collecting nectar. Flower spikes add great interest to the winter landscape.

Leaves are very small, straplike, broad-lanceolate, and inconsequential.

Spike gayfeather is vertical in habit, and reaches 2 to 4 ft. tall with a width of up to 2 ft. The flower spikes add great interest to the winter landscape. This species may require staking after it has established itself in the garden. It is tolerant of many soil conditions, but prefers well-drained sites, and prefers full sun. It thrives in dry, hot conditions. I have grown this plant for over 10 years, and in my garden, it always emerges late in the spring, compared to other perennials. The plants tend to be long lived.

I have not observed any disease or insect problems. Reportedly, Southern root-knot nematode can be a problem in southern areas of the Midwest.

There are several excellent *Liatris spicata* cultivars. 'Alba' has white flowers and grows to 4 ft. or more in height. The white-flowering cultivars usually bloom a couple of weeks later than the mauve-colored cultivars. 'Kobold' is a wonderful selection that is a little shorter than the species; it has mauve-pink flowers.

The unusual flower spikes contrast nicely with other flower shapes. I have used *Liatris spicata* with *Hemerocallis* (daylily), *Leucanthemum* (Shasta daisy), and *Gaillardia* (blanket-flower). The foliage of *Baptisia australis* (false Indigo) also provides a perfect backdrop for *L. spicata*.

Ligularia stenocephala   narrow spiked ligularia   daisy family / Asteraceae

Hardiness: Zones 5a to 8a
Origin: Japan and China
Mature height: 3 to 5 ft. (in flower)
Mature spread: 2 to 4 ft.
Landscape use: Shade garden; woodland garden; near wet areas
Season of bloom: Early to midsummer
Key ornamental characteristics: yellow to orange daisylike flowers; bold foliage

Bold, bright, and beautiful are three words I would use to describe this plant. I became truly aware of the beauty of narrow spiked ligularia when I worked at the Royal Horticultural Society's Wisley Gardens in the late 1980s. And the plant has continued to be one of my favorites.

Gorgeous, bright, lemon-yellow flowers that are approximately 1 in. across occur in racemes. They are densely packed for 18 to 24 in. at the apex of a spike that rises 2 to 4 ft. above the foliage. They make a dramatic statement in dappled shade. The flower stems have a dark purplish color.

Leaves are heart shaped to triangular, coarsely toothed, and up to 1 ft. long and wide. Alternate in arrangement, they are light green in color. Foliage is mostly basal, which gives the plant a mounded habit. Although the flowers are the highlight of the plant, the leaves offer ornamental value.

Ligularia stenocephala can be particular about cultural conditions. It requires organically rich, moderately wet to wet soils that do not dry out. It performs best in dappled shade. Too much sun, even if soil conditions are met, causes the leaves to wilt during the day before becoming turgid again at night. The plant likes zones that have relatively cool nights. Too much

Ligularia 'The Rocket'

shade will result in the flower spikes leaning toward brighter light, which detracts from the ornamental value of the vertical flowers.

Snails and slugs like to munch on the foliage, especially in the spring and early summer. There are no serious disease or insect problems.

Propagation can be accomplished by seed or division. But division is seldom needed. If you want to propagate cultivars, I recommend division to ensure true-to-type reproduction.

'The Rocket' is usually listed as a cultivar of *Ligularia*. It is also occasionally listed as a cultivar of *L. przewalskii* (Shavalski's ligularia). Or it may be a hybrid of these two related species. 'The Rocket' is a marvelous plant with flower spikes reaching up to 6 ft. *Ligularia dentata* (leopard plant, Zones 4 to 8) is a related species with yellow, daisylike flowers. It has large leaves and grows 3 to 4 ft. tall.

Narrow spiked ligularia is ideal for a moist to wet shade or woodland garden. If you have a stream or pond, this plant will steal the show when placed around it. It would also love being sited in a bog garden. *Aruncus dioicus* (goat's beard), *Astilbe*, *Chelone lyonii* (pink turtlehead), and *Hosta* all contrast nicely with the coarseness of *Ligularia*. I also like it with the fine-textured foliage of *Dicentra* (bleeding heart). Narrow spiked ligularia is excellent as a specimen or in small groupings.

Lilium   lily   lily family / Liliaceae

Asiatic lily

Hardiness: Zones 5a to 9a
Origin: Hybrid
Mature height: 2 to 6 ft.
Mature spread: 12 to 16 in.
Landscape use: Mid border; specimen
Season of bloom: Summer
Key ornamental characteristics: Showy flowers in a
    wide range of colors

Highly valued for their exotic-looking flowers, lilies have been a source of fascination for millenia. Most lilies sold in mail order catalogs today are products of hybridization. There is a large number of species to select from. Lilies have been placed in 9 divisions, based on plant parentage, flower shape, and flower position (nodding or upright). Two of the more popular divisions are Asiatic and oriental hybrids.

Flower colors range from shades of orange, red, pink, and purple, to yellow and white. Lilies are available in every color but blue. Asiatic hybrids usually bloom in early to midsummer and are unscented. Oriental hybrids typically have larger blooms that are heavily scented. They usually bloom from mid to late summer. If flowers are cut, do not remove more than ⅓ of the stem. The leaves and stems produce food for the following year's flowers, and if heavily cut back, subsequent flower production may be poor.

Lilies typically have many leaves coming off an erect stem. They are lanceolate, 2 to 6 in. long, and ⅓ to ¾ in. wide. Asiatic hybrids' leaves are smaller than those of oriental hybrids. Asiatic hybrids are also typically shorter than oriental hybrids, ranging from 1 to 3 ft.

Lilies tolerate a wide range of soils, but prefer organically rich soils that are not overly wet. They prefer full sun but withstand light shade. A layer of summer mulch is ideal to help keep the roots cool. Lily bulbs should be planted at a depth that is 2 to 3 times their diameter.

A number of diseases can be problems for lilies. Basal bulb rot infects the bulbs, causing them to rot. It tends to occur in poorly drained soils in warmer regions. Botrytis can affect the leaves, causing them to fall off. Aphids cause lily mosaic virus by carrying it from one plant to another. The leaves become distorted and have yellow streaks; the flowers also may become distorted. This virus can also be transmitted from tulips, specifically Rembrandt types, so be careful when planting tulips and lilies next to each other.

Propagation is by division, scales, bulbils, or seed. Divide the clumps in fall and split them into single bulbs. Scale propagation is done in the summer. Remove the outer scales of the bulb and peel off the inner scales for propagation. Dip the cut end in a fungicide, pot in well-drained media, and plant in a greenhouse. Shiny, black bulbils are borne in the leaf axils; remove when ripe (mid to late summer), pot in well-drained media, and place in a cold frame. Seed germination rate is highly variable; you will need patience with some species. Seed should be planted in spring.

This star of the garden is great to use in the mid border. Plant lilies in groupings or as a specimen plant. I like to plant other perennials in close proximity so lily stems will have extra support if needed. The flashy flowers work with all plants. *Foeniculum vulgare* (fennel) provides an excellent backdrop, especially the cultivar 'Purpurescens'.

A list of recommended *Lilium* cultivars or species would be endless. For further information, see the North American Lily Society Web site.

Linum perenne   perennial flax, prairie flax   flax family / Linaceae

Hardiness: Zones 5a to 8b
Origin: Europe
Mature height: 18 to 24 in.
Mature spread: 1 to 2 ft.
Landscape use: Mid border; rock garden
Season of bloom: Late spring through summer
Key ornamental characteristics: Delicate, sky blue
  flowers; attractive foliage

Linum perenne

Perennial flax is a charming plant with delicate, sky blue flowers. The plant is fairly short lived, but it freely self-seeds, and will pop up in unexpected places in the garden from year to year if the conditions are right. Native to much of Europe, the annual species *Linum usitatissimum* is grown for linseed oil and flax fiber.

Linum perenne flowers are approximately 1 in. across. Like daylilies, the flowers last one day, but are borne so profusely that the plant is always in bloom from late spring through summer. Cutting the plant back after flowering in the summer will promote more blooms later in the season.

Leaves are linear to lanceolate, and alternate in arrangement, and stems are thin and wiry. Leaves and stems are pale greenish-blue. The plant has a fine-textured appearance, but it is tougher than it looks.

Linum perenne is easy to grow and tolerant of a wide range of conditions. It prefers full sun and light, well-drained soil. It tends to root shallowly in heavy, clay soils, which can result in decreased winter survival, especially if the soil is overly wet. It performs with gusto in warmer regions, thriving in heat and humidity while being drought tolerant.

There are no serious insect or disease problems with perennial flax. Cutworms and grasshoppers are occasional pests.

Propagation is best done by seed, which germinates rapidly. Cuttings can be taken in the summer. Division is difficult (the root system tends to be very fibrous) and probably not worth the effort, given the ease of viable seed.

Linum perenne 'Blau Saphir' ('Blue Sapphire') is a cultivar with sapphire-blue flowers; it grows to 1 ft. in height. 'Diamant' has white blooms and grows to approximately 15 in. *Linum perenne* subsp. *lewisii* 'Appar' (Zones 5 to 8) is a closely related species with sky blue flowers and lovely bluish-green foliage. It was named to honor the explorer Meriwether Lewis, who collected it on Lewis and Clark's journey to the Pacific Northwest.

Perennial flax works best when planted in mass, so drifts of blue or white flowers can make a strong impact. Great for the mid border of a cottage garden, it can also be used in meadows or wildflower gardens.

Liriope spicata   lilyturf   lily-of-the-valley family / Convallariaceae

Hardiness: Zones 4a to 10a
Origin: China and Japan
Mature height: 8 to 15 in.
Mature spread: Indefinite
Landscape use: Ground cover; edging
Season of bloom: Summer
Key ornamental characteristics: Grasslike foliage; spikes of white or lavender
    flowers; purplish-black fruits

A member of the same family as lily-of-the-valley, lilyturf is primarily grown for its glossy, grasslike foliage. Evergreen in southern zones, it may turn yellow-brownish-green in all regions of the Midwest. Just set the mower on low in early spring, and cut it to spruce up the plant! The arching, dark green leaves are ¼ in. wide and up to 18 in. long. Lilyturf forms a clump and spreads via underground rhizomes.

Flowers are either white or pale lavender and rise to the top of the foliage. They are small at ¼ in. wide, and occur in terminal racemes. The subsequent fruit is a purplish-black berry that is visible in the fall. Flowers and fruit are understated and attractive.

Lilyturf prefers light shade, but it can also be sited in full sun or partial shade. For optimum growth, it requires evenly moist, fertile soils, but it will tolerate dry sites as well. It is a tough plant.

There are no serious insect or disease problems associated with lilyturf. But be alert for snails and slugs. The dense foliage can hide those pests, but fortunately it also hides their damage.

The best method of propagating lilyturf is to divide it in spring.

The related species *Liriope muscari* (blue lilyturf, Zones 6 to 10) has wider, longer leaves than *L. spicata*. This plant is not as winter hardy as *L. spicata*, however, with Zone 6 being its typical northern limit.

You can use lilyturf in the front border to provide texture. It spreads, so you better plant it in a sunken pot. It is charming when incorporated into small courtyards. It forms a dense ground cover, and it can be used under trees, even trees with shallow roots. I tend to regard the plant as appropriate for use in a formal landscape. I often see it planted along a sidewalk, which is a good idea, since the concrete helps to stop the rhizomes from spreading underground. Use a root barrier on the other side, to keep it from mixing with the lawn or other plants.

Liriope spicata in foreground. Global Book Publishing Photo Library

Lobelia cardinalis cardinal flower campanula family / Lobeliaceae

Hardiness: Zones 3b to 9a
Origin: Eastern North America
Mature height: 3 to 4 ft.
Mature spread: 2 ft.
Landscape use: Mid to back border; shade or
    woodland garden; near wet areas
Season of bloom: Late summer to fall
Key ornamental characteristics: Brilliant scarlet
    flowers

Lobelia cardinalis

Brilliant, scarlet flowers are the highlight of this species. The erect racemes can reach 2 ft. in height, and bear many tubular-shaped, 2-lipped flowers. The lower lip of each flower has 3 prominent lobes, while the upper lip has 2 lobes. If you want to attract butterflies and humming-birds to your garden, plant cardinal flower.

The leaves are medium to dark green, oblong-lanceo-late, and finely toothed. Serrations can be irregular, and leaves can be up to 4 in. long. Leaf arrangement is alternate and stems are not branched.

Lobelia cardinalis (also known as *L. fulgens*) is easy to grow in organically rich, moist to wet soil. It prefers partial shade but will perform well in full sun if summer temperatures are cool and the soil is kept moist; it appreciates a layer of summer mulch. The plant tends to have a short life span.

There are no serious disease or insect problems associated with this native plant.

Propagation can be done by dividing clumps in spring. Seed is also viable, and in ideal growing conditions this plant will self-sow. Soak the roots of a potted plant in water for a half day before digging it into the garden.

Two *Lobelia cardinalis* cultivars are especially attractive. *Lobelia cardinalis* f. *alba* has white flowers, and *L. cardinalis* f. *rosea* has pink flowers. The species *L.* ×*speciosa* (Zones 3 to 8) comprises many hybrids of *L. cardinalis*, *L. siphilitica*, and *L. splendens*. These hybrids tend to have larger flowers and greater height. They also tend to be fairly long lived, compared to many species in this genus, which may only live 2 to 3 years.

The eye-catching, scarlet blossoms of cardinal flower light up shade areas like a torch.

The plant also is effective when placed next to ponds, streams, or wet areas. Try using it with hostas and ferns. *Eupatorium purpureum* subsp. *maculatum* (Joe-Pye weed) also is an excellent companion for cardinal flower.

Lobelia siphilitica   big blue lobelia, blue cardinal flower   campanula family / Campanulaceae

Hardiness: Zones 4a to 8a
Origin: Eastern North America
Mature height: 2 to 3 ft.
Mature spread: 12 to 18 in.
Landscape use: Mid border; native or woodland garden; next to ponds or streams
Season of bloom: Late summer
Key ornamental characteristics: Late-blooming blue flowers

Lobelia siphilitica

There are numerous species of *Lobelia*, and big blue lobelia is a fine late-season bloomer. Don't be afraid to experiment with this out-of-the-ordinary plant.

The species name *siphilitica* came from this plant's reported use as a medicinal treatment for syphilis.

Light to dark blue blooms are tubular in shape, 2-lipped, and 1 to 1½ in. long. Flowers are surrounded by leafy green bracts and borne in dense, unbranched racemes that range from 6 to 20 in. long. Big blue lobelia makes a pleasant show in the garden, and its flowers also make a nice floral arrangement.

Leaves are light green, ovate to lanceolate, finely serrate, and 4 to 6 in. long.

Big blue lobelia is easy to cultivate in organically rich, moderately wet to wet soils. It requires consistently moist soil conditions. It prefers partial shade but will adjust to full sun in the cooler regions of the upper Midwest. The plant appreciates a layer of summer mulch in all hardiness zones.

There are no serious disease or insect problems associated with big blue lobelia.

Propagation may be achieved by division or seed. Divide clumps of this species in the spring. Seed is readily viable. Under ideal conditions, this plant will freely self-sow and can form large colonies, but it is not aggressive in spreading.

The cultivar *Lobelia siphilitica* 'Alba' has white blooms. It reaches 2 to 3 ft. in height. 'Blue Select' has bright blue flowers and reaches 3 ft. tall. All *L. siphilitica* cultivars should be propagated by division or stem cuttings. Plants with the parents *L. siphilitica* and *L. cardinalis* are known as *L. ×speciosa* (also known as *L. ×gerardii).* The cultivar *L. ×speciosa* 'Vedrariensis' has dark green leaves, violet-purple flowers, and a mature height of 4 ft.

Big blue lobelia is great to use in the mid border, in a native or woodland garden, and next to ponds and streams. Try it with the native *Rudeckia fulgida* (black-eyed Susan) or *Eupatorium purpureum* subsp. *maculatum* (Joe-Pye weed).

Lychnis chalcedonica Maltese cross, Jerusalem cross   carnation family / Carophyllaceae

Hardiness: Zones 3b to 8b
Origin: European Russia
Mature height: 2 to 4 ft.
Mature spread: 1 ft.
Landscape use: Mid or back border
Season of bloom: Early to midsummer
Key ornamental characteristics: Attractive clusters of scarlet, pink, or white flowers

Lychnis chalcedonica

Species in the genus *Lychnis* often have brightly colored flowers. *Lychnis chalcedonica* is an old favorite that easily upholds that reputation with intense, scarlet blooms.

A rounded, terminal, flower head is 2 to 4 in. in diameter and is made up of 10 to 40 blooms. Despite having 5 petals like all members of this genus, the flowers of this species appear to have a cross shape. Flower petals also have a deep notch.

Leaves are dark green, lanceolate to ovate, and clasp the erect, hispid stem. They are opposite in arrangement and 2 to 3 in. long. The leaf base is cordate or rounded.

Members of this genus tend to be short lived. Maltese cross is one of the longer lived species if cultural conditions are met. This plant prefers well-drained, fertile, evenly moist soils. Root rot will quickly occur in soils that are poorly drained. The plant prefers full sun but will withstand partial shade. It may need staking, and benefits from being placed in a wind-protected site.

There are several disease problems associated with Maltese cross. Leaf spot, rust, and smut can afflict this wonderful species. You can help prevent many of these diseases by providing the optimal cultural conditions for the plant. There are no significant insect issues.

Propagation is easy by seed, and Maltese cross may freely self-sow. But the plant is not aggressive. Plant seeds in winter or very early spring. Division is best done every 3 or 4 years in the spring or fall.

A few *Lychnis chalcedonica* cultivars are available. 'Alba Plena' has white flowers. 'Rosea' has rosy-pink flowers. 'Rubra Plena' has intense, scarlet, double flowers.

Ideal for the mid or back border, Maltese cross looks fantastic with blue flowers and yellow flowers. Try planting it behind *Nepeta ×faassenii* (catmint). Yellow-flowered *Coreopsis grandiflora* (tickseed) also works nicely with Maltese cross.

Lychnis coronaria rose campion carnation family / Carophyllaceae

Hardiness: Zones 4a to 9a (perhaps 10a)
Origin: Southern Europe
Mature height: 2 to 3 ft.
Mature spread: 18 in.
Landscape use: Mid border accent; cottage garden
Season of bloom: Late spring to early summer
Key ornamental characteristics: Crimson-purple, pink, or white flowers; silver-white foliage

Lychnis coronaria is an ideal perennial for informal gardens. Because of its short life span, the plant should be treated as an annual or biennial in the Midwest. Commonly known as rose campion, the plant freely seeds itself in the garden without being overly aggressive. It also blooms the first year. Deadheading spent blooms prevents any unwanted seedlings the following year.

The genus name is derived from the Greek *lychnos*, meaning "lamp," which alludes to the showy, bright flowers. Rose campion has single, crimson-purplish flowers borne at the tip of a peduncle. This species will bloom in abundance in all Midwest hardiness zones where it can grow successfully.

The oblong, pubescent, silvery-white leaves remind me of *Stachys byzantina* (lamb's ear) foliage. Basal leaves are

Lychnis coronaria

larger than stem leaves. Upper leaves are sessile and lower leaves are petioled. The plant may be grown just for its attractive foliage.

Rose campion has an upright habit and is heavily branched. It prefers full sun for optimum growth but tolerates afternoon shade. It prefers well-drained soil but performs admirably in dry sites.

There are no serious disease or insect problems associated with rose campion.

Propagation is very easy from seed and does not require any type of pretreatment. Division can also occur in the spring or fall.

Several *Lychnis coronaria* cultivars are available. Two of my favorites are 'Abbotswood Rose', a compact plant bearing pale pink blooms, and 'Alba', which produces white flowers that blend perfectly with the silvery-white foliage.

Because of its intense flower color, rose campion is best used in the mid border as an accent or specimen. Because the plant seeds so freely, it is best used in a cottage-style garden where it has freedom to roam.

Lychnis coronaria can be a bit difficult to color coordinate with other plants. But the bright flowers and gorgeous foliage make it a worthwhile inclusion in your garden. The species adds distinctive character and interest to any garden or landscape.

Macleaya cordata plume poppy poppy family / Papaveraceae

Hardiness: Zones 3b to 8a
Origin: China and Japan
Mature height: 6 to 10 ft.
Mature spread: 3 to 6 ft.
Landscape use: Back border; specimen
Season of bloom: Summer
Key ornamental characteristics: Bold foliage; plumelike, creamy white flowers; height

This handsome plant can grow up to an amazing 10 ft. tall and rarely needs staking. Formerly known as *Bocconia cordata*, surprisingly it is part of the poppy family. The plant brings impressive ornamental and architectural value to the garden.

Subtle, apetalous flowers are creamy white and occur in panicles up to 1 ft. long. The blooms add great interest to a fresh cut arrangement.

Leaves have an attractive, cool, silvery-blue-green cast on the upper side and white pubescence on the underside. Leaves have approximately 7 lobes that are dentate or sinuate, and the leaf base is cordate. Up to 8 in. wide, leaves are somewhat heart shaped, and the plant has an overall coarse texture. If the stems are broken, clear yellow sap will flow, which is a characteristic of many members of the poppy family.

Plume poppy thrives in full sun. It prefers moist soil but can withstand slightly dry conditions. If sited in light shade and rich soil, plume poppy can spread quickly by roots. I have grown this plant for several years and never found it to be as aggressive as some claim. But I have it placed in clay soil that is relatively dry. If you wish to contain this plant, put it in a large container that you sink in the ground.

The only disease problem with plume poppy is anthracnose, which may occur during warm, wet weather. There are no serious insect problems.

Propagation can easily be accomplished by division. Seed can also be planted in spring. This plant self-sows.

The cultivar *Macleaya cordata* 'Alba' has white flowers. *Macleaya* ×*kewensis* 'Flamingo' (Zones 4 to 9), a related species, has pinkish flowers. *Macleaya microcarpa*, also a related species, has pinkish flowers. It is similar in appearance but more invasive than *M. cordata*.

The extreme height of plume poppy makes it ideal for the back border or the center of an island bed. The visual impact this grand plant brings to the garden makes it ideal as a specimen. I have used it around shrubs such as *Syringa* (lilac) and *Fothergilla gardenii* (dwarf fothergilla) to add contrast. If you have a large area and want to make an imposing display of large perennials, plant it with *Helianthus* (sunflower), *Eupatorium purpureum* subsp. *maculatum* (Joe-Pye weed), and *Foeniculum vulgare* (fennel).

Macleaya cordata

Malva alcea   hollyhock mallow   mallow family / Malvaceae

Hardiness: Zones 4a to 8a
Origin: Southern Europe
Mature height: 3 to 4 ft.
Mature spread: 18 in.
Landscape use: Mid border; specimen; cottage
    garden
Season of bloom: Late spring through summer
Key ornamental characteristics: Attractive lavender,
    pink, or white flowers

Malva alcea

I planted hollyhock mallow in my mother's garden more than 15 years ago. It has come back every year since. It self-seeds and turns up in different places each year, which is part of its charm. It provides carefree flower display all summer long, so it works well in a cottage garden.

The hollyhocklike flowers are approximately 1½ in. across, and come in shades of lavender, pink, and white. The singly produced flowers are borne in the leaf axils. Flowers have 5 petals with a noticeable notch at the apex. Removing spent flowers will encourage later blooming.

Light green, pubescent stem leaves are alternate in arrangement with 3 to 5 palmate lobes. Leaves are much larger toward the base of the plant than at the top.

Hollyhock mallow grows in full sun or partial shade. It prefers slightly alkaline soil, but will adapt to a variety of soils as long as it gets good drainage. A big advantage to this plant is its drought tolerance. If the plant starts to look ragged, cut it back to the basal foliage or pull it up.

Japanese beetle, thrips, and spider mites can be problems with this plant. But I have not encountered those pests on my plants. I have had a minor problem with this plant getting foliar leaf spot; hollyhock mallow is prone to fungal diseases.

Propagation is easy from seed and is your best bet. Terminal cuttings can be taken in the spring, and established plants can be divided at that time of year.

Malva alcea var. *fastigiata* is more erect than the species. It produces many ascending branches and has rose-pink flowers. This plant is the one frequently found in nurseries.

Hollyhock mallow is great to use in the mid border of a cottage or meadow garden.

Because the plant is short lived, I usually let it self-sow and grow where it wishes, unless it interferes with certain special plants.

Marrubium vulgare   horehound; white horehound   mint family / Lamiaceae

Hardiness: Zones 4a to 9a
Origin: Europe, Asia, and North Africa
Mature height: 18 in. to 4 ft.
Mature spread: 12 to 18 in.
Landscape use: Back to mid border; herb garden;
    filler plant
Season of bloom: Summer
Key ornamental characteristics: Woolly leaves;
    subtle white flowers

Marrubium vulgare

This plant's botanical name is derived from the Hebrew *marrob*, which means "bitter juice." Its common name comes from the Old English *har hune*, which means "downy plant." Horehound is an old-fashioned candy and cough syrup flavoring. An herbal remedy uses horehound tea with honey to relieve cold symptoms.

Flowers are small, white, and subtly attractive. They are densely borne in whorls atop the plant stems. Not showy, they are greatly appreciated by bees.

Leaves are ovate, medium green, sessile, wrinkly, and opposite in arrangement. The leaves and stems have a heavy, white pubescence, giving the foliage a woolly, soft texture that contributes visual interest to the garden. When crushed, leaves emit a mintlike aroma.

Black horehound (*Ballota nigra*) should not be confused with white horehound (*Marrubium vulgare*). Black horehound has a scent and taste unpalatable even to cows and other farm animals.

Horehound tolerates a wide range of soils and even does well in dry situations. It thrives in alkaline soils. Preferring full sun, it grows even taller in partial shade. Plants may need staking if they reach 4 ft. in height.

There are no disease or insect problems associated with this species. The plant may rot if sited in conditions that are too wet and cold in the winter.

Propagation is by seed, division in the spring, or cuttings taken from new growth in the summer. Horehound can be somewhat invasive; it spreads by runners, but is easy to pull up. Remove flower heads, since the plant freely self-sows.

Marrubium vulgare is a natural in the herb garden. I like to use it in the back border of the perennial garden since it makes a great filler plant. Its erect habit provides the perfect foil among showier specimens.

Mertensia virginica   Virginia bluebells, cowslip, bluebells   borage family / Boraginaceae

Mertensia virginica

Hardiness: Zones 3a to 9a
Origin: Eastern North America
Mature height: 1 to 18 in.
Mature spread: 1 ft.
Landscape use: Shade garden; woodland garden; rock garden
Season of bloom: Early spring
Key ornamental characteristics: Beautiful, blue, nodding flowers; blue-gray foliage

Virginia bluebells is a graceful, upright, clump-forming plant that is a true harbinger of spring. Buds and emerging funnel-shaped, pendulous flowers are pink before turning bluish-lavender as they mature. Flowers are up to 1 in. long and borne in clusters at the apex of the stem.

Bluish-green, glabrous leaves are up to 6 in. long and 2 to 4 in. wide. Leaves have noticeable veins and are alternate in arrangement. Stem leaves are smaller and nearly sessile. *Mertensia virginica*, like *Papaver orientale* (oriental poppy), starts to go dormant in midsummer if not sooner, so foliage turns yellow and dies.

Cultural requirements include well-drained, moist, rich soils. This plant naturally occurs in woodlands, so it prefers partial to full shade.

I have not witnessed any insect or disease problems with this plant. But fungal problems may occur occasionally.

Propagation is best done by seed. The seeds require cool, moist conditions, so just sow seeds outside in early summer. Although the plants prefer to be undisturbed, division can be done in spring after the plants have developed into a small colony. Use care with the plants, and get them quickly planted in their new site.

The cultivar *Mertensia virginica* 'Alba' has white flowers and is less vigorous than the species. 'Rubra' has pink flowers. I much prefer the straight species.

Clumps of Virginia bluebells are great to scatter in shade, woodland, or rock gardens. But since the plants go dormant in summer, they should be overplanted with annuals or used in conjunction with other thriving perennials. Virginia bluebells is a good companion for *Asarum* spp. (wild ginger), *Dicentra* spp. (bleeding heart), hostas, and ferns.

Miscanthus sinensis   eulalia, Japanese silver grass, miscanthus   grass family / Poaceae

Hardiness: Zones 5b to 9a
Origin: Asia
Mature height: 3 to 8 ft.
Mature spread: 3 to 4 ft.
Landscape use: Specimen; screen; mass; around ponds
Season of bloom: Fall (blooms last over winter)
Key ornamental characteristics: Plumelike flowers; foliage; winter interest

Miscanthus sinensis

When I think of ornamental grasses, this species is one of the first that comes to mind. Easily recognizable by its growth habit and flowers, this king of grasses provides great year-round ornamental value in the landscape, especially in winter. The way snow settles on the plant makes a pleasing sight.

The flowers of *Miscanthus sinensis* have a pale pink to reddish cast and are borne in 8- to 10-in. panicles in the fall. Turning tan during the winter, they are wonderful inclusions in dried flower arrangements.

Serrate foliage rises from a clump, and each leaf is 3 to 4 ft. long and approximately ½ in. wide. This plant needs plenty of room to grow: the clumps slowly expand in circumference by short rhizomes. Providing great texture during the growing season, the foliage should be left standing not only for winter interest but to provide protection for the crowns. Cut the foliage back to the ground in late winter or early spring just before new shoots appear.

Eulalia is a warm-season grass that tolerates a wide range of soil types from clay to sand. It prefers evenly moist, well-drained sites, and thrives in full sun. It also grows well in heat and humidity. It tolerates partial shade, but then growth rate and flowering can be retarded.

There are no major insect or disease problems with eulalia. Miscanthus mealybug is on the increase, and it can cause stunted growth. This pest lives in the stems and is difficult to control. Fungal problems such as blight are also on the rise with *Miscanthus sinensis*. Rust may also be an occasional problem.

The species may self-sow once established, but seedlings will not necessarily resemble the parent plant. If seedlings appear in large numbers, make sure they do not spread to uncultivated areas. Division should take place in the spring. Cultivars should be divided to propagate the plants.

There are many *Miscanthus sinensis* cultivars available, with the differences being height, foliage color, and flower color. 'Adagio' has a compact habit, growing 2 to 3 ft. tall. Flowers are tinged pink before turning creamy white. The foliage turns yellow in fall. 'Variegatus' has beautiful, green and creamy white striped leaves. It grows to 4 to 6 ft. and may flop. An old cultivar, it is a great choice to consider.

Miscanthus sinensis is an excellent specimen for the back border. Its upright, fountainlike habit provides a good backdrop for just about any plant. Try it with plants that have an erect habit such as *Hibiscus moscheutos* (rose mallow), *Perovskia atriplicifolia* (Russian sage), or *Rudbeckia fulgida* (black-eyed Susan). It can also be used as a utility screen for trashcans or walls. If you have a large area, plant miscanthus in mass. It also looks perfect around ponds and other water features.

If you have never planted ornamental grasses, this plant would be a good first choice. Compact cultivars are available for smaller gardens, if you don't have room for the larger specimens.

Monarda didyma   bee balm, Oswego tea, monarda   mint family / Lamiaceae

Hardiness: Zones 4a to 9a
Origin: Eastern North America
Mature height: 2 to 4 ft.
Mature spread: 2 to 3 ft.
Landscape use: Mid border; specimen; naturalized garden
Season of bloom: Summer
Key ornamental characteristics: Bright red, pink, or white flowers

Monarda didyma

Brilliant, red flowers of *Monarda didyma* put on a spectacular show when plants are in full bloom. Blossoms are 2 to 3 in. in diameter and borne in single- or double-whorled clusters. Resembling an unkempt mop, the plentiful, red flowers attract bees, butterflies, and hummingbirds; this plant is a favorite of nectar-gathering creatures. Cutting back spent blooms will encourage flowering later in the season.

Leaves are ovate to ovate-lanceolate, toothed, and opposite in arrangement. Stems are square. The foliage is hairy, and when crushed emits a strong, minty aroma. The leaves are used to make tea and other herbal remedies. This species was first recorded as growing near Oswego, New York, thus the common name Oswego tea.

Monarda didyma requires full sun and even soil moisture. Overly wet winter soils can lead to this plant's demise. It does not stand up very well to drought.

Bee balm is prone to the fungal problem known as powdery mildew. Although it can become infected in the wild, it is more susceptible in a garden setting. Rust can also occur. Growing bee balm in dry or crowded conditions increases the likelihood for disease problems. A foliar spray program can be carried out in late spring, which is a lot of work. If you have stands of powdery mildew–infested bee balm by late summer, you may want to simply pull the plants out. This plant seems to prefer full sun or partial shade, moist soils, and the cooler Upper Midwest climate.

Propagation is best by division. In fact, it will enhance plant health if you divide it every 2 or 3 years because the center can become thin. Seed is also viable, and softwood cuttings can be taken in early summer.

Many *Monarda* cultivars exist. Some of them claim to be mildew resistant, but monarda is monarda. 'Blaustrumpf' ('Blue Stocking') has violet-blue flowers and is reasonably heat and drought tolerant. 'Cambridge Scarlet' is an old favorite with scarlet flowers. 'Gardenview Scarlet' has scarlet flowers and is supposedly highly mildew resistant. 'Marshall's Delight' has pink flowers and claims mildew resistance. 'Squaw' has dark red flowers. *Monarda fistulosa* (wild bee balm, Zones 3 to 9) is a related species often seen growing along country roads. Up to 4 ft. in height, it has lavender-pink flowers.

Bee balm is clump forming and works well in the mid border. It is also perfect in a naturalized setting. It can be invasive in optimal conditions. The plant works with any companion and can make a dramatic effect in the garden. Try it with *Coreopsis grandiflora* (tickseed) or *Leucanthemum ×superbum* (Shasta daisy).

Nepeta ×faassenii   Faassen catmint   mint family / Lamiaceae

Hardiness: Zones 3b to 7b
Origin: Hybrid
Mature height: 18 to 24 in.
Mature spread: 18 in.
Landscape use: Front border to mid border; specimen; mass
Season of bloom: Late spring to midsummer
Key ornamental characteristics: Abundant lavender-blue flowers; pubescent, silver-gray foliage

In my experience, cats are highly attracted to *Nepeta ×faassenii*. And it is a lovely perennial to incorporate into the garden. Catmint's sprawling-erect habit lends itself to informal garden settings. The attractive silver-gray foliage and delicate lavender-blue flowers put on a subtle but stunning show. Catmint is a hybrid of *N. racemosa* and *N. nepetella*.

Leaves are pubescent and opposite in arrangement. When crushed, the foliage smells minty. The stems are square, which is a signature characteristic of plants in the mint family.

The blooms are small, at up to approximately ¼ in. long, and are shaped like a trumpet. Flowers appear in late spring and usually last to midsummer. If catmint is cut

Nepeta ×faassenii

back halfway after initial flowering, it will bloom again later in the season. Each floret is 2-lipped; the upper lip is 2-lobed, the lower lip is 3-lobed. Flowers are insignificant individually, but when plants bloom in mass, they make a beautiful display.

Nepeta ×faassenii will grow in a variety of soil conditions and thrives in full sun. I have not encountered any disease or insect problems with this species. The plant can become leggy, so just cut it back to encourage new growth and tidiness.

Nepeta ×faassenii is sterile and must be propagated by division, preferably in the spring.

There are several wonderful *Nepeta* cultivars. *Nepeta* 'Six Hills Giant' (also known as *N. gigantea*) is much larger and more sprawling than the species. Leaves are greener, and the plant flowers later than the species. *Nepeta racemosa* (Zones 4 to 8) is a related species; the cultivar *N. racemosa* 'Walker's Low' was the Perennial Plant Association's Plant of the Year for 2007. It is similar to *N. ×faassenii*, except that it is lower in habit and more sprawling at 8 to 12 in. tall. *Nepeta racemosa* 'Little Titch' is also a smaller cultivar at 8 to 12 in. tall. *Nepeta sibirica* (Siberian catmint, Zones 3 to 7) is upright rather than sprawling, and grows up to 3 ft. It has apple-green leaves, and flowers are the classic blue of *Nepeta*.

Catmint complements most plants, and I use it heavily in my garden. It looks particularly attractive when placed near white, pink, yellow, or dark purple–flowering plants. It also works well with species that have round flowers. For an interesting combination, try it with *Campanula punctata* (spotted bellflower).

Every garden needs a cat, so you may want to incorporate this wonderful plant in your garden.

Oenothera macrocarpa   Ozark sundrops, evening primrose
evening primrose family / Onagraceae

Hardiness: Zones 3b to 7b
Origin: United States
Mature height: 8 to 12 in.
Mature spread: 1 ft.
Landscape use: Front border; rock garden; slope
Season of bloom: Late spring to midsummer
Key ornamental characteristics: Large, bright yellow flowers

If you want bright yellow flowers in the garden, look no farther than Ozark sundrops. This plant brings cheer to any landscape. The species was formerly called and is still often sold as *Oenothera missouriensis*.

The gorgeous, mildly fragrant flowers, ranging from 3 to 5 in. in diameter, open in the afternoon and remain open until the next morning, thus the common name evening prim-

Oenothera macrocarpa

rose. Singly borne, flowers have 4 petals that are paper thin and shallowly toothed. The fruit is a woody, winged pod 2 to 4 in. long.

Leaves are lanceolate, with entire margins, and alternate in arrangement. The stems have coarse, appressed hairs. Foliage is late to appear in spring.

Ozark sundrops grows easily in a wide range of soil types, even poor-quality and dry soils. It is also tolerant of drought. But the soil must be well drained. It thrives in full sun and prefers light shade in the lower Midwest. The plant appreciates a layer of winter mulch in northern climates.

There are no major disease or insect problems associated with this plant. Root rot may be a problem in wet, poorly drained soils.

Propagation is easily accomplished by seed, and ozark sundrops will self-sow under ideal growing conditions. Division can be done in the spring or fall.

Oenothera macrocarpa 'Greencourt Lemon' is a cultivar with pale yellow flowers. *Oenothera fruticosa* (common sundrops, Zones 4 to 8) is a wonderful related species with bright yellow flowers. *Oenothera speciosa* (showy primrose, Zones 5 to 8) is a related species with whitish-pink flowers. This plant can be quite invasive, but it is ideal for low-quality soils where many other plants will not grow.

Oenothera macrocarpa is a beautiful complement for blue or blue-lavender–flowering plants like *Nepeta* ×*faassenii* (catmint) or *Linum perenne* (perennial flax). For an eye-catching show, try planting it with *Lychnis coronaria* (rose campion). For a more subtle display, plant it with small shrubs or ornamental grasses. It is also well sited along a terraced hill or embankment, and is a natural for the front border or rock garden.

Paeonia hybrids   peony   buttercup family / Ranunculaceae

Hardiness: Zones 3a to 8a
Origin: Asia and Eurasia; hybrid
Mature height: 30 in. to 3 ft.
Mature spread: 2 to 3 ft.
Landscape use: Mid border; groupings; specimen
Season of bloom: Late spring to early summer
Key ornamental characteristics: Large, showy flowers in a variety of colors;
   attractive foliage

Great diversity exists with the flowers of herbaceous peonies. (Herbaceous peonies die back to the ground in the fall. Tree peonies are shrubs that have persistent woody stems and often grow larger than herbaceous peonies.) No matter which *Paeonia* cultivar you select, it will be showy.

Peony flowers come in shades of red, pink, salmon, yellow, and white. Blooms last approximately 7 to 10 days and should be removed once spent. Cultivars are classified as early, mid-

Herbaceous peony

season, or late blooming. Purchase cultivars with different bloom times to extend floral display. There are 4 different forms of flowers: single, Japanese, semidouble, and double. Peony flowers can have a heavy, sweet fragrance. They make fabulous fresh-cut arrangements.

In spring, emerging shoots have a reddish cast that turns dark green in summer. The leaves are alternate in arrangement. The leaflets are biternate and divided into oval or lanceolate segments that are entire or lobed. The plant's habit is noticeably rounded. Cut the plant back to the ground in late fall after frost. Do not add peony foliage to your compost pile, because you run the risk of spreading foliar diseases throughout your garden.

Peonies will withstand partial shade but they require full sun to flower at their best. They are easy to grow, and prefer rich, fertile, well-drained soils. Peony will benefit from compost added at planting.

Botrytis and phytophthora are the main disease problems with peony, but the two blights do not occur often. Ants frequently crawl on the plant seeking the flower nectar, but they are harmless. If plants do not flower, some causes include: (1) planted too deep or shallow, (2) receives too much shade, (3) late frost killed flower buds, (4) plant is too young or old, (5) plant has been recently moved or disturbed, or (6) excessive heat has strained flower development. Contact the American Peony Society for additional information.

Propagation is by stem cuttings taken in spring or early summer. Use a rooting powder to increase success. Division can be done in spring. But peonies do not need frequent division, despite being long-lived plants, and typically like to grow undisturbed. Seeds are viable, but it takes a number of years for the plant to mature before flowering, and the resulting plants may not resemble the parent.

Peonies are an old-fashioned favorite for the perennial border, both in groups and as a specimen. They are often used to line a driveway or sidewalk, or to create an informal early summer property fence. Peonies can be used in many other creative ways in the garden or landscape. After spent flowers are removed, the foliage provides an excellent backdrop for other flowering plants.

Papaver orientale   oriental poppy   poppy family / Papaveraceae

Hardiness: Zones 3a to 7a
Origin: Mediterranean region
Mature height: 2 to 4 ft.
Mature spread: 2 to 3 ft.
Landscape use: Mid border; specimen; small groupings
Season of bloom: Spring
Key ornamental characteristics: Large, showy flowers in brilliant colors

Oriental poppy has large, brilliant-colored flowers in shades of orange, red, pink and white. The petals have dark splotches at the base, and have an unusual crepe paper appearance. The cup-shaped flowers have dark purple stamens, are 4 to 6 in. across, and are borne on long stalks that rise above the foliage.

Leaves are dark green, up to 1 in. long, and sharply toothed. They are lanceolate and pinnately dissected. The leaves have a rough (hispid) texture. This upright, clump-forming plant tends to sprawl and the leaves will flop unless staked. When snapped, stems bleed white, milky sap. Foliage turns yellow and withers shortly after the flowers are spent, leaving a hole in the garden. But low-growing, new leaves appear in fall until spring, when the foliage puts on a growth spurt until the flowers bloom.

Papaver orientale prefers organically rich soils that have medium amounts of moisture. But it performs well in average soils as long as it gets good drainage. It thrives in full sun, and appreciates a layer of winter mulch. This is a plant for northern climates (the upper Midwest), because it needs a period of winter dormancy. Oriental poppies typically do not grow well south of USDA Zone 7.

Papaver orientale

There are few insect and disease problems associated with *Papaver orientale*. Root rot may occur in poorly drained soils. Powdery mildew and botrytis may occur on occasion.

Propagation can be accomplished by taking 4- to 6-in. root cuttings in the mid to late summer. Division can also be accomplished in the fall. Seeds germinate readily, but many cultivars will not come true and flowering will occur in the second year of growth. Once established, oriental poppy likes to be left undisturbed.

Papaver orientale cultivars are plentiful and some are hybrids with other species. 'Allegro' is a dwarf form that only grows to 18 in. tall. It features large, scarlet flowers. 'Big Jim' has dark red flowers and grows up to 3 ft. in height. 'Bonfire' lives up to its name, with fiery red blooms. 'China Boy' has orange flowers with creamy white bases. 'Glowing Rose' has watermelon-pink flowers.

Oriental poppy is best used in single clumps or small groups in borders. *Gypsophila* (baby's breath) and *Boltonia asteroides* (boltonia) have foliage that expands as the summer progresses and may be effectively interplanted with oriental poppies to fill the void when they go dormant.

Pennisetum alopecuroides   perennial fountain grass   grass family / Poaceae

Hardiness: Zones 5b to 9b
Origin: East Asia
Mature height: 3 to 4 ft.
Mature spread: 3 to 4 ft.
Landscape use: Back border; specimen; mass
Season of bloom: Late summer to fall
Key ornamental characteristics: Feathery flower spikes; fine foliage; winter
   interest

Perennial fountain grass has many qualities that make it a valued part of any garden or landscape. The foliage and handsome flower spikes provide excellent texture, color, and contrast. They sway in a light breeze, providing a pleasing effect.

   The flower spikes are noticeable, feathery, and resemble a bottlebrush that is approximately 7 in. long. Protruding from the foliage in late summer like water spraying from a

Pennisetum alopecuroides

fountain, they have a silvery-pinkish-white cast. As the flowers mature, they turn reddish-brown. The fresh flowers make an interesting contribution in summer bouquets. Unlike many other ornamental grasses, which have flowers that persist through winter, perennial fountain grass's flowers shatter early in winter.

The arching, flat leaves of this grass are approximately 2 to 3 ft. long. Only ¼ in. wide, they add a fine texture. Bright green in color during the spring and summer, they become yellow in early fall and golden brown in late fall. The foliage provides winter interest; it should be cut back to the ground in late winter.

Perennial fountain grass prefers rich soils, but performs well in most typical garden soils if good drainage is provided. It prefers moist to wet conditions. The plant performs best in full sun but tolerates partial shade. The amount of flowers can be reduced if the plant is sited in too much shade. Perennial fountain grass may not be reliably hardy in the northernmost zone of its range. Placing it in a protected site is advisable in USDA Zone 5.

There are no serious disease or insect problems associated with *Pennisetum alope-curoides*.

Propagation of cultivars can be accomplished by division. Species seed is viable and perennial fountain grass frequently self-sows.

There are several *Pennisetum alopecuroides* cultivars available with a variety of heights and colors of flowers and fall foliage. 'Cassian's Choice' is a shorter cultivar that grows to 30 in. It has beautiful, golden yellow fall color. 'Hameln' has very fine-textured foliage and silvery-white flowers. It is a popular cultivar in the nursery trade. 'Little Bunny' is only 1 ft. tall. Flowers are silvery-white. It is ideal for small gardens or rock gardens.

This warm-season ornamental grass is great to use in a variety of situations, from focal specimen to small groupings or massed. It also works well around ponds and streams. It is attractive with the rich yellow flowers of *Rudbeckia fulgida* (black-eyed Susan).

Penstemon cobaea   showy beardtongue   figwort family / Scrophulariaceae

Hardiness: Zones 5a to 9a
Origin: Central United States
Mature height: 1 to 3 ft.
Mature spread: 8 in. to 2 ft.
Landscape use: Mid border; prairie, wildflower, or native plant garden
Season of bloom: Mid-spring to early summer
Key ornamental characteristics: Showy purple to white flowers

This truly striking species may have the largest flowers in the genus *Penstemon*. Gorgeous, tubular-shaped blooms are borne on upright, pubescent stems. Flowers are approximately 2

Penstemon cobaea

in. long and occur in shades of purple, lavender, and white. The Greek word *penstemon* means "5 stamens." One of the stamens is sterile and tufted with hairs, thus the common name beardtongue.

The medium to dark green leaves are opposite in arrangement and sessile, or clasping the stem. Lower leaves are spatulate and dentate, becoming ovate as they ascend the stem. They are typically glabrous, but a light layer of pubescence may occur, especially on lower leaves.

Showy beardtongue is easy to grow in dry to moderately moist, very well-drained soil. Overly wet and poorly drained soil conditions will lead to quick death. This native plant must have full sun to thrive. The clump-forming plant is short lived and it benefits from a layer of winter mulch.

There are no serious disease or insect problems with showy beardtongue. Powdery mildew, rust, or leaf spot may occur on occasion. Root rot may also occur in poorly drained sites.

Propagation can be accomplished by seed, cuttings, or division. Sow seed in early spring; by this method, it may take 2 or 3 years before plants flower. Cuttings may be taken in early summer. Division is best done in spring.

Penstemon barbatus (bearded penstemon, Zones 3 to 8), a related species, is fairly cold and heat tolerant. It produces red to pink flowers and grows up to 3 ft. tall.

Penstemon cobaea is a wonderful plant. It is ideal for a prairie, wildflower, or native plant garden. Try it in the mid border of a cottage garden. Plant it with *Gaura lindheimeri* (white gaura) or *Perovskia atriplicifolia* (Russian sage). Come on! This plant is waiting for you.

Penstemon digitalis 'Husker Red'   Husker red foxglove penstemon, beardtongue   figwort family / Scrophulariaceae

Hardiness: Zones 3a to 8a
Origin: Hybrid
Mature height: 2 to 3 ft.
Mature spread: 24 to 30 in.
Landscape use: Mid border; specimen; small
    groupings
Season of bloom: Mid-spring to early summer
Key ornamental characteristics: Whitish-pink
    flowers; maroon foliage

Penstemon digitalis 'Husker Red'

This plant appeared more than 10 years ago and is still extremely popular today. It was named the Perennial Plant Association's Plant of the Year for 1996. With a name like Husker red foxglove penstemon, it is clear this plant was developed at the University of Nebraska. The flowers are gorgeous, and the foliage is a distinctive highlight for any garden.

The plant features white flowers that often have a pale pink cast. Tubular in shape and 2-lipped, blooms are borne in upright panicles that rise above the foliage. Flowering can be so heavy that the plant may need staking. Penstemon is sometimes called beardtongue because the sterile stamen (of 5) has a tuft of small hairs.

The flowers are set off by outstanding maroon-colored foliage, thus the common name. The more sun the plant receives, the more maroon the leaves are; the less sun it receives, the more green they are. My plant receives full sun until approximately 2:00 p.m. all summer, and the leaves keep a dark maroon cast. Basal leaves are elliptic, and stem leaves are lanceolate to oblong, and opposite in arrangement. This penstemon is an upright, clump-forming plant.

Penstemon digitalis 'Husker Red' grows in a wide range of soil conditions from dry to average to slightly wet. Like most members of this genus, it does not like overly wet conditions. It prefers full sun but withstands partial shade.

I have grown the same plant for approximately 10 years and have never witnessed any disease or insect problems. Root rot can be a problem in wet, poorly drained soils, as for most members in this genus. Leaf spot can also be an occasional problem.

Propagation is best by division. Cuttings can be taken during the spring before the plant flowers.

This product of middle-American ingenuity is highly effective as an accent or specimen plant in the mid border. The maroon foliage contrasts boldly with plants that have silvery foliage, such as *Artemisia schmidtiana* 'Nana' (silvermound) or *Perovskia atriplicifolia* (Russian sage). Or let it be the star of a sunny border and plant it in small groups.

Perovskia atriplicifolia   Russian sage   mint family / Lamiaceae

Perovskia atriplicifolia

Hardiness: Zones 5a to 9a
Origin: Central Asia
Mature height: 3 to 4 ft.
Mature spread: 3 to 4 ft.
Landscape use: Back border; specimen; mass
Season of bloom: Midsummer to fall
Key ornamental characteristics: Lavender-blue
    flowers; pubescent silver-gray foliage

This aromatic plant is technically a subshrub, but it is sold as a perennial. The Perennial Plant Association named *Perovskia atriplicifolia* Perennial Plant of the Year for 1995.

Individually the flowers are small and not showy, but there are so many blooms per panicle that they have the appearance of a misty cloud, making a stunning impact. Lavender-blue flowers are 2-lipped, borne in 12- to 15-in. panicles, and arranged in an interrupted spire that rises above the foliage. Having a fine texture, Russian sage provides a graceful, vertical shape in the garden.

Leaves and stems have a grayish-white cast that adds interest to the winter garden. The stems are square, while foliage is noticeably dissected and opposite in arrangement.

Perovskia atriplicifolia is most happy in full sun and tends to flop if sited in shade. It tolerates many soil conditions but prefers well-drained sites. It also performs better in cooler climates; it tends to have a slightly washed-out appearance in regions with long, hot summers. Once established, the plant's base is woody. To insure the best growth, Russian sage should be cut back to within a few inches of the ground in the spring.

I have grown this plant for over 15 years and have never experienced any disease or insect problems.

Propagation is best accomplished by taking softwood cuttings in the summer.

Perovskia atriplicifolia 'Blue Mist' is a cultivar that flowers sooner and has lighter colored flowers than the species. 'Little Spire' has a mature height of 2 ft. and is ideal along pathways and in small gardens. 'Blue Spire' is a cultivar with dark violet flowers and foliage that is more heavily dissected than the species.

Russian sage works very well with almost any plant. It is excellent in the back border or as a specimen throughout the garden. It also is gorgeous when used in mass. I use it in conjunction with *Agastache rupestris* (threadleaf giant hyssop), *Boltonia asteroides* (white boltonia), and round-flowering plants like *Echinacea purpurea* (purple coneflower). It also will blend nicely in a shrub border. Despite its height and width, it does not dominate the garden; rather it performs harmoniously in any situation.

Persicaria amplexicaulis   mountain fleeceflower   knotweed family / Polygonaceae

Hardiness: Zones 4b to 7b
Origin: Asia and Himalayas
Mature height: 3 to 4 ft.
Mature spread: 2 to 4 ft. (more over time)
Landscape use: Back border; wet areas
Season of bloom: Midsummer to fall
Key ornamental characteristics: Attractive, spiky, red to pink flowers

When I think of the genus *Persicaria*, I think of rampant weeds. But a few species in this genus have terrific garden value, and *Persicaria amplexicaulis* (also known as *Polygonum amplexicaulis*) is one of them. Mountain fleeceflower has a long flowering time, making this plant a good one for a perennial garden. The genus is used frequently in Europe, and it is just waiting to be discovered by more American gardeners.

Red, purple, pink, or white flowers rise just above the foliage on spikes that are 4 to 6 in. long. Each flower is approximately ¼ in. long and somewhat resembles a bell. The floral spikes look like thin bottlebrushes. It is not uncommon for the flowers to last until the first frost.

Persicaria amplexicaulis

The foliage is dark green, ovate or heart shaped with a pointed apex, and alternate in arrangement. *Amplexicaulis* means "leaves that clasp the stem," referring to one of the identifying features of this species.

Persicaria amplexicaulis is easy to grow in well-drained, moderately wet to wet soils. It prefers full sun for optimal flower production. It also easily withstands partial shade, and in fact performs better in the lower Midwest if given some shade. Mountain fleeceflower needs some room to spread out. The species does not spread nearly as aggressively, however, as many others in this genus.

There are no serious insect or disease problems associated with this plant.

Propagation is best accomplished by division in the spring.

The cultivar *Persicaria amplexicaulis* 'Atrosanguinea' has dark crimson blooms. 'Firetail' is an outstanding cultivar with crimson flowers. Both cultivars grow to 4 ft. in height. The related species *P. bistorta* (European bistort, Zones 3 to 8) has the cultivar 'Superba', which has large, pink, flower spikes. It is 2 to 3 ft. tall and is a good plant for the upper Midwest.

Mountain fleeceflower is an excellent plant for those moist to wet areas. Try using it next to ponds, streams, or water gardens. Its clump-forming, bushy habit makes it useful in front of small trees or large shrubs. Try it in the back of the perennial border.

Phlox paniculata   garden phlox   phlox family / Polemoniaceae

Hardiness: Zones 4a to 8a
Origin: Eastern United States
Mature height: 2 to 4 ft.
Mature spread: 2 to 3 ft.
Landscape use: Mid to back border; specimen; small groupings
Season of bloom: Summer to early fall
Key ornamental characteristics: Dense panicles of flowers in a variety of brilliant colors

Phlox paniculata 'Robert Poore'

Phlox paniculata is an old-time favorite because of its showy, long-lasting blooms. The plant makes a bold statement in any garden.

Flower colors come in shades of red, pink, purple, lavender, blue, and white. Individual, disk-shaped flowers are densely clustered in large panicles 6 to 12 in. long. Garden phlox is highly attractive to hummingbirds and other birds. The flowers make excellent cut flowers.

Leaves are opposite in arrangement, oblong-lanceolate to ovate-lanceolate, and 3 to 5 in. long. They are noticeably thin and pointed at the apex. Garden phlox's habit is upright and clump forming.

Garden phlox does well in moderately fertile, medium wet, well-drained soil. But it prefers soils that are rich and moist, and is intolerant of dry locations. It thrives in full sun. Plants need good air circulation to help prevent powdery mildew, so do not hesitate to thin plants. Apply a layer of mulch for the summer to help keep the root zone cool. Remove spent blooms to increase flowering, and to prevent seedlings that may not be true in color.

Garden phlox is not an easy plant to grow. Powdery mildew can be a major problem. You can help prevent the spread of powdery mildew spores if you water at ground level so the leaves do not get wet. Spider mites can be a problem in hot, dry conditions. Spraying may alleviate these problems but is a chore. Root rot can also be a problem as the heat of summer wears on. Despite these issues, this species is worth the effort because of its magnificent blooms.

Phlox paniculata is best propagated by division in spring or fall. Basal cuttings can be taken in spring, and root cuttings can be taken in the fall.

There are many *Phlox paniculata* cultivars available that are more disease resistant and produce larger, more colorful flowers. But many of them are also prone to powdery mildew. 'Bright Eyes' has pink flowers with a crimson eye and grows to 2 ft. 'David' is a gorgeous, white-flowering plant that is highly resistant to mildew. 'Robert Poore' has violet-pink flowers, grows 3 to 4 ft. tall, and is highly resistant to powdery mildew.

Utilize *Phlox paniculata* in the back or mid border. It is very attractive with *Perovskia atriplicifolia* (Russian sage) and *Echinacea purpurea* (purple coneflower).

Phlox subulata   moss phlox   phlox family / Polemoniaceae

Hardiness: Zones 3♂ to 8♂
Origin: Eastern United States
Mature height: 4 to 8 in.
Mature spread: 1 to 2 ft.
Landscape use: Rock garden; pathways; slopes; walls
Season of bloom: Early spring
Key ornamental characteristics: Dense panicles of bright flowers

Moss phlox is as synonymous with spring as tulips and daffodils. It is a very popular plant for the landscape. When planted in mass, the brilliantly colored flowers make a stunning splash in the landscape.

Flowers come in various shades of pink, purple, blue, reddish-purple, or white, and the center, or throat, of the flower is a darker shade of the same color. Flowers are approximately 1/2 in. across and are borne in cymes just above the foliage. The corolla lobes are often notched at the apex.

Leaves are stiff, linear, and needlelike, 1/2 in. long, and opposite in arrangement. Foliage should be sheared back halfway after flowering to encourage thick growth over the summer and perhaps a spattering of blooms later in the year. You can also set a lawn mower on high to shear the plants back. Unlike the other members of this genus, which are relatively tall, moss phlox forms a dense, low-growing, mounded mat. It spreads by stoliniferous, creeping stems.

Moss phlox prefers well-drained soils that are sandy or gravelly. It also performs well in

Phlox subulata

average soil with moderate amounts of moisture. It needs full sun to thrive and tolerates hot, dry sites better than most species of phlox.

Phlox is usually prone to powdery mildew, but that does not apply to *P. subulata*. Spider mites and rust are occasional problems with this species.

Propagation can be accomplished by layering or division after flowering. Layering can be successful by taking a nonflowering stem and covering it with soil. Keep the soil moist until the stem develops roots. For division, cut back the foliage before digging and be careful of the shallow, fragile, root system. Cuttings can also be taken in late summer and fall.

There are many *Phlox subulata* cultivars to select from. Just choose a color. 'Blue Hills' has fantastic, dark blue flowers. 'Crackerjack' has bright reddish-purple flowers. 'Emerald Cushion Pink' has pink flowers. 'Snowflake' produces large amounts of gorgeous white flowers.

Phlox subulata is perfect for use in a rock garden or along pathways. It also is excellent on slopes or hills. My favorite way to use the plant is to let it cascade down a stone wall. It is very attractive with spring flowering bulbs. It also looks wonderful in flower when planted around the shrub *Prunus glandulosa* (dwarf flowering almond). However you utilize this reliable favorite, plant it in mass to create a spectacular show in spring.

Physostegia virginiana   obedient plant, false snapdragon   mint family / Lamiaceae

Hardiness: Zones 3a to 9a
Origin: Eastern United States
Mature height: 2 to 4 ft.
Mature spread: 2 to 3 ft. (can be invasive)
Landscape use: Mid border; mass; wildflower
   garden
Season of bloom: Midsummer to early fall
Key ornamental characteristics: Attractive pink or
   white flowers

Obedient plant gets its common name from the fact that each individual flower will, if turned in any direction, temporarily remain in the new position. Another common name, false snapdragon, refers to the snapdragonlike flowers. Obedient plant is as beautiful as it is tough. If you are looking to add a splash of color to the midsummer border, this plant is ideal.

Borne in spikes from the bottom to the top, the flowers are a soft pink color. In addition to decorating the landscape, the flowers make excellent cut arrangements.

Physostegia virginiana features leaves that are lanceolate with sharply serrate margins. The foliage is medium to dark green, and the stems are square, which is typical of many members of the mint family.

Physostegia virginiana

This plant grows best in moist, well-drained, acidic soil. It prefers full sun, but performs well in partial shade. It is tolerant of a wide range of environmental conditions. I have seen this plant flourishing in a dry, sun-baked street median polluted with car exhaust fumes.

Obedient plant is erect and grows 2 to 4 ft. tall. Like many members of the mint family, the plant can spread aggressively. Dividing obedient plant every 1 to 2 years helps keep it from overtaking an area. It is such a vigorous plant that I just pull out unwanted clumps. If grown in fertile soils, it may need staking.

I have not experienced insect or disease problems with this plant. Rust could be a slight problem.

Obedient plant is easy to propagate by seed and cuttings as well as division. Seed does not need pretreatment, and cuttings root fairly easily, but you might want to use a rooting powder.

Physostegia virginiana 'Alba' is an excellent white cultivar that adds flash to any garden. 'Miss Manners' also has white flowers, with the added attraction that it does not spread.

Best used in the mid border, the plant is very effective in mass. It works nicely with *Artemisia ludoviciana* 'Silver King' ('Silver King' white sage) and *Heliopsis* (sunflower heliopsis). It is also attractive in a naturalized or wildflower garden.

Platycodon grandiflorus balloon flower campanula family / Campanulaceae

Hardiness: Zones 3b to 8a
Origin: Eastern Asia
Mature height: 2 to 3 ft.
Mature spread: 18 in. to 2 ft.
Landscape use: Front or mid border; rock garden
Season of bloom: Summer
Key ornamental characteristics: Beautiful blue, white, or pink flowers

Platycodon grandiflorus 'Hakone Blue'

Platycodon grandiflorus flower buds have the shape of a hot air balloon, and when they open, they pop. Or you can squeeze the mature buds, popping them yourself. This plant is a terrific one for introducing children, or anyone, to gardening. The beauty of the blooms makes this plant a valuable one for any garden.

The 5-lobed flowers are generally blue, but can also be pink or white. They come in single or double forms. Dead-heading spent flowers will promote further flowering all summer long.

Bluish-green leaves are ovate-lanceolate, sharply dentate, about 1 to 3 in. long, and alternate in arrangement. They are unequally spaced on the top half of the stem and frequently whorled toward the base. The plant has a clump-forming habit.

Platycodon grandiflorus prefers full sun in northern climates and partial shade in the south. It prefers well-drained soils that are not wet. It will perform better in soils that are slightly acidic. Like *Asclepias tuberosa* (butterfly weed), the plant is slow to emerge from winter sleep. I advise retaining the previous year's growth until new leaves appear in spring, so you will know where the plant is and not damage it while cultivating the garden in early spring.

A carefree plant, balloon flower has no insect or disease problems. In warmer climates, it may flop and need staking.

Propagation can be accomplished by division, but take care with the fragile, fleshy root system of these plants. Perhaps you should leave these plants undisturbed once established. Seed germinates easily with warm temperatures and moisture.

Several *Platycodon grandiflorus* cultivars exist. 'Hakone Blue' has gorgeous, deep blue, double flowers (2 to 3 in. across) that appear singly or in small clusters atop stems typically growing 18 in. to 2 ft. tall. 'Sentimental Blue' is a dwarf that grows to 6 to 10 in. and has blue flowers. 'Shell Pink' grows to 2 ft. and has soft pink flowers.

I have planted balloon flower with *Leucanthemum* ×*superbum* (Shasta daisy) and *Heuchera sanguinea* (coral bells). It works well with many plants in the front or mid border. It also is happy in rock gardens.

Polemonium caeruleum   Jacob's ladder   phlox family / Polemoniaceae

Hardiness: Zones 3a to 7a
Origin: North America
Mature height: 18 in. to 2 ft.
Mature spread: 18 in.
Landscape use: Front border; woodland or shade garden; rock garden
Season of bloom: Late spring to early summer
Key ornamental characteristics: Delicate, blue, lavender, or white flowers; attractive foliage

The leaflets of this plant look like a ladder leading up the center stem of each leaf, thus the common name. This plant has highly attractive foliage.

Flowers are soft to dark blue with yellow stamens. They occur in clusters in loose terminal cymes. The individual flowers are reminiscent of the blooms of the tropical houseplant Persian violet (*Exacum affine*). Cut the spent blossoms back to prevent unwanted seedlings and to encourage flowering later in the growing season.

The foliage has a delicate, relatively bright green color. Leaflets are ½ to 1 in. long and almost sessile. Leaves are odd-pinnate and alternate in arrangement. Basal leaves are produced in upright mounds. Stem leaves are smaller than basal leaves.

Jacob's ladder prefers partial shade and needs full shade in the extreme lower Midwest. It can tolerate full sun in regions with cool summers. The species prefers the cooler temperatures of the upper Midwest. It requires evenly moist, humus-rich soil conditions. If the soil is too dry, the leaflet tips will turn brown.

Powdery mildew, leaf spot, and rust can be problems, especially in hot, humid regions. But these problems typically are not serious. Snails and slugs may visit on occasion. Otherwise, there are no major disease or insect problems with Jacob's ladder.

Propagation can be accomplished by division, cuttings, or seed. Divide mature plants at summer's end. Cuttings can be taken during the summer. Seeds will germinate in approximately 4 weeks during the warm days of spring. This species tends to be short lived. But if grown in ideal conditions, it will continue to reseed itself.

Several cultivars are available. *Polemonium caeruleum* 'Blanjou' (or Brise d'Anjou) has variegated green and creamy white foliage, blue flowers, and a height and width of 18 to 24 in. *Polemonium caeruleum* subsp. *himalayanum* (also known as *P. himalayanum*) has dark blue flowers that are slightly larger than those of the species. 'Album' has attractive white flowers.

Polemonium caeruleum 'Blanjou'.
Global Book Publishing Photo Library

Use Jacob's ladder in the front border, rock garden, or in a woodland setting. The foliage reminds me of ferns, so it is an excellent companion to *Aquilegia* spp. (columbine), hostas, and *Pulmonaria saccharata* (Bethlehem sage).

Pulmonaria saccharata Bethlehem sage, lungwort borage family / Boraginaceae

Hardiness: Zones 3a to 8a
Origin: Europe
Mature height: 12 to 18 in.
Mature spread: 18 in. to 2 ft.
Landscape use: Front or mid border of a shade garden; woodland or shade garden
Season of bloom: Early to mid-spring
Key ornamental characteristics: Handsome blue to pink flowers; highly attractive spotted foliage

Bethlehem sage is a highly valuable plant for the shade garden. The funnel-shaped flowers are attractive, but the plant is prized for the foliage. The unique spotting of the leaves really lights up a shaded area. Foliage is mostly basal clumps of fuzzy, dark green leaves up to 1 ft. long with silver spots. The stem leaves are smaller and alternate in arrangement. The common name lungwort comes from the leaves supposedly resembling a diseased lung.

Pulmonaria saccharata

The drooping flowers are very noticeable and an added bonus. Pink buds emerge into pink flowers that turn blue as they mature.

Pulmonaria saccharata is easy to grow in cool, moist, well-drained soils rich in organic matter. Overly wet soil, especially in the winter, will lead to this plant's death. It does not tolerate dry soils. To keep the plant truly happy, it needs partial or full shade. Bethlehem sage spreads slowly by creeping roots, but it is not aggressive.

There are no serious disease or insect problems with Bethlehem sage. Slugs and powdery mildew can be slight problems on occasion. Leaves can suffer considerably in extremely hot, sunny weather.

Propagation is by division. Since the plant emerges in early spring, divide it in the fall and supply adequate amounts of water to transplanted plants. If spring division is preferred, wait until after the plant has flowered. Seeds can be planted in the spring.

The cultivar *Pulmonaria saccharata* 'Mrs Moon' is an old favorite and sets a standard for other cultivars. It has pink flowers that turn blue, with silvery-white spots on the leaves. *Pulmonaria* 'Margery Fish' has large spots on the foliage. 'Sissinghurst White' has gorgeous white flowers that complement the spotted leaves. The related species *Pulmonaria longifolia* (long-leafed lungwort, Zones 3 to 8) has narrower leaves than the species, and its flowers open just before or when the foliage emerges.

Bethlehem sage is a natural to use with hostas, which have the same cultural requirements. It is also ideal when massed in a woodland or shade garden. Try it with *Heuchera sanguinea* (coral bells) for an attractive display of contrasting foliage.

Pulsatilla vulgaris   pasque flower   buttercup family / Ranunculaceae

Hardiness: Zones 5a to 8a
Origin: Europe
Mature height: 8 to 12 in.
Mature spread: 1 ft.
Landscape use: Front border; rock garden
Season of bloom: Early to mid-spring
Key ornamental characteristics: Silky flowers; foliage; fluffy seed heads

This gorgeous, sensuous plant was formerly known as *Anemone pulsatilla*. It blooms around Easter, thus the common name pasque flower.

Beautiful, urn-shaped flowers are borne on erect stems before the foliage is fully developed. Flower color varies from deep maroon-purple to blue, with a noticeable circle of yellow stamens in the center. Flowers have 6 sepals (not petals) covered with pubescence, and they are up to 2½ in. across. The resulting showy seed heads are white with a downy, feathery appearance.

Pulsatilla vulgaris

The basal foliage emerges after the flowers have faded. Leaves are medium green and deeply cut. Basal leaves can be up to 6 in. long and stem leaves are smaller. The leaves, stems, and buds have a silky, glistening pubescence.

Pasque flower prefers full sun in northern regions and partial shade in southern zones. The plant is easy to grow in a variety of well-drained soils. This species performs best in rich, humus-rich soils. It is somewhat drought tolerant but appreciates supplemental water in hot climates. Although short lived, the plant's distinctive, ornamental value is a special contribution to the garden.

There are no serious disease or insect problems associated with pasque flower.

Propagation is best by seed, but fresh seed is required because seed becomes dormant with age. Division can also take place in spring with established plants, but plants tend not to transplant well.

There are several *Pulsatilla vulgaris* cultivars available. 'Alba' has off-white flowers and grows up to 10 in. tall. 'Barton's Pink' has pink flowers. *Pulsatilla vulgaris* subsp. *grandis* is like the species but a bit larger in size. *Pulsatilla vulgaris* var. *rubra* has wine-red flowers.

The luscious flower color, deeply divided leaves, and later, downy seed heads make *Pulsatilla vulgaris* an extraordinarily appealing plant. It is a perfect complement for spring flowering bulbs. Its low growth habit makes it ideal for the front border, and it is excellent in a rock garden. Plant it as a specimen or in mass.

Ratibida columnifera   Mexican hat, prairie coneflower   daisy family / Asteraceae

Hardiness: Zones 4a to 8b
Origin: Southwestern Canada to northern Mexico
Mature height: 3 ft.
Mature spread: 18 in.
Landscape use: Mid border; meadow garden
Season of bloom: Early summer to early autumn
Key ornamental characteristics: Attractive red and yellow flowers; finely divided foliage

Once you discover this little-known gem, you will want it in your garden. I grow over 100 different perennial species and cultivars in my garden, and of them all, Mexican hat has the longest bloom period. The shear natural beauty of *Ratibida columnifera* will charm you for months on end.

Drooping, disk-shaped flowers are mahogany-red edged in yellow; they resemble a brightly colored sombrero. The tan to dark gray cone is up to ½ in. tall. The species name *columnifera* refers to the flower's center cone. Flowers appear in early summer and last until early autumn. Once established, a single plant will bloom heavily.

The leaves are alternate in arrangement, pinnately divided, deeply cut, and hairy. The foliage looks almost delicate, adding a lacy texture to the garden.

Native to the prairies of the United States, Mexican hat is drought tolerant. It prefers full sun and well-drained soils. The plant is tolerant of light shade. It prefers cool climates but performs admirably in warmer regions. The plant has an upright but floppy growth habit, and stems tend to twist. It may need a little support.

I have not observed any disease or insect problems with this plant.

Propagation is best by seed. Division can take place in the spring.

Cultivars of *Ratibida columnifera* include 'Buttons and Bows', a prolific bloomer with mahogany-red disk flowers

Ratibida columnifera

edged with yellow, and 'Yellow', which has yellow flowers. A related species *R. pinnata* (grayhead coneflower, Zones 3 to 10) has drooping, yellow ray florets and reddish-brown disk florets. This native prairie plant grows to 4 ft. in height and has a wild, unkempt appearance.

Mexican hat is wonderful in the mid border or in a meadow garden. I have used it with two other native plants, *Gaillardia* (blanket flower) and *Liatris* (spike gayfeather). I think it would complement almost any plant.

Rudbeckia fulgida black-eyed Susan, yellow coneflower daisy family / Asteraceae

Hardiness: Zones 3a to 9a
Origin: United States
Mature height: 18 in. to 3 ft.
Mature spread: 2 ft.
Landscape use: Mid border; meadow garden; mass
Season of bloom: Midsummer to frost
Key ornamental characteristics: Vibrant yellow-orange flowers with a dark center; winter interest

Rudbeckia fulgida var. *sullivantii* 'Goldsturm'

I love black-eyed Susan. The plant is beautiful, reliable, and a must in every garden. It is tough but spectacular while putting on its summer show.

Flowers are 2 to 3 in. across, yellow-orange, and occur from midsummer until frost. Flower petals surround a dark brown to black center. Flowers can be used in fresh or dried arrangements. The plant also adds interest to the winter landscape.

This species has rough, hairy foliage. The dark green basal leaves are up to 5 in. long and typically are twice as long as they are wide. They are oblong to lanceolate and have 3 noticeable veins. Stems have many branches, allowing for an abundance of blooms.

This upright plant will quickly make itself at home in the garden. It will grow in a wide variety of soil conditions. The plant is extremely heat and drought tolerant. It is not invasive, but spreads by rhizomes and forms clumps after a few years, especially if sited in fertile soil. I have used black-eyed Susan in full sun to medium shade and it always performs. I put a few spare plants under a lilac shrub in my garden, and they have thrived for years.

Unlike a few species in this genus that can have mildew problems, this native plant is free of disease and insect problems.

The plant can be easily propagated by division or seed in the spring. Terminal cuttings may also be taken.

The cultivar *Rudbeckia fulgida* var. *sullivantii* 'Goldsturm' is probably the best known, having flowers up to 4 in. in diameter. *Rudbeckia fulgida* var. *deamii* grows to about 2 ft. tall and produces even more flowers than the species.

I have placed *Rudbeckia fulgida* in several places in my garden, which tends to unify the overall impression. I have planted it with *Perovskia atriplicifolia* (Russian sage), *Macleaya cordata* (plume poppy), *Physostegia virginiana* (obedient plant), and *Nepeta ×faassenii* (catmint), just to name a few options. It looks terrific in the mid border of a cottage garden, meadow garden, or massed by itself. In one corner of my garden, it does not receive sun after 3:00 p.m. The rich, yellow flowers light up that corner as the evening sets in.

Ruta graveolens   rue, herb of grace   citrus family / Rutaceae

Hardiness: Zones 4a to 8b
Origin: Southern Europe
Mature height: 1 to 3 ft.
Mature spread: 18 to 30 in.
Landscape use: Front to mid border; herb garden
Season of bloom: Summer
Key ornamental characteristics: Attractive blue-
    green foliage

Ruta graveolens

Rue has a long and varied history of reported medicinal applications, including an antidote for snakebite, preserving eyesight, and treating high blood pressure. Rue's other common name, herb of grace, refers to its historic role as an addition to holy water. It also was believed to provide protection from witchcraft. Rue is traditionally found in the herb garden. But its style and beauty make it an ideal candidate for the perennial garden.

Flowers are muted mustard-yellow, ½ to ¾ in. across, and borne in terminal corymbs that are moderately showy.

This plant's foliage is what makes it valuable in the landscape. The leaves are oblong or spatulate and alternate in arrangement. They have a highly attractive bluish-green color, and are pinnately dissected, giving the plant a fine texture. Be careful handling the foliage, since it can cause minor skin irritation, especially during the heat of summer. The foliage is also aromatic.

Rue requires full sun and well-drained soils to thrive. It actually enjoys being sited in poor soils and prefers slightly alkaline conditions. Overly wet conditions will lead to this plant's demise. It is considered a subshrub: the plant base becomes woody. It should be cut back to just a few inches above ground every spring. In its colder hardiness zones, the plant benefits from a layer of winter mulch.

I have grown this species for years and it seldom has any disease or insect problems. It is susceptible to root rot on occasion. White fly may also be an occasional pest.

Propagation can be accomplished by cuttings or seed. Cuttings of new shoots may be taken in spring or early summer. Cuttings may also be taken in late summer. Seed germinates quickly.

Several *Ruta graveolens* cultivars are available. 'Blue Beauty' has beautiful, bluish-green leaves and a mounded habit. It grows to 18 in. tall. 'Jackman's Blue' is a popular cultivar with waxy, blue-green leaves. It grows up to 2 ft. in height and like many cultivars can be propagated only by cuttings. 'Variegata' has creamy white blotches on the leaves. The foliage may have the tendency to revert to bluish-green in color, so prune it in early summer to encourage new variegated growth.

Rue blends well with many plants. The blue-green leaves provide a cooling effect when planted with warm-colored flowers of other perennials. It also is a perfect companion for *Lavandula angustifolia* (common lavender) in the herb garden. Try it in the mid border of a perennial bed. Because of its upright habit, it easily fits into a knot garden or a formal garden.

Salvia azurea   azure sage, blue sage   mint family / Lamiaceae

Hardiness: Zones 5a to 9b
Origin: Southeastern United States
Mature height: 3 to 4 ft.
Mature spread: 4 ft.
Landscape use: Mid to back border
Season of bloom: Midsummer to fall
Key ornamental characteristics: Sky blue flowers

Salvia azurea produces breathtaking sky blue flowers. You need only 1 or 2 plants for the flowers to steal the show in your garden.

Heavily produced on spikes, flower display begins in midsummer. Flowers are 1/2 to 3/4 in. in length. Removal of the spent flower spikes may encourage additional flowering. Butterflies and bees are attracted to the blooms.

The medium green, pubescent leaves are lanceolate. Lower leaves are approximately 3 in. long; leaves become smaller as they ascend the stem. If the foliage gets ragged in the summer, cut it back after flowering. Once the plant has reached its mature height, it may become leggy and need support. To promote a fuller, more compact plant in spring cut back the foliage halfway.

Salvia azurea is easy to grow in a wide range of soil types that have dry to medium amounts of moisture. It prefers sandy to gravelly soils that are well drained, or the roots may rot. It tolerates heat, humidity, and drought. This plant requires full sun to thrive but it will withstand partial, light shade. Plants benefit from a layer of winter mulch in colder climates.

There are no serious insect or disease problems associated with this native plant. Rust and leaf spot can be minor nuisances.

Propagation of *Salvia azurea* is best done by seed or division in the spring.

Salvia azurea var. *grandiflora* (also known as *S. pitcheri*) is a cultivar native to the Midwest and Great Plains. It primarily differs from the species by having hairy stems and larger flowers. *Salvia azurea* 'Nekan' ('Nekan' is an abbreviation of Nebraska and Kansas) is a seed strain that was found growing wild in the Nebraska-Kansas region. It has larger flowers and is more cold hardy than the species.

Azure sage is an excellent choice for the mid or back border of a perennial or cottage garden and is a natural for a wildflower or prairie garden. The combination of yellow-flowered plants such as *Heliopsis helianthoides* var. *scabra* (sunflower heliopsis) or *Rudbeckia fulgida* (black-eyed Susan) is stunning with the sky blue blossoms of azure sage.

Salvia azurea

Salvia officinalis   common sage   mint family / Lamiaceae

Hardiness: Zones 4a to 8a
Origin: Mediterranean region
Mature height: 18 to 24 in.
Mature spread: 2 ft.
Landscape use: Mid border; specimen
Season of bloom: Late spring to early summer
Key ornamental characteristics: Attractive gray-green leaves that can be used in cooking; lavender-blue flowers

Salvia officinalis

I initially planted common sage in my garden for culinary reasons. It is a wonderful herb for grilled salmon and Thanksgiving turkey stuffing, among other foods. But common sage is also a truly beautiful plant for the perennial garden.

Flowers are an attractive lavender-blue and appear from late spring to early summer. Blooming in whorls on an erect raceme, they rise slightly above the foliage.

Moderately pubescent on both sides, the gray-green leaves provide the perfect complement for the blooms. Leaves can be harvested at any time for culinary use. I have a plant situated in a protected part of my garden. It never dies all the way back (in Zone 5b), and I often harvest leaves in midwinter. Leaves are 3 to 4 in. long, approximately 1 in. wide, and opposite in arrangement. Being a member of the mint family, the stems are square.

Salvia officinalis needs full sun and well-drained soils that are not heavy. It tends to die from root rot if placed in overly wet soils. This plant is a subshrub but is sold as a perennial. Older stems will become markedly woody. Common sage can become a little sprawling over time and should be pruned back periodically to help keep its shape.

I have grown this plant for too many years to count and have never witnessed any disease or insect problems.

The species is propagated by seed. Cultivars that have colored leaves are propagated by stem or basal cuttings.

Several cultivars are worth noting. 'Purpurascens' has purple foliage. 'Tricolor' is an attractive plant with mottled white, purple, and pink leaves.

A small portion of my garden is dedicated to herbs, and common sage is at the focal center. I placed it in front of fennel (*Foeniculum vulgare*), creating a handsome contrast of leaf textures and colors. It also looks wonderful if intermixed with rose bushes. Or place it in the mid border as a specimen plant. Even if you never use sage as an herb, this plant adds aesthetic value to any garden.

Salvia ×superba   perennial salvia   mint family / Lamiaceae

Hardiness: Zones 3a to 8a
Origin: Hybrid
Mature height: 2 to 3 ft.
Mature spread: 2 ft.
Landscape use: Mid border; mass
Season of bloom: Summer
Key ornamental characteristics: Abundant purple-
    blue flowers

Salvia ×superba

Perennial salvia is a familiar plant in the landscape. I just recently incorporated it into my garden, and I regret waiting so long.

Salvia ×superba is a consistent bloomer throughout the summer. Spikelike racemes 4 to 8 in. long carry purple-blue flowers. Even more blooms can be produced by deadheading.

Gray-green leaves are lanceolate to oblong and opposite in arrangement. Basal leaves have short petioles, while stem leaves are sessile. Foliage is slightly crinkly.

Salvia ×superba thrives in the heat of summer. It prefers moist soils but will easily withstand dry conditions, even drought. Relatively cool evenings, like in the upper Midwest, will enhance flower color intensity and bloom period.

Perennial salvia is mildly susceptible to leaf spot and rust. Scale and white fly can be occasional problems.

Perennial salvia is propogated by stem cuttings and division. Seeds are sterile. Division should take place in the spring from well-established plants. Separated clumps can be slow to get established.

Several outstanding cultivars exist. *Salvia ×sylvestris* 'Mainacht' ('May Night') is a popular cultivar that was introduced by German plant breeder Karl Foerster. It stands 18 in. tall and has deep purple-lavender blooms. *Salvia nemorosa* 'Ostfriesland' ('East Friesland') is a many-branched selection that has dark violet flowers and reaches a mature height of 18 in.

This plant is an excellent choice for the mid border. Planting in mass will create a vibrant impact. I currently use perennial salvia in front of *Perovskia atriplicifolia* (Russian sage) and intermixed with *Leucanthemum ×superbum* (Shasta daisy). It particularly complements blue- or white-flowering plants.

Santolina chamaecyparissus   lavender cotton   daisy family / Asteraceae

Hardiness: Zones 6a to 8a
Origin: Mediterranean region
Mature height: 18 to 24 in.
Mature spread: 18 to 24 in.
Landscape use: Edging; accent; rock garden
Season of bloom: Mid to late summer
Key ornamental characteristics: Silvery-gray foliage

Santolina chamaecyparissus

The handsome, silvery-gray foliage of this perennial is its star characteristic. The scented, pubescent leaves are pinnately divided into small segments, giving the plant a tight appearance. Foliage takes on a whitish cast when it receives more sun. The base of the plant can become woody; this species is also considered a subshrub.

Round, bright yellow flowers are buttonlike, up to ¾ in. in diameter, and borne in summer. Some people remove the flowers because they prefer the aesthetic quality of the foliage. The plant may need light pruning periodically anyway, to maintain its compact habit.

Santolina chamaecyparissus thrives in full sun. It requires soil that is well drained and likes its site to be a bit dry. The plant will survive better in its colder hardiness zones if you give it an application of winter mulch. This versatile plant has a relatively narrow hardiness range. It is fairly short lived in my Zone 5b garden, even though I have placed it in a wind-protected location. But lavender cotton can be simply treated as an annual in all parts of the Midwest except the extreme southern portion.

There are no serious disease or insect problems with this plant. But hot, wet summers can lead to fungal problems, which will open up the center of the plant, leaving it looking tired and ragged.

Propagation is best by stem cuttings in the spring, although they can be taken and often successfully rooted during the summer. Seeds tend to be inconsistent in germination.

There are a few cultivars available in the nursery trade. *Santolina chamaecyparissus* var. *nana* includes smaller plants like 'Weston' and *S. chamaecyparissus* 'Small-Ness'. They grow to a mature height of approximately 10 in. *Santolina chamaecyparissus* 'Lambrook Silver' has silvery-gray foliage.

Lavender cotton's foliage color and texture makes it an excellent accent plant. It is particularly effective when planted in small groupings. Plant it with *Dianthus* (pink) or plants with maroon foliage like *Penstemon digitalis* 'Husker Red' (Husker red foxglove penstemon). You can easily shear this plant to create a low-growing hedge. And since it tolerates pruning so well, it can be used in a knot garden. Lavender cotton is also ideal to use as an edging or in a rock garden.

Saponaria ocymoides   rock soapwort   carnation family / Caryophyllaceae

Hardiness: Zones 3a to 7a
Origin: Southern and central Europe
Mature height: 4 to 8 in.
Mature spread: 10 in. to 2 ft.
Landscape use: Rock garden; walls
Season of bloom: Late spring to early summer
Key ornamental characteristics: Abundant, pink or white flowers

Rock soapwort's common name refers to the fact that the roots of most plants in this genus can be boiled to produce a soaplike lather to wash clothing.

The 5-petaled, dark pink blooms of *Saponaria ocymoides* are borne in mass at the ends of the branches, making quite an impact in the garden. The plant is most floriferous in late spring and early summer, but pruning after flowering will encourage some additional blooms later in the summer.

Leaves are medium green, up to 1 in. long, spatulate or elliptic, simple, and hairy. The lower leaves have short petioles while the upper leaves are sessile. Stems have many branches and a red cast. The plant should be cut back hard to encourage new growth and to keep it from becoming leggy and sprawling. Once established, the plant forms a dense mat.

Saponaria ocymoides

Saponaria ocymoides is tolerant of cold temperatures and does not do well in hot, humid climates, so it is better suited to the upper Midwest. Preferring full sun for best performance, it tolerates poor soils as long as they are well drained and neutral to slightly alkaline. I have attempted to grow this attractive plant in my Zone 5b garden several times, but by the end of summer it has a pitiful appearance and does not survive the winter.

There are no serious disease or insect problems associated with *Saponaria ocymoides*. Snails and slugs may visit occasionally.

Propagation is best by seed, and the plant will germinate in a couple of weeks. Once established in the garden, the plant will freely self-seed. Division can also be accomplished, but it is difficult to do without damaging the stems. Cuttings can also be easily propagated.

Saponaria ocymoides 'Alba' is a white cultivar that is very floriferous. 'Floribunda' produces large numbers of pale pink blooms.

Rock soapwort is ideal for a rock garden. It also makes a stunning effect along a pathway or growing out of crevices in a rock wall. Use it with *Salvia ×sylvestris* 'Mainacht' ('May Night', perennial salvia) to create a beautiful show of pink and purple. It also beautifully complements shrub roses.

Scabiosa columbaria   pincushion flower   teasel family / Dipsacaceae

Hardiness: Zones 5a to 9a
Origin: Europe and western Asia
Mature height: 12 to 18 in.
Mature spread: 12 to 18 in.
Landscape use: Front or mid border; rock garden; edging; mass
Season of bloom: Late spring to fall
Key ornamental characteristics: Soft pale blue or pinkish-blue flowers

Pincushion flower is a subtle beauty in the garden. The genus name *Scabiosa* comes from the Latin *scabies*, referring to an itchy ailment this plant reportedly was used to cure.

Scabiosa 'Butterfly Blue'

Dome-shaped, pale blue or pinkish-blue flowers are approximately 2 in. in diameter. The common name refers to the cushion with protruding stamens that looks like a pincushion with pins in it. Flowers are singly borne on thin, wiry stems above the foliage. They last throughout a good portion of the growing season. Remove spent flowers to encourage additional blooming.

Green-gray leaves are slightly hairy. Basal foliage is oblanceolate and dissected. Upper leaves are smaller and cut into linear segments.

Pincushion flower is easy to grow in a variety of well-drained soils in full sun. Tolerating part shade, particularly in the hot summer climates of the lower Midwest, it prefers soils with a neutral to slightly alkaline pH. It is not tolerant of wet soils, especially in winter.

No serious disease or insect problems occur with this plant.

Scabiosa is best divided in spring. Basal cuttings can also be taken at that time.

Two excellent, popular cultivars exist. *Scabiosa* 'Butterfly Blue' stands 15 in. tall, with the same spread as the species, and has soft blue flowers. It was named Perennial Plant of the Year for 2000. 'Pink Mist' is the same size and has pale lavender-pink blooms.

Scabiosa columbaria blends easily into any garden situation. I have used it with another member of the teasel family, *Knautia macedonica* (knautia); it has the same flower shape, but a dark crimson flower color. Or, try it with *Veronica spicata* (spiked speedwell). Use it in the front or mid border. It also works well in rock gardens or as an edging. Grouping at least three plants will enhance the pleasing effect this plant brings to the garden.

Sedum spectabile   showy stonecrop, sedum   orpine family / Crassulaceae

Hardiness: Zones 3a to10a
Origin: Japan
Mature height: 18 to 24 in.
Mature spread: 18 in.
Landscape use: Mid border; rock garden; mass; specimen
Season of bloom: Late summer to frost
Key ornamental characteristics: Pinkish flowers; succulent foliage; winter interest

When the flowers of *Sedum spectabile* (also known as *Hylotelephium spectabile*) start to bloom, the end of summer is not far away.

Flowers occur in dense heads 3 to 6 in. in diameter. They are made up of smaller blossoms and usually come in shades of pink, but shades of red and white are also available. The flowers are a favorite of bees and butterflies. Blooms are set in midsummer and the flowers persist in late summer until frost, keeping the garden alive before the chill of fall sets in. If left standing, the dead flower heads and foliage will add great ornamental interest to the winter landscape.

Light green, fleshy foliage has a succulent appearance, giving the plant an exotic look. The

Sedum spectabile

leaves are obovate, with toothed margins, approximately 3 in. long, and opposite in arrangement. The plant has an attractive mounded habit. The foliage of *Sedum spectabile* adds interesting texture and color to the garden during the growing season.

Showy stonecrop sedum thrives in full sun and any soil that is well drained. It will tolerate dry soils. If planted in too much shade, stems become weak and unable to support the
flower heads. Plants sited in partial shade will produce fewer blooms.

I have grown this plant for years and have not witnessed any disease or insect problems.

Propagation is by division in the spring. But the plant does not need to be divided frequently. Stem cuttings can be taken in the summer.

Several excellent *Sedum spectabile* cultivars exist. 'Carmen' is a wonderful selection and
has carmine-pink flowers. 'Iceberg' has white flowers. *Sedum* 'Indian Chief' has red flowers
that fade to pink. 'Autumn Joy' is a related hybrid with pinkish flowers that many people
prefer. It is probably a cross of *S. spectabile* and *S. telephium*.

Many plants work well with showy stonecrop sedum. I like it with *Aster ×frikartii* (Frikart's
aster), *Aster novi-belgii* (New York aster), and *Rudbeckia fulgida* (black-eyed Susan), which
flower at the same time. Also consider planting it with other perennials that bloom earlier in
the year, for the complementary texture and color of its foliage.

Sedum spurium   two-row stonecrop   orpine family / Crassulaceae

Hardiness: Zones 3a to 7b
Origin: Caucasus
Mature height: 2 to 6 in.
Mature spread: 12 to 24 in.
Landscape use: Ground cover; rock garden; stone wall
Season of bloom: Midsummer
Key ornamental characteristics: Apple-green foliage; pinkish star-shaped flowers

---

The genus *Sedum* is notable for including both taller, border perennials and low-growing
ground covers. In fact, there are several species that grow no more than a few inches in height.
Of these, *S. spurium* is a tough plant with showy flowers. It thrives more in the cooler, upper
Midwest than in warmer regions.

Star-shaped flowers are ½ to 1 in. wide and can be profusely borne in dense clusters at
the stem tip. They are typically pinkish-red but can also be pinkish-purple or white.

The semievergreen foliage is apple green in color. Leaves are ½ to 1 in. long and oblong
with toothed margins. Leaf margins are slightly tinged with red, and the entire leaf turns red
in fall and winter. Stems root at leaf nodes, allowing the species to spread rapidly. Leaves are

Sedum spurium 'John Creech'

opposite in arrangement and occur in 2 distinct rows along the stem, thus the common name two-row stonecrop. Older leaves are deciduous while younger leaves are evergreen.

Two-row stonecrop adapts to a wide range of soil types, even poor-quality soils, but requires well-drained sites. It prefers moist soils that are not overly wet, but it withstands drought. The plant prefers full sun for best growth, but it tolerates partial shade. It is vigorous and can be slightly invasive under the right conditions.

There are no serious insect or disease problems associated with two-row stonecrop.

Propagation is easy to accomplish. Division can be done at anytime during the growing season. Cuttings can also be taken at anytime during the summer.

Several cultivars are available. *Sedum spurium* 'Schorbuser Blut' ('Dragon's Blood') has purple-bronze foliage and produces red flowers. 'John Creech' is named after a former director of the United States National Arboretum. He reportedly collected the plant at the Central Siberian Botanic garden. It grows to only 2 in. tall and has dark pink flowers. 'Purpurteppich' ('Purple Carpet') has purple foliage. 'Variegatum' has green leaves with creamy pink margins and pink flowers. It can also produce green foliage.

Two-row stonecrop is ideal for use as a ground cover or in the rock garden. It can add character to stone walls when placed in the crevices.

Sempervivum tectorum hen and chicks, houseleek orpine family / Crassulaceae

Hardiness: Zones 3a to 8b
Origin: Europe
Mature height: 2 to 3 in.
Mature spread: 1 to 4 in.
Landscape use: Rock garden; wall; front border; rocks; pots
Season of bloom: Summer
Key ornamental characteristics: Succulent foliage that grows in a rosette

Sempervivum tectorum

The name of this plant comes from the Latin *semper,* meaning "always," and *vivo,* meaning "live," and *Sempervivum tectorum* does seem to live forever. There is a large, porous rock in our garden, and hen and chicks has always grown on it. In Europe, hen and chicks is often seen growing on tiled roofs. Folklore says it guards against lightning and prevents fires, thus the common name houseleek. I have fond memories of this fascinating plant from when I was a little boy. It is perfect for a children's garden.

Flowers appear in summer and rise up to 1 ft. above the foliage. Usually red, they can also be green, purple, yellow, or white. They are secondary to the foliage and growth habit.

Succulent, thick and fleshy, bright green leaves frequently have a reddish-purple cast at the apex. Leaves are flat on the top and slightly curved on the underside. Foliage rosettes are 1 to 4 in. in diameter. This plant remains evergreen in all climates.

Hen and chicks thrives in full sun and easily tolerates partial shade. It prefers dry, rocky soil that is poor in quality and well drained. It will even grow in a small crack in concrete. Rich soil will cause its demise.

Crown rot and rust are the major disease problems associated with *Sempervivum tectorum.* There are no serious insect problems.

Hen and chicks spreads by stolons, and the new plants, or chicks, nestle against the parent plant, or hen. Removing and replanting the chicks is the easiest form of propagation. The plant may also be grown from seed.

This species has been sold under a vast array of names, many of which are incorrect. *Sempervivum tectorum* var. *calcareum* (Zones 3 to 8) has smooth leaves that have red-brown tips at the apex. The leaves of *S. arachnoideum* are connected by strands; it goes by the common name cobweb hen and chicks.

This plant is excellent to use in areas where many other plants would never grow. It is a natural for the rock garden. Grow it in cracks of rock walls to add interest. Try planting it in terra-cotta strawberry pots and placing the pots throughout the garden.

Silene regia   royal catchfly   carnation family / Carophyllaceae

Silene regia

Hardiness: Zones 5a to 8a
Origin: Eastern United States
Mature height: 3 to 4 ft.
Mature spread: 15 to 24 in.
Landscape use: Mid border; cottage garden;
    woodland or wildflower garden
Season of bloom: Mid to late summer
Key ornamental characteristics: Bright scarlet
    flowers

Silene regia caught my attention a few years ago. Belonging to the same family as *Lychnis* (campion) and *Dianthus* (pink), this native plant has striking, showy flowers that are highly attractive to hummingbirds.

Spectacular, scarlet flowers occur in the heat of summer. They have 5 petals and are 1 to 2 in. in diameter. Petals may or may not be notched at the apex. The calyx is sticky and often traps small insects, thus the common name royal catchfly.

Leaves are medium green, 1 to 3 in. long, ovate, entire, and opposite in arrangement. Leaves and stems are slightly pubescent. Upright in habit, royal catchfly is clump forming. Taller plants may need support.

Royal catchfly is tolerant of a wide range of soil types, but it prefers well-drained, sandy, or loamy conditions. It also prefers moderately even soil moisture, and once established is tolerant of dry sites. Preferring dappled shade, royal catchfly also performs well in full sun.

I have not experienced any insect or disease problems with royal catchfly. Slugs, snails, whitefly, and aphids can be occasional pests. Rust and smut may also occur.

Seeds can be planted in the fall or spring. Division can be difficult since this species has a deep root system. If you must divide royal catchfly, do so in fall.

Silene regia 'Prairie Fire' is an excellent cultivar with scarlet flowers. It grows 3 to 4 ft. tall. The related species *S. dioica* (red campion, Zones 6 to 9) has reddish-purple blooms. It grows 2 to 3 ft. in height. *Silene virginica* (fire pink, Zones 4 to 7) is shorter than the species at 1 to 2 ft., has crimson blooms, and is short lived.

Silene regia is an excellent plant for the mid border or a cottage garden. It provides a splash of vibrant scarlet in woodland or wildflower gardens. Try it with *Rudbeckia fulgida* (black-eyed Susan), *Leucanthemum ×superbum* (Shasta daisy), or in front of ornamental grasses.

Silphium perfoliatum cup plant daisy family / Asteraceae

Hardiness: Zones 4a to 9a
Origin: Eastern and central United States
Mature height: 4 to 7 ft.
Mature spread: 3 ft.
Landscape use: Prairie or native plant garden; near ponds; back border
Season of bloom: Mid to late summer
Key ornamental characteristics: Yellow, daisylike flowers; unusual foliage

Silphium perfoliatum has an untamed beauty. It is a large plant, with flowers 3 to 4 in. in diameter. Flowers have pale yellow rays and a darker yellow center. Blooms appear in midsummer and last for several weeks.

Leaves are medium to dark green, triangular-ovate, coarsely serrate, and opposite in arrangement. Cup plant has square stems; it is the only member of the genus *Silphium* to have square stems. Lower leaves on the stem are up to 14 in. long and united at the petioles. As leaves ascend the stem, they lack petioles, and the leaf pairs are joined at the base, forming a cup, thus the common name. The leaf cups collect water. When snapped, stems bleed a slightly pungent, resinous sap, which is a characteristic of this genus.

Cup plant is a rugged native of the prairies. It thrives in moist to wet soils that are rich with organic matter. But once it has taken a foothold, it will withstand drought conditions. Full sun is a must.

Downy mildew and rust can be occasional problems. I have not encountered any insect problems with this species.

Propagation is by seed or division. Sow seed in containers; they can be slow to germinate. This species will freely self-sow if grown under ideal conditions. Divide in spring.

Silphium perfoliatum

Silphium laciniatum (compass plant, Zones 5 to 9), a related species, has hairy stems and large, finely divided leaves that resemble oak leaves. The leaves grow vertically on the stem, and the leaf edges point north and south, hence the common name. The plant does this to minimize its direct exposure to the sun. Growing to 8 ft. tall, it also has yellow flowers. *Silphium integrifolium* (wholeleaf rosinweed, Zones 4 to 7) has yellow flowers 2 to 3 in. in diameter. Mature height is 4 ft., which is small for the genus.

This big plant has a very coarse texture. It is ideal for prairie or native plant gardens where it can assume its preferred habit. It also grows well around wet areas like ponds. If you have a sufficiently large garden, enjoy cup plant as a backdrop in the back border.

Sisyrinchium angustifolium   blue-eyed grass   iris family / Iridaceae

Hardiness: Zones 3a to 8b
Origin: Eastern United States
Mature height: 8 to 12 in.
Mature spread: 8 to 12 in.
Landscape use: Front border; naturalized areas; rock garden; along pathways;
   mass
Season of bloom: Mid spring to midsummer
Key ornamental characteristics: Attractive purplish-blue, yellow-throated flowers;
   grasslike foliage

Sisyrinchium is a relatively little-known genus that is becoming more popular in the perennial nursery industry. The subtle beauty of blue-eyed grass adds an element of understated charm to any garden. Although it may not appear to be, *Sisyrinchium angustifolium* is a member of the iris family.

Sisyrinchium angustifolium

Blue-eyed grass truly lives up to its common name, with modest, purplish-blue flowers with a yellow throat. Flowers appear slightly above the grassy foliage. The star-shaped flowers are ¼ to ½ in. across. They occur from mid-spring to midsummer, and are showy if the plant blooms in mass. Flowers open when the sun shines but stay closed in the morning and evening and on overcast days.

The plant has linear, flat, bluish-green, semievergreen leaves. The foliage is very handsome, and reminds me of low-growing, ornamental grass. Plants may remain evergreen throughout the winter in the lower Midwest, if placed in a protected site.

Blue-eyed grass performs best in moist locations and neutral to slightly alkaline soils. But it adapts easily to a range of soil conditions. It tends to languish and quickly die in heavy clay soils or in soils that are overly wet during winter. It prefers full sun to light shade. Partial shade should be provided in the warmer regions of the Midwest.

I have grown this plant for several years and have not encountered any associated disease or insect problems.

Blue-eyed grass is a low-maintenance plant. It is not aggressive, but it may freely self-seed. Plant seed in the fall if kept in a greenhouse, and in spring if sown outdoors. Divide plants in spring every 2 to 3 years to help keep the plant healthy.

The cultivar *Sisyrinchium angustifolium* 'Lucerne' has larger flowers than the species. The related species *S. striatum* (Argentine blue-eyed grass, Zones 4 to 8) is larger than *S. angustifolium*, reaching 2 ft. in height with a spread of 18 in. The leaves are green and look even more grasslike.

Blue-eyed grass is effective in a variety of garden situations. It is ideal for the front border, rock garden, or along a pathway. Naturalized or woodland gardens are also excellent situations for this plant. Use it in mass to achieve the potential impact of the plant. I have used it with great visual success in combination with *Artemisia schmidtiana* 'Nana' (silvermound), *Heuchera sanguinea* (coral bells), *Nepeta* ×*faassenii* (catmint), and *Stachys byzantina* (lamb's ear).

Solidago hybrids   goldenrod   daisy family / Asteraceae

Hardiness: Zones 2a to 8b
Origin: United States; hybrids
Mature height: 2 to 3 ft.
Mature spread: 1 to 2 ft.
Landscape use: Mid or back border; mass; native plant garden
Season of bloom: Midsummer to fall
Key ornamental characteristics: Bright yellow flowers

Numerous species of goldenrod are scattered throughout the United States, adding bright yellow masses to the roadside vista from midsummer to fall. Goldenrod has been falsely accused of causing hay fever, whereas the culprit is the pollen of other plants that bloom at the same time, such as ragweed.

Goldenrod has tiny, yellow flowers borne profusely in large panicles. They appear in rows on one side of the plume (branch). Bees and butterflies are drawn to this plant. Flowers are excellent for fresh or dried arrangements.

The leaves are linear-lanceolate to elliptic-lanceolate, and range from 2 to 6 in. long. They can be glabrous or scabrous, and are alternate in arrangement.

Goldenrod prefers full sun but also does well in light shade. It is tolerant of poor-quality, dry soils. Taller cultivars may need staking.

There are no serious insect or disease problems with this perennial. Rust may occur on occasion. Powdery mildew and leaf spot can also be occasional minor problems.

Propagation of goldenrod hybrids is easy by division in spring. Stem cuttings can also be successfully rooted if taken in early summer. The species can be grown from seed.

Much hybridization of *Solidago* has taken place, resulting in shorter, more compact plants with improved flowers. There are many interesting goldenrod cultivars, most

Solidago

with obscure parentage. *Solidago* 'Crown of Rays' is 2 ft. tall with brilliant yellow flowers. 'Goldkind' ('Golden Baby') is approximately 2 ft. in height with bright yellow flowers. 'Golden Shower' is 3 to 4 ft. tall with yellow flowers. Many of the species, and some hybrids, are invasive. *Solidago odora* (sweet goldenrod, Zones 3 to 9), however, is not overly aggressive. This species' leaves smell like anise when crushed and can be used to make tea. It is 2 to 4 ft. tall with bright yellow flowers.

Goldenrod is excellent for native plant gardens. But do not stop there. This handsome plant is perfect for the mid or back border of the perennial garden. Plant it with *Sedum spectabile* (showy stonecrop sedum), *Eupatorium purpureum* subsp. *maculatum* (Joe-Pye weed), and the subshrub *Buddleja davidii* (butterfly bush) to create a feeding ground for butterflies and other insects at the end of the growing season.

Sphaeralcea munroana   orange globe mallow   mallow family / Malvaceae

Hardiness: Zones 4b to 9a
Origin: Western United States
Mature height: 2 to 3 ft.
Mature spread: 18 in. to 2 ft.
Landscape use: Mid border
Season of bloom: Midsummer to end of season
Key ornamental characteristics: Attractive apricot-
    orange flowers; gray-green foliage

Sphaeralcea munroana

If you are looking for something different, *Sphaeralcea munroana* may be the plant. Native to the western United States, orange globe mallow has made itself at home in my lower midwestern garden and quickly charmed me.

Orange globe mallow is in the mallow family, which includes hollyhock, and the flowers look like small hollyhock blossoms. Flowers are approximately ¾ in. in diameter with beautiful apricot-orange petals and yellow anthers. They are borne on gray, upright, branchless stems that rise 2 to 3 ft. in height. Flowers appear from midsummer to the end of the season.

Leaves are light green-gray, have 3 to 5 shallow lobes and a fine layer of pubescence, and are alternate in arrangement. The pale foliage color is attractive in its own right: it provides the perfect backdrop for the flowers while complementing the darker green foliage of other species in the garden.

Orange globe mallow has a mature spread of 18 in. to 2 ft., and it may spread by underground runners (it has a deep root system) but is not aggressive. It is tolerant of a wide range of soils and thrives in heavy clay. Its natural habitat is dry, open space, so it is drought resistant and prefers full sun. It may need staking over the course of the summer.

Few disease and insect problems exist with this plant. Leaf rust may be a slight problem.

Propagation is by seed. Unlike members of the mallow family, such as *Alcea rosea* (hollyhock) and *Malva alcea* (hollyhock mallow), my plants have not produced any unwanted seedlings.

Sphaeralcea munroana is perfect for the mid border. It makes an impact in small groupings or as a specimen plant. It will fit right into a meadow, wildflower, or desert garden. Its upright habit and flower and leaf color complement the floppy, mounded habit of catmint (*Nepeta* spp.) and the sprawling ground-cover habit of poppy mallow (*Callirhoe involucrata*).

Spigelia marilandica   Indian pink, pinkroot   pinkroot family / Loganiaceae

Hardiness: Zones 5b to 9a
Origin: Southeastern United States
Mature height: 12 to 18 in.
Mature spread: 12 to 18 in.
Landscape use: Front border; woodland, shade, or
    native garden; by ponds or streams
Season of bloom: Late spring to early summer
Key ornamental characteristics: Eye-catching
    trumpet-shaped, red flowers

Spigelia marilandica

This magnificent plant has bright red, trumpet-shaped flowers. The upright, 2-in.-long blooms reveal a flashy, star-shaped yellow throat. Occurring above the foliage in 1-sided cymes, the flowers of this native plant have an attention-grabbing, tropical look. The flowers of Indian pink are a favorite of hummingbirds. Indigenous peoples reportedly used extracts from the roots to treat parasites. Western medicine also reportedly has used the plant for the same reason. Indian pink is a star waiting to be discovered by the gardening world.

The glossy, dark green leaves are ovate, entire, sessile, 3 to 4 in. long, and opposite in arrangement.

Spigelia marilandica is a clump-forming plant that grows easily in moist, well-drained soils that are rich in organic matter. It requires partial to full shade. If the summer is cool and you provide plenty of organic matter and moist conditions, the plant may withstand full sun. It is best suited for the relatively milder winters of the lower Midwest.

There are no serious insect or disease problems associated with Indian pink.

Propagation can be a bit challenging, as is often the case with woodland plants. The best bet is by seed. Stem and tip cuttings can also be taken from plants that have not yet flowered that season. Division may be done in spring with fully established plants.

Spigelia marilandica 'Little Redhead' is a compact, red-flowered cultivar that reaches a maximum height of 12 in.

When in bloom, Indian pink lights up any shaded area of the garden. Try placing it among native ferns and hostas. It puts on a show if used as a specimen or is planted in drifts. Site it in a woodland or shade garden. It does well when placed next to streams and ponds.

Stachys byzantina   lamb's ear, woolly woundwort   mint family / Lamiaceae

Hardiness: Zones 4a to 7a
Origin: Southwestern Asia
Mature height: 6 to 12 in.
Mature spread: 12 to 18 in.
Landscape use: Front border; rock garden; ground cover; mass
Season of bloom: Summer to fall
Key ornamental characteristics: Attractive fuzzy, white-green foliage

Stachys byzantina is a perennial that is typically grown just for its foliage. The soft, tomentose, white leaves and stems are highly attractive. In fact, the fuzzy texture of the leaves, which are oblong-elliptic and up to 4 in. long, gives the plant its common name lamb's ear. It is also called woolly woundwort, because the plant was used by soldiers in the Civil War to bandage minor wounds. The intriguing name and soft leaves of this plant make it a favorite of children.

Stachys byzantina

The flowers are of minor ornamental value; they occur from summer to fall. Purplish-pink blooms are borne in spikes that rise 4 to 6 in. above the foliage. They often flop over after a rain, and many gardeners remove the flowers to eliminate distraction from the foliage.

Lamb's ear prefers full sun in low-fertility soils. In the lower Midwest, the plant will find partial shade acceptable. In hot, humid regions, the plant will be healthiest in well-drained soils. *Stachys byzantina* readily spreads without choking out other plants and will eventually form a carpetlike mat. This species performs well in the spring, tends to look a bit shabby in summer, and returns to form in the fall. When irrigating, try to keep leaves dry, or water the plant in the morning.

The only insect or disease problem I have encountered with this species is leaf rot. If this disease does occur, just pull off the infected leaves.

Propagation is easy. Division can be done during the spring or fall, and the plant separates readily.

Stachys byzantina 'Cotton Boll' is a compact cultivar that produces woolly clusters rather than flowers. 'Big Ears' ('Countess Helen von Stein') has large leaves and few flowers. 'Silver Carpet' does not produce flowers.

Use lamb's ear in the front border or along a pathway. The white-silvery-green foliage works with any plant and adds coolness to the garden.

Stachys macrantha   big betony   mint family / Lamiaceae

Hardiness: Zones 3a to 8a
Origin: Asia
Mature height: 8 in. (18 in. when in bloom)
Mature spread: 12 in.
Landscape use: Front border; pathways; mass; specimen
Season of bloom: Summer
Key ornamental characteristics: Mauve-purple flowers; dark green, crinkly leaves

There are more than 200 species of *Stachys*, but only a few are commonly used. The genus name *Stachys* may make you think of the fuzzy leaves of lamb's ear (*S. byzantina*). *Stachys macrantha* bears little resemblance to that species, but is also of great value in the garden.

Handsome, cylindrical, mauve-purple flowers are up to 1 in. long and are arranged in whorls on stems that rise to 18 in., or 8 to 10 in. above the foliage. The upper lip of the flower is 2-lobed while the lower lip is 3-lobed.

Big betony is a clump-forming plant that has rosettes of attractive, dark green, heart-shaped to ovate leaves. Leaves are slightly hairy, crinkly, and coarsely serrate. Uppermost

Stachys macrantha

leaves on the stem are smaller than basal leaves. A member of the mint family, the plant's stems are square.

In the upper Midwest, big betony thrives in full sun and well-drained soils. Gardeners in the lower Midwest should site this plant in partial shade. The species tends to bloom more prolifically in cooler climates, and flowers tend to last longer in partial shade. In overly hot conditions, big betony benefits from additional irrigation.

There are no serious disease or insect problems associated with this species.

Propagation is best by division in the spring. The plant can also be reproduced by seed.

The cultivar *Stachys macrantha* 'Alba' has white blooms. 'Rosea' has rosy-red flowers. 'Superba' is an excellent cultivar; its rosy-lavender flowers reach up to 2 ft. A related species *Stachys officinalis* (wood betony, Zones 4 to 8) is similar in appearance, but it prefers more sun than *S. macrantha*.

Big betony is a perfect candidate for the front border. I have also placed it along pathways. It makes an attractive statement if used in mass or as a specimen. It is a lovely companion for plants with light green foliage, such as *Alchemilla mollis* (lady's mantle).

Stokesia laevis   Stokes' aster   daisy family / Asteraceae

Hardiness: Zones 5a to 9a
Origin: Southeastern United States
Mature height: 1 to 2 ft.
Mature spread: 12 to 18 in.
Landscape use: Front or mid border; small groupings
Season of bloom: Summer
Key ornamental characteristics: Large pale blue, purple, white, or pale yellow
    flowers

The only species in this genus, *Stokesia laevis* is native to the southeastern United States. It was named after English physician and botanist Jonathan Stokes. At quick glance, the flowers are reminiscent of *Centaurea montana* (perennial bachelor's button) blooms.

In the wild, flowers are up to 1 in. in diameter. Through breeding programs, cultivar flowers are up to 4 in. in diameter. Borne on upright stems, the soft blue flowers have a feathery appearance. The flower stems may flop, especially after heavy rain or strong winds. Deadhead spent flowers (and stems) to encourage further flowering. The quiet blue flowers make an excellent addition in fresh cut arrangements.

Basal leaves are oblong-lanceolate, up to 8 in. long, and alternate in arrangement. Leaves have a noticeable white midrib and become smaller and stalkless as they ascend the tomentose stem. Basal rosettes can remain evergreen in warmer zones.

Stokes' aster prefers full sun and tolerates light shade. It likes moist, well-drained soils but is tolerant of drought conditions. The plant prefers slightly acidic soil conditions. Overly wet soils in winter will likely cause this plant's demise. In northern zones, the plant benefits from a layer of winter mulch. I have successfully grown this species in my Zone 5b garden for more than 10 years.

There are no serious disease or insect problems associated with this species.

Propagation is by division or cuttings in spring. Seed can also be planted but germination is slow.

Stokesia laevis

Several *Stachys laevis* cultivars exist. 'Alba' has white flowers but does not produce as many blooms as the blue-flowering cultivars. 'Blue Danube' has lavender-blue flowers that are up to 5 in. in diameter. 'Wyoming' probably has the darkest blue flowers of any *Stachys* cultivar and blooms profusely. Newer introductions include 'Mary Gregory', a surprising clear yellow; 'Honeysong Purple', a compact plant with dark purple flowers; and 'Peachie's Pick', to 20 in., with profuse blue flowers.

Stokes' aster is excellent for the front or mid border. The soft blue of the flowers complements just about any other species. Plant it in small groups of three or more to achieve a graceful impact in the garden. Try placing it behind *Stachys byzantina* (lamb's ear) and in front of *Coreopsis grandiflora* (coreopsis).

Teucrium chamaedrys   wall germander   mint family / Lamiaceae

Hardiness: Zones 4b to 9a
Origin: Europe and southwest Asia
Mature height: 10 to 16 in.
Mature spread: 12 to 16 in.
Landscape use: Front border; herb garden; rock garden; hedges; knot gardens
Season of bloom: Summer
Key ornamental characteristics: Dark green, shiny foliage; pale pink to purple
    flowers

The Latin genus *Teucrium* was reportedly named after Teucer, the first king of Troy. The species *chamaedrys* is the ancient Greek word for "ground oak"; wall germander's leaves resemble those of an oak tree. The aromatic leaves of this subtly attractive plant had a variety of medicinal applications in medieval times.

Flowers are pale pink to purple and 2-lipped. The lower lip is much larger than the upper

Teucrium chamaedrys

lip, with the entire flower being approximately ½ in. long. Flowers are borne in whorls, and usually are not produced in abundance.

Leaves are dark green, shiny, oblong-ovate, usually serrate but also entire, up to ¾ in. long, and opposite in arrangement. After flowering, you may cut back the plant to promote a bushy, compact habit. I prefer not to shear this plant and to let its mounded habit and ascending stems grow as they may.

Teucrium chamaedrys thrives in dry to moderately moist soils. It likes slightly alkaline conditions, but tolerates a wide range of soil types as long as good drainage is provided. Full sun is a must. Evergreen in many climates, wall germander is also considered a subshrub. It may die back to the ground in colder regions or during harsh winters. Winter protection is advised.

There are no serious insect or disease problems associated with wall germander. Powdery and downy mildew, leaf spot, rust, and spider mites may occur from time to time.

Propagation can be done by seed, cuttings, or division. Seed may be planted in spring, but germination is variable. Take cuttings in spring or summer. Division is easy because of wall germander's creeping roots; divide plants in spring.

Teucrium chamaedrys 'Nanum' ('Prostratum'), a short cultivar at 6 to 10 in., has pink flowers. 'Variegatum' has pale pink to purple flowers and green and creamy white foliage.

Often used as a low, clipped hedge or to form a knot garden, wall germander is also ideal in the front border, herb garden, or rock garden. The dark green foliage provides the perfect complement for silver-leaved plants like *Artemisia* (wormwood), *Lavandula angustifolia* (common lavender), or *Santolina chamaecyparissus* (lavender cotton). Its fine-textured foliage also goes well with plants that have coarse texture.

Thalictrum rochebruneanum   lavender mist meadow rue
buttercup family / Ranunculaceae

Hardiness: Zones 3a to 7a
Origin: Japan
Mature height: 4 to 6 ft.
Mature spread: 2 ft.
Landscape use: Back border; along a fence or wall; dappled shade gardens
Season of bloom: Summer
Key ornamental characteristics: Lavender flowers; attractive foliage; architectural height

Thalictrum rochebruneanum is not as widely known in American gardens as it deserves to be. There are several excellent *Thalictrum* species, but *T. rochebrunianum* is my favorite. I first encountered this species in 1988 while working at the Royal Horticulture Society's Wisley

Thalictrum rochebruneanum

Gardens. It is not flashy by any means, yet I continue to consider it one of the most beautiful plants I know.

The delicate-looking, small, pendulous, lavender-violet flowers do not have true petals, only petal-like sepals and yellow stamens. Blooms are borne on dark green-purple stems that rise above the foliage. When the plants are grouped, the flowers create an atmosphere of lavender-violet mist.

The foliage is also very pleasing. Graceful bluish-green, pinnately compound leaves are alternate in arrangement. Leaves are 3 to 4 ternate, which means they are divided into threes, giving the foliage a fine, fernlike texture.

Lavender mist meadow rue grows in average, medium-wet, well-drained soil in full sun to partial shade. It prefers humus-rich soil and light shade. In the lower Midwest, partial to dappled shade is a must. The plant is intolerant of hot and humid summers. It may require staking, especially if sited in a place that is windy.

I have grown this plant in my garden for over 10 years and I have not witnessed any disease or insect problems. Powdery mildew, rust, and smut can be occasional problems.

Propagation is best done by dividing fully established plants in spring. Seed can also be sowed in the spring.

Thalictrum delavayi (Yunnan meadow rue, Zones 4 to 7) is a related species that grows to 5 ft. and has lavender flowers. The stems of this species are very thin and will require staking. It also likes shade and moist, humus-rich soils.

I use this plant in the back border or along a fence or wall. Its fine texture, lovely flowers, and great height make a magnificent statement in the garden.

Thymus serpyllum   mother-of-thyme, creeping thyme   mint family / Lamiaceae

Hardiness: Zones 3a to 8a
Origin: Europe
Mature height: 3 to 6 in.
Mature spread: 6 to 12 in.
Landscape use: Front border; rock garden, ground cover; herb garden; among stepping-stones
Season of bloom: Late spring to early summer
Key ornamental characteristics: Attractive pale pink flowers; aromatic foliage

Thyme has great ornamental value in any garden. It is a must for the herb garden. In herbal medicine, thyme has been used to alleviate numerous ailments, including spasms and coughing.

Tubular, pale pink flowers are borne in clusters on spikes that are ¼ to ½ in. long. The blooms are fragrant and highly attractive to bees.

Leaves are tiny, elliptic to oblong, and opposite in arrangement. They are bright green, aromatic, and have a scent that is somewhat minty. The strength of the scent varies from

Thymus serpyllum

one season to the next. Stems can be cut back as needed to maintain plant growth and appearance.

Thymus serpyllum prefers full sun but will tolerate light shade. It must have well-drained soil that is not wet or the roots will quickly rot. It prefers sandy or rocky soil. Tolerant of drought and low-fertility soils, this plant performs best in cooler climates. High heat and humidity may leave creeping thyme looking tattered and tired. If so, just trim the plant back hard and it should recover.

There are no serious disease or insect problems associated with this species. It is susceptible to root rot if not grown in proper soil conditions.

Propagation is by seed. Division can also be done in the spring.

The cultivar *Thymus* 'Aureus' has pink flowers and a prostrate growth habit. *Thymus serpyllum* 'Goldstream' has lilac flowers with yellow and green foliage. A related species *Thymus pseudolanuginosus* (woolly thyme, Zones 5 to 8) has woolly leaves and a very low, prostrate habit. This wonderful plant adds great interest to the garden. It must have excellent drainage or it will decline and die. *Thymus vulgaris* (common thyme, Zones 4 to 8) grows to 1 ft. and is the species commonly used to flavor foods.

Thyme adds a touch of elegance when used as a small-area ground cover, or when allowed to fill gaps between stepping-stones along a pathway. Let it sprawl over small rocks or ledges in the rock garden. Or plant thyme in a container with other plants and let it flow over the edge.

Tiarella cordifolia   foamflower   saxifrage family / Saxifragaceae

Hardiness: Zones 3a to 8a
Origin: Eastern United States
Mature height: 6 to 12 in.
Mature spread: 1 to 2 ft.
Landscape use: Front border; rock garden; ground cover; mass
Season of bloom: Early spring
Key ornamental characteristics: Fluffy, white flowers; attractive foliage

Tiarella cordifolia is a handsome plant. The flowers have an appealing, fluffy appearance. Creamy white blooms appear out of pink-tinged buds to usher in spring. Flowers are borne in a raceme 4 to 8 in. long; individual flowers have 5 petals and 10 stamens.

Basal leaves are green, attractive, hairy, ovate-cordate, and have 3 to 5 lobes. Leaves are similar to those of *Heuchera sanguinea* (coral bells) or a stereotypical maple leaf. Foliage turns a slight red-bronze once cold weather arrives. In mild climates, the foliage is evergreen.

To thrive, *Tiarella cordifolia* requires moist soils rich in organic matter and a shady loca-

Tiarella 'Spring Symphony'. Global Book Publishing Photo Library

tion; otherwise it requires little maintenance. It spreads by runners, and over time will form a low-growing mat. The plant is not aggressive.

I have grown this species for over 10 years and have not encountered any disease or insect problems.

Propagation is by seed or division in the spring. Seeds will germinate best if sowed in a cold frame.

Many *Tiarella cordifolia* cultivars have been developed, and some have noticeable leaf differences. 'Purpurea' has purple-tinged foliage and pale pink flowers. 'Eco Red Heart' has red-veined leaves with pale pink flowers. *Tiarella* 'Spring Symphony' is very floriferous and has pale pink flowers. The leaves have a black midrib, are deeply cut, and look like turkey feet. I have also grown the species *T. wherryi* (Wherry's foamflower, Zones 5 to 9), which is similar to *T. cordifolia* but is clump forming (it does not spread by runners) and slightly taller.

Foamflower grows well in a shady area, and in a woodland or rock garden. The white flowers blend nicely with other plants that require the same cultural conditions. Try it with astilbe, ferns, and hellebore.

Tradescantia **Andersoniana Group**   spiderwort   spiderwort family / Commelinaceae

Hardiness: Zones 3b to 9a
Origin: Central United States; hybrid
Mature height: 18 to 24 in.
Mature spread: 2 ft.
Landscape use: Front border; mid border; moist areas; woodland garden; meadow garden
Season of bloom: Mid-spring to midsummer, maybe into fall
Key ornamental characteristics: Vivid blue, purple, pink, red, or white flowers; straplike foliage

This perennial bears many flower buds and has a long blooming period. Violet-blue or sometimes white, pink, or red flowers occur from mid-spring to midsummer and sometimes into

Tradescantia Andersoniana Group

fall if the summer is not too hot or dry. Blooms last for one day, and deadheading is not required since spent flowers dissolve. Flower parts appear in threes: 3 sepals, 3 petals, and 6 stamens form a bloom that is 1 to 3 in. across.

Leaves are dark green with a noticeable midrib on the underside, similar to daylily leaves. The plant forms a dense clump.

Spiderwort can be grown easily. It prefers full sun in the upper Midwest, and partial shade in the lower Midwest. The plant bears more flowers when it receives more sun in the upper Midwest. Soils should be moist and well drained. If your plant's foliage expends itself by midsummer, cut it back to promote new growth. In my Zone 5b garden, my spiderwort's foliage persists through the summer.

Botrytis blight can be a slight problem with spiderwort, but otherwise this plant is insect and disease free.

Propagation is best done by division of the clumps in the spring or fall.

Tradescantia Andersoniana Group was named for a supposed cross of *T. ohiensis*, *T. subaspera*, and *T. virginiana*. Numerous hybrids exist. *Tradescantia* 'Blue Stone' has violet-blue flowers. 'Iris Pritchard' has white flowers tinted with violet-blue. 'Sweet Kate' (or 'Blue and Gold') has striking, bright golden foliage and deep purple-blue flowers.

I have frequently planted spiderwort with ferns, hostas, and other woodland or shade-loving plants. It also works nicely in the front or mid border, and is at home in a woodland or meadow garden. It adds textural contrast in the garden.

Veronica prostrata   harebell speedwell   figwort family / Scrophulariaceae

Hardiness: Zones 4b to 8a
Origin: Europe
Mature height: 4 to 8 in.
Mature spread: 8 to 12 in.
Landscape use: Front border; rock garden; along pathways
Season of bloom: Late spring to early summer
Key ornamental characteristics: Spikelike blue to pink flowers

I originally bought *Veronica prostrata* on a whim some seven years ago. The plant was charming, but it looked delicate, and I assumed it might not live long in my garden. Fortunately I was wrong. This little gem has proven to be as tough as it is beautiful.

Flowers are dark blue, approximately ¼ in. in diameter, and are borne in racemes that rise above the foliage. Flower stems grow 4 to 8 in. tall. Despite being small, flowers are profuse and eye catching.

Leaves are ovate to linear, serrate, mildly pubescent, and opposite in arrangement. The

Veronica prostrata 'Trehane'

leaves provide the perfect foil for the flowers. The sterile, prostrate, flowering stems form mats of creeping foliage, which you can trim back if growth is too invasive.

Harebell speedwell adapts to a wide range of well-drained soil types. It thrives in full sun and performs well in light shade.

There are no serious disease or insect problems with harebell speedwell. Downy mildew and leaf spot can be occasional, mild problems.

Propagation can be by division after flowering in the early summer. Cuttings can also be taken from the sterile stems.

Several *Veronica prostrata* cultivars exist. 'Blue Sheen' has lilac-blue flowers. 'Heavenly Blue' has dark blue flowers and grows up to 4 in. 'Mrs Holt' has pink flowers and grows to 6 in. 'Trehane' is an excellent cultivar, with yellow-green foliage that contrasts nicely with the deep blue flowers. The foliage adds a spark in the garden long after the flowers have faded.

Harebell speedwell is perfect for the front border. It also works well in the rock garden. Try it along a pathway. I place it in front of *Euphorbia epithymoides* (cushion spurge), because there is an overlap in flowering time. It also works nicely with *Aquilegia* (columbine).

Veronica spicata   spiked speedwell   figwort family / Scrophulariaceae

Hardiness: Zones 3b to 8a
Origin: Europe and Asia
Mature height: 1 to 3 ft.
Mature spread: 18 to 24 in.
Landscape use: Front border; mid border;
    specimen; mass
Season of bloom: Summer
Key ornamental characteristics: Beautiful blue,
    pink, or white flowering racemes; glossy
    foliage

Veronica 'Sunny Border Blue'

Spiked speedwell is one of the best available blue-flowering summer perennials. The plant's erect habit offers elegant line and shape in the garden. The spectacular blue flowers offer a cooling effect in the heat of summer and are a perfect complement to any color scheme.

Flowers may occur in pink and white, depending on the cultivar, but most are a shade of blue. Borne in dense, terminal racemes, the blooms rise 8 in. to 2 ft. above the foliage. They last from 4 to 8 weeks, and removing spent flower spikes will encourage additional bloom. They are a wonderful cut flower.

Leaves are medium green, glossy, lanceolate, 2 in. long, and opposite in arrangement. Leaf margins are crenate to serrulate except at the base and apex.

Spiked speedwell is easily grown in well-drained soil. The plant especially requires well-drained soil in winter and consistent moisture. It performs best in full sun. It tolerates partial shade but does not flower as profusely.

There are few disease or insect problems with spiked speedwell. My plants may have leaf spot by late summer if we have had a very humid, wet season. Root rot may also occur in wet, poorly drained soils.

Propagation is best from seed, and this species may self-seed. Terminal cuttings and division are the best methods to propagate cultivars.

Many *Veronica spicata* cultivars exist. 'Alba' has white flowers and grows 18 in. to 2 ft. tall.

'Blue Charm' is tall at 3 ft. and produces lavender-blue flowers. 'Rotfuchs' ('Red Fox') has dark rosy-pink flowers and grows up to 15 in. A related plant *Veronica* 'Sunny Border Blue' (Zones 4 to 8) comes from varieties of *V. spicata* and *V. longifolia* (long-leaf veronica). It has outstanding dark blue flowers and crinkled leaves, and grows 18 in. to 2 ft. It was named Perennial Plant of the Year for 1993.

Spiked speedwell is a natural in the front or mid border, depending on the cultivar, and works well with many species. It particularly complements plants with round flowers. I enjoy it with *Asclepias tuberosa* (butterfly weed), *Leucanthemum ×superbum* (Shasta daisy), *Rudbeckia fulgida* (black-eyed Susan), and *Scabiosa columbaria* (pincushion flower).

Resources

Illinois

Chicago Botanic Garden
1000 Lake Cook Road
Glencoe, IL 60022
847-835-5440
www.chicagobotanic.org

Garden Illinois (Illinois Nurserymen's
    Association)
www.gardenillinois.com

Illinois' Best Plants
www.bestplants.org

Indiana

Indianapolis Museum of Art and the
    Oldfields–Lilly House & Gardens
1200 West 38th Street
Indianapolis, IN 46208-4196
317-923-1331
www.ima-art.org

Purdue Extension Garden Tips
www.ces.purdue.edu/gardenTIPS

Purdue University Horticulture Gardens
Department of Horticulture and Landscape
    Architecture
625 Agriculture Mall Drive
West Lafayette, IN 47906-2010
www.hort.purdue.edu/ext/hort_gardens.html

Iowa

Des Moines Botanical Center
909 Robert D. Ray Drive
Des Moines, IA 50316
515-323-6290
www.botanicalcenter.com

Dubuque Arboretum and Botanical Gardens
3800 Arboretum Drive
Dubuque, IA 52001
563-556-2100
www.dubuquearboretum.com

Iowa Arboretum
1875 Peach Avenue
Madrid, IA 50156
515-795-3216
www.iowaarboretum.org

Iowa State University
www.hort.iastate.edu
www.yardandgarden.extension.iastate.edu

Michigan

Cranbrook House and Gardens
380 Lone Pine Road
Bloomfield Hills, MI 48303-0801
248-645-3147
www.cranbrook.edu/housegardens

Fernwood Botanical Garden & Nature Preserve
13988 Range Line Road
Niles, MI 49120
269-695-6491
www.fernwoodbotanical.org

W. J. Beal Botanical Garden
Michigan State University
East Lansing, MI 48824-1047
517-355-9582
www.cpa.msu.edu/beal/

Minnesota

Minnesota Landscape Arboretum
3675 Arboretum Drive
Chaska, MN 55318
952-443-1400
www.arboretum.umn.edu

Public Gardens of Minnesota
horticulture.coafes.umn.edu/gardens/
    home.htm

University of Minnesota Extension Service
www.extension.umn.edu/yardandgarden
www.extension.umn.edu/topics.html?topic=5

Missouri

Kemper Center for Home Gardening
www.mobot.org/gardeninghelp/
    plantfinder/Alpha.asp

Missouri Botanic Garden
4344 Shaw Boulevard
Saint Louis, MO 63110
314-577-9400
www.mobot.org

Missouri Environment and Garden
ppp.missouri.edu/newsletters/megindex.htm

Ohio

Cleveland Botanic Garden
11030 East Boulevard
Cleveland, OH 44106
216-721-1600
www.cbgarden.org

Holden Arboretum
9500 Sperry Road
Kirtland, OH 44094
440-946-4400
www.holdenarb.org

Ohio State University WebGarden
www.webgarden.osu.edu

Wisconsin

Boerner Botanical Garden
9400 Boerner Drive
Hales Corners, WI 53130
414-525-5600
www.boernerbotanicalgardens.org

Olbrich Botanical Gardens
3330 Atwood Avenue
Madison, WI 53704
608-246-4550
www.ci.madison.wi.us/olbrich

University of Wisconsin Extension
Urban Horticulture
http://www.uwex.edu/ces/wihort/

Glossary

alternate: Arrangement of leaves, with only one leaf occurring at each node on the stem.

anther: The pollen-bearing portion of the stamen.

apetalous: Without petals.

apex: The tip or terminal end.

appressed: Pressed close or lying flat against a stem or leaf.

auriculate: With small, ear-shaped lobes.

axil: Angle between a plant part and the stem that bears it.

basal: At the base of a plant.

bipinnately compound: In leaves, where both primary and secondary divisions are pinnate.

biternate: Twice divided into threes.

bract: Modified leaf at the base of flower or flowerhead, usually scalelike.

bulbil: A small bulb that forms along the stems of certain plants.

bulblet: A small bulb borne at the base of the parent bulb that can be removed to propagate additional plants.

calyx: Sepals that form the outer whorl of the perianth.

cordate: Heart shaped, with a notch at the base.

corolla: The flower petals as a group.

corymb: A flat-topped or domed inflorescence where the outer flowers open first.

crenate: With rounded teeth on the leaf margin.

crown: A central growing point of a perennial under or near the ground surface.

cultivar: A plant within a species that originates under cultivation; it is distinguished from the species by one or more characteristics, and when the plant is reproduced sexually or asexually, it retains those distinct characteristics.

cyathium: An inflorescence in which a cuplike involucre surrounds a single pistil and several male flowers with a single stamen.

cyme: A flat-topped or round-topped inflorescence whose terminal flowers open first.

cymose: Arranged in cymes.

dentate: Toothed; the teeth are perpendicular to the margin.

dioecious: With male and female staminate and pistillate flowers on different plants.

disk flower: A tubular flower in the center of a flower of the aster family.

dissected: Divided into many narrow segments.

dormancy: The period when perennials are asleep, in winter.

downy: Having soft, fine hairs.

elliptic: With an oval shape that is narrow or rounded on the ends and broader in the middle.

entire: A leaf margin that is smooth, with no teeth, serrations, notches, or divisions.

fan: A single daylily plant, which emerges in a fan consisting of leaves, a crown, and roots.

floret: A small flower; an individual flower in a dense inflorescence.

floriferous: Flower bearing.

foliar: Relating to leaves.

glabrous: Without hairs; smooth.

hispid: Having bristly hairs.

hybrid: A plant produced by the cross-breeding of two or more parent plants of different varieties, subspecies, species, or genera.

involucre: A whorl of small leaves or bracts below a flower or inflorescence.

knot garden: A garden with a formal design like an intricately woven knot.

lanceolate: Spear shaped; longer than wide and tapering at the apex.

layering: To form roots where a stem comes in contact with the ground.

leaflet: One unit of a compound leaf.

linear: Shaped like a line; long and narrow.

lobe: A rounded segment of a leaf or flower that is cut back about halfway between the margin and the middle.

midrib: The middle vein or rib of a leaf or leaflet.

node: A joint on a stem where leaves or branches arise.

oblanceolate: Inversely lanceolate.

oblong: Longer than broad, somewhat rectangular in shape.

obovate: Broadest above the middle portion.

opposite: Arrangement of leaves where two leaves occur across from each other at each node.

orbicular: Rounded or circular.

ovate: Broadest below the middle portion; egg shaped.

palmate: Arising from a common point and fanning out, like fingers on a hand.

panicle: A branched inflorescence where the branches are usually racemes or corymbs.

paniculate: Having panicles.

peduncle: The stalk of a single flower or cluster of flowers.

pendulous: Drooping or hanging downward.

petiole: The leaf stalk.

pinnate: Compounded with leaflets along each side of an axis, like a feather.

pistillate: Having a pistil or pistils, but no stamens.

plume: A feathery shape.

pod: A dry fruit that opens at maturity.

prostrate: Lying flat on the ground.

pseudobulb: A swollen, bulblike stem.

pubescent: Having short, soft hairs.

raceme: An elongated inflorescence with pedicelled flowers maturing from the bottom upward.

rhizomatous: Having, resembling, or being a rhizome.

rhizome: An underground stem distinguished from a root by having nodes, buds, or similar structures.

rosette: A crown of leaves at or just above the ground surface.

scabrous: Having a rough, gritty feeling when touched.

scale: A thin layer of a bulb; an insect that sucks the juices of plants, sometimes a serious pest.

scape: A leafless peduncle arising from a basal rosette; bractlike leaves may be present.

sepal: Part of the calyx.

serrate: Toothed along the margin of the leaf; teeth point forward.

serrulate: Finely serrate.

sessile: Without a petiole; stalkless.

shatter: To break apart, dropping the fruit.

sinuate: Having a wavy margin.

spatulate: Shaped like a spoon.

spike: An unbranched inflorescence with sessile flowers.

spikelet: One of the spikes that make up the inflorescence of many grasses or sedges.

spine: A stiff, sharp-pointed growth on a leaf, stem, or other part of a plant.

sport: A mutation that deviates from type.

stamen: The male portion of a flower that consists of an anther and filament.

staminate: Relating to stamens.

stolon: A horizontal stem that roots at the tip and forms a new plant.

stoloniferous: Having thin stems that grow on or just below the ground and are capable of rooting.

subshrub: A perennial plant that can be woody at the base.

terminal: The end.

ternate: Occur in threes.

tomentose: Fuzzy; covered with short, soft hairs.

toothed: With small, serrate shapes along the margin.

tripinnate: When leaflets are pinnately compound once, then twice, then three times.

tubular: A flower that is trumpet shaped.

umbel: A domed or flat-shaped inflorescence where the florets arise from the same point.

whorled: Arranged in a ringlike formation.

References

The American Horticultural Society. 1996. *A–Z Encyclopedia of Garden Plants*. New York: DK Publishing.

Armitage, Allan M. 1997. *Herbaceous Perennial Plants: A Treatise on Their Identification, Culture, and Garden Attributes*. Champaign, Illinois: Stipes Publishing.

Bremness, Lesley. 1994. *The Complete Book of Herbs: A Practical Guide to Growing and Using Herbs*. New York: Penguin Books.

Coombs, Allen J. 1999. *Dictionary of Plant Names*. Portland, Oregon: Timber Press.

Haggard, Ezra. 1996. *Perennials for the Lower Midwest*. Bloomington: Indiana University Press.

Hodgson, Larry. 2000. *Perennials for Every Purpose*. Emmaus, Pennsylvania: Rodale.

Ingwersen, Will. 1986. *Manual of Alpine Plants*. Twickenham, England: Collingridge Books.

Lloyd, Christopher. 2000. *Garden Flowers*. Portland, Oregon: Timber Press.

McVicar, Jekka. 1994. *Herbs for the Home*. New York: Viking Studio Books.

Patent, Dorothy Hinshaw. 2003. *Plants on the Trail with Lewis and Clark*. New York: Clarion Books.

Perennials. 2000. New York: DK Publishing.

Phillips, H. Wayne. 2003. *Plants of the Lewis and Clark Expedition*. Missoula, Montana: Mountain Press.

Still, Steven M. 1994. *Manual of Herbaceous Ornamental Plants*. Champaign, Illinois: Stipes Publishing.

Thomas, Graham Stuart. 1986. *Perennial Garden Plants or The Modern Florilgium*. London, England: J. M. Dent and Sons.

Woods, Christopher. 1992. *Encyclopedia of Perennials: A Gardener's Guide*. New York: Facts on File.

Index